WHITENESS ON THE BORDER

NATION OF NATIONS:
IMMIGRANT HISTORY AS AMERICAN HISTORY

General Editors: Rachel Buff, Matthew Jacobson, and Werner Sollors

Whiteness on the Border

Mapping the U.S. Racial Imagination in Brown and White

Lee Bebout

NEW YORK UNIVERSITY PRESS
New York

NEW YORK UNIVERSITY PRESS
New York
www.nyupress.org

References to Internet websites (URLs) were accurate at the time of writing.
Neither the author nor New York University Press is responsible for URLs that
may have expired or changed since the manuscript was prepared.

ISBN: 978-1-4798-8534-3 (hardback)
ISBN: 978-1-4798-5853-8 (paperback)

For Library of Congress Cataloging-in-Publication data, please contact the
Library of Congress.

New York University Press books are printed on acid-free paper,
and their binding materials are chosen for strength and durability.
We strive to use environmentally responsible suppliers and materials
to the greatest extent possible in publishing our books.

Manufactured in the United States of America

10 9 8 7 6 5 4 3 2 1

Also available as an ebook

For Michael Bebout-Vega

We actively struggle for a more just world
because the other alternatives
are simply not acceptable.

CONTENTS

NOTE ON TERMINOLOGY

Social identity labels can be both elucidating and confusing. At the level of academic discourse, scholars often strive for simplicity and clarity. For example, "Mexicans," "Mexican immigrants," and "Mexican Americans" may be used to reference three distinct groups of people. However, beyond the pages of academe, the world and words are messier. "Mexican" may be a label of racial, ethnic, or national identification. And "Mexican" is not alone. Consider how "American" may refer not just to a U.S. citizen or someone from the Americas if we are to think hemispherically. Rather, in popular discourse "American" can be used to reference white U.S. citizens exclusively or non-Latinos more generally. Often this is not purposeful, for the unstated, normalized category of white occupies central positioning in the term "American." This is not happenstance or inconsequential. In many ways, this slippage between national and ethnoracial categories is the central thread of this book. In the following pages, I strive for simplicity and clarity, marking the distinction between Mexicans, Mexican Americans, and Anglo-Americans. At points, I deploy "Chicana/o," "Latina/o," and "Mexican American" to signal their historical and political differences, but at other times I use Chicana/o transhistorically as has become common in the field of Chicana/o studies. Readers will notice other moments in the text when there is slippage between "Mexican" and "Mexican American" as well as between "American" and "Anglo-American." These are not moments of laziness or inadvertent mistakes. They are purposeful acts of signification, for the dynamic tension and play between ethnoracial and national categories is the very heart of the matter.

Perhaps, at some point, all scholarship has its root in the autobiographical. This book certainly feels so. I was born outside of Chicago, Illinois, two hundred years after the United States declared independence, over one hundred years after the end of slavery, approximately thirty years after the defeat of Nazi fascism in Europe, a few years after the end of mass protests that marked the freedom struggles of the 1950s, 1960s, and 1970s, at the cusp of neoliberalism, soft multiculturalism, and color blindness. All this to say, like many others, I was born into white supremacy in a time like today when many whites sought a clean break from the past, a chance to baptize themselves in dreams of innocence.

Raised by my mother, I was taught that racism is wrong. This is a value that is imparted by many white parents today. Knowing this is not enough. Knowing that racism is wrong does not account for what racism is or what it does. Knowing that racism is wrong does not arm oneself with strategies for combating injustice. These two gaps create significant challenges today as racism is popularly conflated with outward expressions of personal prejudice and the solution is simply to "don't say things like that." Like many white families, mine rarely spoke of race and racial difference, and when it did, race was coded below the surface of politeness.

Growing up in the western suburbs of Chicago in the 1980s, my conscious introduction to the U.S. racial imagination was largely through television and racial comments by friends and adults outside my family. The targets of jokes would be Polish Americans or black people—*what do you do when a Polack throws a hand grenade at you?* When the pretense of humor was absent, the comments were always about black folk. In first grade, I watched television as the sitter casually told her friend about the laziness of black people, how they should go back to Africa. The same year my best friend's dad repeatedly went on violent screeds about black folks ruining the country. Lacking the language then, I only recently spoke with my mother about these experiences and others.

In 1989, something strange happened. We moved to Texas, altering the terrain of the racial imagination tremendously. Jokes about Polish Americans were replaced with Aggie jokes, targeting students of Texas A&M University as well as rural Texans: *What do you do when an Aggie throws a hand grenade at you?* I did not know what an Aggie was. Derisive attitudes and jokes about black people remained, but I was also introduced to anti-Mexican attitudes and humor: *Why do Mexicans eat tamales at Christmas?* I did not know the answer, and when I learned it, I did not get the joke. I did not know what tamales were, nor did I have the wide array of racial and social codes to "know" what a "Mexican" was. But over the years I learned; I learned to be white. As my wife and partner Sujey Vega as well as many colleagues in Chicana/o studies would surely point out, there has been a Mexican American presence in Chicago and other parts of the Midwest for a hundred years. However, in the 1980s, living in the suburbs with few Mexican Americans, my understanding of race was largely black and white. Moving to Texas changed things, exposing me to and inviting me to participate in a racial imagination also mapped in brown and white. This book marks a similar shift. While U.S. whiteness has largely been examined against the experiences and representations of black Americans, this project maps the ways representations of Mexico, Mexicans, and Mexican Americans forge aspects of white Americanness.

It would be unfair and inaccurate to suggest that all U.S. white attitudes toward and depictions of Mexico and people of Mexican descent are pejorative or derisive. The brown-white binary does not work that way. White supremacy does not work that way. As I came of age in Texas and traveled through out the Southwest, I became immersed in seemingly more positive depictions of Mexicanness. For me, this often came through my growing love for Texas country music. In his classic "Pancho and Lefty," Townes Van Zandt sings of a Mexican bandit named Pancho and his gringo friend Lefty who betrays Pancho to the *federales*. In his "Gallo del Cielo," Tom Russell sings of the Mexican Carlos Zaragoza who steals a one-eyed rooster named Gallo del Cielo, travels to the United States to win enough money through cockfighting in order to buy back his family's land, and loses everything never to return. In too

many songs, one finds the ubiquitous eroticized, desirable, and desiring Mexicana. Here, I must note that these attitudes and depictions—
negative and seemingly positive—do not always exist in discrete worlds.
Over the years, I have heard those who lament the browning of America
or bond racially through anti-Mexican humor also proclaim their love
of all things Mexican through music and other cultural productions.
As a scholar of Chicana/o studies and American studies, as a white
man raised within this discursive and ideological system, the question
emerged and haunted me: what cultural work is performed by these various iterations of Mexicanness? The answer: representations of Mexico,
Mexicans, and Mexican Americans are deployed to forge whiteness and
Americanness.

* * *

If scholarship often has a root in the autobiographical, sometimes it
comes back a bit too close. In January 2015, I had drafted half of the
manuscript that would become this book and had just begun teaching
an undergraduate course titled "U.S. Race Theory and the Problem of
Whiteness." Unbeknownst to me, a conservative student-blogger who
was not enrolled in the class found out about the course, read the title
and the titles of some of the required texts, and on January 22 published
an article that couched the ensuing controversy in a discourse of white
victimization: "They would never allow a class talking about the problem of 'blackness.' And if they did, there would be an uproar about it.
But you can certainly harass people for their apparent whiteness."[1] I discovered the initial article only after I had been contacted with requests
to do radio interviews and began receiving emails that were less than
supportive. The next day, the student-blogger appeared on the *Fox &
Friends* morning show with Elisabeth Hasselbeck to bemoan the state
of higher education, claimed that the course, via its readings in critical whiteness studies, blames all white people for social injustice in
the United States, and wondered "what students . . . are taking out of
this course when they learn all about negative racial tension."[2] And so
began a semester-long drama that I lovingly and jokingly call "my whiteness kerfuffle." Across three months, the situation involved unwanted
media attention, a significant amount of hate mail, a white supremacist
group distributing leaflets in my neighborhood and on campus, white

supremacists uploading pictures of my family with overtly racist captions, a teach-in in support of my class, and protests and counterprotests regarding the neo-Nazi presence on campus and Arizona State University's silence on the matter. All the while, ASU asked that I not talk to the media. I had inadvertently become the subject of my object of study. This, dear reader, is not how one wishes to spend the semester in which one waits to hear if one is going to receive tenure. I do not tell this story to elicit sympathy or attention. Rather, I tell it because as the situation unfolded while I was drafting this book, it confirmed my suspicions about how white supremacy operates today as well as reinforced my sense of urgency in combating it.

Almost immediately, I was struck by the way in which race and my whiteness became manifested within and constrained through the rhetorical maneuvers of the hate mail. Several writers proclaimed themselves not to be racist and simultaneously declared me to be a race traitor filled with white guilt and racial self-loathing. They kindly suggested ways my suffering might end. Notably, they did not write with potential antiwhite stereotypes. They asserted, rather, that I was insufficiently white. For some, such missives were not enough, and they resorted to questioning my masculinity and sexuality. Here several aspects should be evident. Embedded within the logic of these letters, whiteness occupies a position of the ideal. The potential insult is that one fails in one's whiteness. Moreover, in an era that feigns color blindness and postracism, declarations that one is a race traitor do not have much cache outside explicitly white supremacist circles. Furthermore, one must note race, gender, and sexuality are overlaid—one's "failure" in whiteness is quickly translated to "failures" toward heteropatriarchy.

Yet whiteness was neither the sole nor the desired locus of attack. Many writers sought to show me the light by trotting out numerous antiblack stereotypes, videos, and "news" articles. Importantly, however, the hate mail did not adhere to a rigid black-white binary. Several letters and online comments about the course on whiteness took aim at U.S. Latinas/os and immigrants. For example, one letter from a resident of Winslow, Arizona, stated, "the problem with whiteness is we are becoming a minority because white people are having less children. all the illegals come here and have big families and go on welfare or take jobs from americans but because where white were supposed to be quiet and let it happen. i read a story about an illegal guy that had a fantasitic job with a roofing company nice house. his wife also illegal had a good job." This letter readily evidences how representations of immigrants and Latinas/os are deployed to shore up whiteness and its benefits as the author feels them under siege.

My inadvertent brush with white supremacy fame also made legible how extremist groups and elements of the political mainstream are not in opposition as some may wish to believe. Rather, explicit white supremacy and everyday whiteness are mutually interdependent. The National Youth Front, the National Socialist Movement, and other seemingly fringe groups relied upon and latched onto the popular claims of legitimacy of Fox News, Campus Reform, and the *Washington Times*.[3] Likewise, media organs like Fox News and others distanced themselves from white supremacist groups in order to assert their belonging in the mainstream. Fighting white supremacy today and in the future requires that scholars and activists recognize, make visible, and strike against the intersections of extremist and everyday whiteness.

But striking out against white supremacy is not always easy, particularly for those who are not used to frank and honest race talk, or those who are in socially and politically precarious positions. I received tremendous individual support at ASU from friends, colleagues, and administrators. Shortly after the *Fox & Friends* segment aired, ASU released a statement defending the course, allowing me to help draft it. I believe this move should be lauded, particularly when compared to other universities' handling of high-profile faculty controversies. However, the university's response was not without weakness. After members of white supremacist organizations distributed leaflets at the end of January and protested on campus at the beginning of March, the lack of university response constituted a resounding silence. Alarmed and outraged by the white supremacist presence and university response, students, faculty, and community members urged ASU to take a vocal stand for racial justice. Nearly two moths later, at the end of April, members of the ASU administration, the Anti-Defamation League, and other community leaders released a formal statement condemning hate speech from the neo-Nazis and local hate preachers. ASU's rhetorical strategy should not be surprising. Considering that the governor and state legislature were contemporaneously debating and cutting nearly a hundred million dollars from state higher education, the approach may well have been judicious. The university's struggle to come out against white supremacy does not simply evidence cowardice, although profiles in courage rarely come through a committee. Rather, in a state that had recently passed the anti-immigrant, anti-Latina/o SB 1070 and the anti–ethnic studies HB 2281, which targeted Mexican American studies in primary and secondary education, the slow response against white supremacists bespeaks a recognition that explicit aspects of white supremacy are part of everyday political culture.

For me, the spring of 2015 was a catalytic moment. Almost immediately, beyond ASU scholars and activists, friends and strangers reached out to offer their support. Their letters far outnumbered the others. Today, as in the past, as likely in the foreseeable future, white supremacy surrounds us. But we are not alone. As George Lipsitz implores us to remember, this is not simply a moment of danger; it is a moment of opportunity.[4]

* * *

The seeds for this book were sewn years ago, and I am tremendously indebted to those who have provided intellectual and psychic nourishment along the way. ASU's Institute for Humanities Research supported me through the 2012–13 IHR Fellows Program. Beyond financial resources and a course release, the IHR offered the opportunity to work with scholars in a yearlong workshop on the Humanities and the Imagination/Imaginary. This experience allowed me to explore disparate threads of the project and begin to discover what I was writing. In 2015 the IHR also awarded a subvention grant to support this book. The Newberry Library Borderlands and Latino Studies Seminar was fundamental in developing the book's narrative arc as well as teasing out the argument's relationship to history. I am particularly appreciative of the feedback from John Mckiernen-González, Jason Ruiz, Benjamin Johnson, Raúl Coronado, Andrae Marak, John Alba Cutler, Carla Della Gatta, and Margaret Power. Portions of chapters 2 and 3 were published in *Latino Studies* and *MELUS*, respectively, where the reviewers and editors offered encouragement and insight. Michael Olivas contacted me out of the blue to let me know about the fascinating case of Macario García, providing critical perspective for the revision of chapter 3. An early portion of chapter 4 was presented at the University of North Carolina at Chapel Hill as part of the Latino Culture(s) Speakers Series. Faculty and students braved a snowstorm to listen to and speak with me about country music, the eroticized Mexicana, and white desire. The insights of María DeGuzmán, Ariana Vigil, Jennifer Ho, Laura Halperin, John Ribó, and other attendees strengthened the chapter.

Several friends have left their marks on this project through conversation as well as through reading and offering feedback on the manuscript. Drew Lopenzina and Daniel Gilfillan offered encouragement and insight, particularly in the early stages of the project when I began to realize that sometimes openly discussing the everyday aspects of white supremacy can make one feel marked and afflicted by a contagious disease. The participants in the critical race theory seminar formed an essential community of learners when doing such work can be an isolating experience. Likewise, the ASU Ethnic Studies Working Group and the Arizona Ethnic Studies Network continually remind me why I came to Arizona in the first place: sites of oppression are simultaneously locations of resistance. Wendy Cheng, Nolan Cabrera, and others have been models for imagining and practicing a locally embedded ethnic studies. Kenneth Ladenburg and I have shared numerous conversations on the rhetorics of white supremacy, the importance of this work, and strategies for working toward racial justice. Travis Franks and I have often spoken about settler colonialism, the moral imperative of standing up against inequality, and our mutual love for music. He turned me onto Jack Ingram's "Inna from Mexico," which is discussed in chapter 4. Drew Lopenzina, Ron Broglio, Eddie Mallot, Louis Mendoza, Angélica Afandor-Pujol, and Jessica Early have been wonderful friends who have helped me balance academic and nonacademic aspects of my life, reminding me that people are and should be multifaceted.

In preparing the manuscript, Susan Curtis and David Vazquez graciously read selections of the book before I sent it out for consideration. I not only appreciate Susan and David's friendship, but I also deeply admire the way they both model an approach to the profession. Adriana Estill and Marzia Milazzo read early drafts of chapters 3 and 4, respectively. Both pushed me to clarify my argument and hone my writing. George Lipsitz and William Nericcio offered tremendous insight and helped frame the project as readers for New York University Press. Long before I completed this project, their work has been foundational to my thinking. I am honored to have the support of those I admire as both scholars and people. After I completed an initial draft of this manuscript, Micha Espinosa invited me to participate in a residency and workshop with Guillermo Gómez-Peña and La Pocha Nostra members Michelle Ceballos Michot and Saul Garía López. It was an amazing experience that helped me understand the role of art in the making of the world. I am indebted to these artists and the other workshop participants. Their influence is felt strongly in the conclusion. Eric Zinner, Alicia Nadkarni, and the editorial team at NYU were a delight to work with. I particularly appreciate their support of my freedom of writerly voice and their belief in what some might consider an odd project that yokes together analysis of political and popular culture. With this book, I owe a tremendous debt to those I have named here as well as those I have inadvertently forgotten. Surely there will be limitations and oversights in this project— those are entirely mine.

Finally, I must acknowledge the impact of my family. Kristine Dutton taught me about struggle and instilled in me a desire for justice, a desire that propels us even when we do not know where it will lead. As usual Sujey Vega read everything, often multiple times, and offered incisive feedback. Her intellectual support for this project is perhaps surpassed only by her emotional support for me as a life partner. Beyond the support, she has reminded me of the necessity of putting one's work on hold so that life can happen and that we must enjoy it. And to my son Michael Bebout-Vega, thank you for teaching me to keep perspective and to look upon the world with fresh eyes. The world will not hand us easy answers to long-enduring challenges, but that does not mean that we shouldn't have fun while calling a new world into being.

Introduction

Chicana/o Studies and the Whiteness Problem; or, Toward a Mapping of Whiteness on the Border

Example 1. A novel, Cormac McCarthy's *Cities of the Plain*: John Grady Cole travels across the border, falls in love with a fourteen-year-old epileptic Mexican prostitute, and dies on the streets of Juarez at the hand of a knife-wielding pachuco pimp who declares, "Your kind cannot bear that the world be ordinary. That it contain nothing save what stands before one. But the Mexican world is a world of adornment only and underneath it is very plain indeed. While your world . . . totters upon an unspoken labyrinth of questions. And we will devour you, my friend. You and all your pale empire."

Example 2. A country song, Roger Creager's "Long Way to Mexico": "I know about this out-of-the-way place. / You can disappear without a trace. / Leave the world behind if only for a while. / You could just get rolling see the winding road / Unfolding feeling better with every passing mile. / Even the getting there makes me smile. . . . / It's a place of señoritas and where mariachis sing. / I know happiness abounds there. / It's a place where I'll soon be."

Example 3. A protest, April 2010: Several thousand gather in Houston, Texas, to protest Arizona's recent anti-immigration bill SB 1070 and the rise in anti-immigrant and anti-Latina/o discourse. They carry U.S. flags. Their signs read "We are all immigrants," "Immigrant Rights = Human Rights," and "Do I look Illegal?" A small counterdemonstration of approximately thirty anti-immigration activists lines the streets periodically. At one corner, a middle-aged couple, white and bedecked in red, white, and blue signifiers of patriotism, yell "Go back home!" A young Latina—a child of immigrants herself and armed with a voice—responds "I am home! I was born here!" For a second, the couple looks dumbstruck, then repeats "Go back home!" and other tautologies such as "Illegal is illegal!" A protest organizer intercedes: "Don't engage them. It's what they want."

At first glance, these three moments may appear as isolated incidents with little cohesion. McCarthy's all-American cowboy crosses the border and falls in love, only to die at the hands of his Mexican nemesis. Backed up by accordions and Mexican *gritos*, Creager croons about the trip to Mexico, leaving his workaday life behind for a temporary escape where Mexican women, music, and tequila can replenish him. Anti-immigrant protestors ascribe foreignness to Latina/o immigration activists, brown skin rendering them questionably American if not perpetually foreign. While these examples emerge from distinct moments and from different contexts, upon closer inspection they share common dynamics resulting in what I call "whiteness on the border."

Whiteness on the border is a discursive and ideological constellation in which representations of Mexico, Mexicans, and Mexican Americans are deployed to construct white identity, or more accurately white identity as American identity. These narratives, tropes, and beliefs work in tandem to order lived experience and naturalize whiteness. Notably, this is nothing new. These examples share a long legacy that is part and parcel of American history. The Mexican Other, real and more often imaginary, has played a significant role in the fashioning of a white identity and U.S. expansion since at least the early nineteenth-century contact narratives of Anglo-American settlers immigrating into the frontier lands of colonial New Spain. In part due to this legacy, these discursive practices have achieved a remarkable and ubiquitous presence, seemingly everywhere as they fly below the critical radar. From these examples and countless others, this critical endeavor engages two interrelated questions: How has whiteness been forged against a Mexican Other embodied in representations of Mexico, Mexicans, and Chicanas/os? How has the Mexican American positioning within the U.S. racial order and dominant imagination enabled and limited the United States to fashion the nation-state as a racial state?

The historical weight of this discursive and ideological constellation gives shape and substance to the nativist protestors' reactions. That is, these anti-immigration activists were merely drawing upon a rich discursive tradition. Despite several centuries of heritage in what is now the United States, including over a hundred years in midwestern cities, Mexican-descent people are all too often rendered "perpetually foreign."[1] Representations of Mexico, Mexicans, and Mexican Americans, however, are scripted as more than simply alien. Indeed, cross-border, cross-cultural imaginings are charged with various, sometimes competing, symbolic meanings such as the escape of romance (often in the arms of a Mexican woman), an ever-encroaching threat to national identity and security (echoes of which reverberate in the words of McCarthy's pachuco pimp), or the potential for unbridled violence and the need for paternalistic protectionism. From the nineteenth century onward, Mexico and Mexican-descent people have become a prosthetic imaginary, a frontier made anew through cultural production at the expansion of and death of the West. Thus, this project widens the gaze beyond the Anglo-American depictions of the Mexican Other to the ways in which these renderings construct whiteness and Americanness, or more aptly whiteness as Americanness.

This broad, ever-sprawling discursive and ideological constellation stretches between and connects lived and textualized experience. Its roots go back to the early nineteenth century, yet it thrives today. *Whiteness on the Border* draws together and advances three critical interventions. First, U.S. whiteness is constructed against a Mexican Other. For example, McCarthy's knife fight functions as a competition of racialized masculinities, and the potential affections of Creager's "señoritas" are constructed solely to fulfill the needs of white male desire. Second, Mexicanness is also juxtaposed to and fashions Americanness. This results in not simply imagining whites to be American but the converse as well: to be American, one must be white. Each of the examples above illustrates a conflation of ethnoracial and national identities wherein whiteness is Americanness and that which is Mexican is rendered Other. Finally, whiteness on the border signals how the ideological and discursive characteristics of whiteness and Americanness are coterminous. Against the Mexican Other, whiteness and Americanness become mutually reinforcing. As such, the innocence, benevolence, fears, anxieties, fantasies, and desires of whiteness may be expressions of not simply a racial imagination but also a nationalist one.

Despite its regional inscription, whiteness on the border pervades the nation. Indeed, the discursive repertoire of cross-border invasions, replete with iconic imagery, has found fertile ground in the anti-immigrant politics of the U.S. heartland. For instance, discourses of borders, security, and invasion permeated the discussion of the 2005 Sensenbrenner anti-immigration bill (HR 4437) in the local politics of the Midwest.[2] Gilberto Rosas has argued that through policing of brown bodies, the border and borderlands have "thickened."[3] Likewise, I contend that the expanded impact of border policing corresponds to a symbolic thickening wherein local demographic changes are ascribed to dynamics of U.S.-Mexico border policy. In this way, whiteness on the border fashions a national fantasy with a localized flare, imagining the geopolitical territory into a racial state. Whether in anti-immigrant polemics of the right or popular country music that imagines Mexico populated with beautiful señoritas who are "hotter than the Mexican sun," the representation of Mexico, Mexicans, and Chicanas/os fashions and reinforces notions of whiteness, often tied to hegemonic structures of nationalism and masculinity.[4] And, as is the case with cultural imaginings, particularly those fashioned and codified by the culture industry, these are not expressions without consequence. The fashioning of the Mexican Other is a critical fulcrum in the machinations of U.S. foreign and domestic social policy. This discursive and ideological constellation undergirds U.S. racial logics, and thus it bears very real, material consequences for the lived experiences of all involved.

Significantly, however, whiteness on the border has not gone without response. Since the first contacts onward, people of Mexican descent have actively positioned themselves in the U.S. racial system and national imagery. At various times claiming whiteness, indigeneity, and mestizaje, Mexican Americans have shaped the discourses of whiteness on the border and their positioning in the U.S. racial imagination. Thus, beyond identifying and theorizing this legacy of the U.S. racial system, this project builds upon these Chicana/o responses in order to make whiteness strange, dislodge it from its normative positioning, and expose it to critique.[5] As Richard Dyer has suggested, such is the critical step in dismantling whiteness from its naturalized center of racial power. Ultimately, I contend that representations of Mexico, Mexicans, and Mexican Americans have been used in various ways, from a threatening menace to a community that must be protected, all of which express national fantasies as racial fantasies, and vice versa. Moreover, Mexican Americans have no simple positioning in the U.S. racial order. Thus, exploring successful and unsuccessful Chicana/o attempts to grapple with white supremacy will contribute to the ongoing scholarly and activist efforts of antiracism and toward the abolition of whiteness.[6] This book explicitly addresses the ways in which U.S. nationalism and the U.S. racial imagination function through anti-Mexican forms of racialization.

For scholars, the theorization and examination of whiteness on the border draw together and work at the intersection of two intellectual and political endeavors: critical whiteness studies and Chicana/o studies. While these fields have undergone rapid growth in recent years and indeed share useful intersections, they have lacked a sustained dialogue. Critical whiteness studies has all too often treated Chicanas/os as either people of color no different from African Americans or white ethnics like Italians, Irish, and other white ethnics before them.[7] Neither of these paradigms is sufficient. In contrast, Chicana/o studies has largely examined the dynamics of Chicana/o legal whiteness and social nonwhiteness, but the field has left underexamined how Chicana/o inequalities and social nonwhiteness foster Anglo-American investment in whiteness. Thus, the next few pages trace the gaps and intersections between critical whiteness studies and Chicana/o studies. Doing so establishes the necessary foundation for mapping whiteness on the border.

Critical Whiteness Studies and the Chicana/o Challenge

While critical whiteness studies has developed as a formalized field of inquiry in recent years, its roots can be traced back to key African American intellectuals such as W. E. B. Du Bois and James Baldwin.[8] These influential thinkers believed that addressing the problem of race required going to the source, understanding the experiences and racial logics that fashion and are reinforced by whiteness. Here, one must think of white supremacy not as people in pointy white hoods or small-town country bigots as is popularly conceptualized, but rather as a system of racial logics and social relations of which we are all inheritors, and that often goes unrecognized as water to fish.[9] Critical whiteness studies has persuasively argued that white supremacy—as structural racial inequality—thrives today not because of the actions and beliefs of fringe, aberrant whites but because of the ideology, actions, and inactions of what Karyn McKinney has termed "everyday whiteness."[10] That is, racial inequality is secured through "commonsense" logics that deny and undergird the status quo.[11] Indeed, John Hope Franklin and others have incisively demonstrated how contemporary articulations of color blindness are both seductive to well-intentioned people and a tremendous obstacle to the freedom movements of African Americans and other peoples of color.[12] Here, I would contend that the investments of "everyday whiteness," color blindness, and aberrant, explicitly supremacist forms of whiteness, are mutually dependent and influencing. Through depictions of aberrant whites (e.g., skinheads and the KKK), everyday whites are able to deny their positioning within a racial system. Likewise, the "possessive investment" of everyday whiteness gives legitimacy and cover to the fears and desires of the more explicit hate groups.

During the African American civil rights movement, critical whiteness studies emerged as part of the curriculum of some freedom schools, rooting the field of inquiry in the struggle for social justice.[13] With the dissolution of the mass movement struggles of the 1960s and 1970s, the rise of Reagan conservatism, and the weakening of social justice gains through politically soft multiculturalism, critical whiteness studies developed along with critical race theory to forge new models of critique. Thus, during the 1990s scholars working with a variety of aggrieved communities—African American studies, labor studies, gender and sexuality studies—began to theorize whiteness in relationship to a wide array of fields. Peggy McIntosh contended that white privilege operates like an "invisible package of unearned assets that I can count on cashing in each day, but about which . . . [white people are] 'meant' to remain oblivious."[14] Toni Morrison argued that literary whiteness has long been fashioned out of the imagined blackness in American literature.[15] David Roediger extended the ideas of Du Bois, arguing that whites earn psychological wages for their race loyalty, integrating systems of race and class oppression.[16] Through ethnographic interviews, Ruth Frankenberg exposed how the lives of white women were shaped by the experience of race, from living segregated lives in their childhood and "unwitnessing" the people of color who entered their social geographies to prohibitions against interracial relationships.[17] Noel Ignatiev demonstrated that white was not a stable racial category by exploring how a previously regarded nonwhite people like the Irish became white and were able to deploy its privileges.[18] Richard Dyer, in an examination of whiteness in visual culture, described how the racial logics of white supremacy are disseminated through the technologies and narratives of the motion picture industry.[19] George Lipsitz forcefully demonstrated how, contrary to popular belief, white people benefit from identity politics.[20] Charles Mills contended that social contract theory and the Enlightenment project that fostered contemporary race-neutral notions of citizenship, history, and personhood are rooted in racial logics that positioned the European and Euro-Americans as the model for the universal man—other peoples subsequently became subpersons.[21] John Hartigan's ethnography of white Detroit complicated previous notions about whiteness, contending that when numerically minoritized white people are quite conscious of their racialization and that race is experienced by them as a daily reality.[22] Karyn McKinney explored the ways in which college youth negotiate and disavow the privileges of whiteness as part of everyday life.[23] Thandeka contended that as children "learn to be white" they are exposed to a form of abuse that strips away other forms of human relations.[24] Joel Olson demonstrated that whiteness is intricately bound to U.S. notions of citizenship, arguing that there is no contradiction between the constitutional ideal of freedom and the peculiar institution of slavery because the freedom of whites has long been made through the unfreedom of others.[25]

The sprawlingly diverse nature of these works suggests two things: the vibrancy of the field and the near universal reach of white supremacy. That is, over the past two decades whiteness has become a critical analytic, prying open new sites of inquiry within traditionally recognized disciplines. Moreover, the power and effects of white supremacy are not exceptions to the rule. Rather, they are the often-unseen cornerstone of cultural production, legitimized epistemologies, and the experience of everyday life.

While it developed out of various ethnic, gender, and class studies, critical whiteness studies is strikingly different from these fields. In contrast to efforts that work to examine marginalized communities and provide a corrective to histories of oppression, critical whiteness studies is a complementary force, what one may call a form of privilege studies, looking to how, without conscious recognition, race shapes the experiences and imaginings of whites. This difference between critical whiteness studies and traditional ethnic, gender, and class studies cannot be overlooked. Critical whiteness studies has developed a set of tenets that can work in tandem with the goals of these other fields. Perhaps first and foremost, whiteness has been positioned as the norm against which other social positions are measured, judged, and often found wanting. For instance, consider how European and Euro-American histories and cultural traditions form the basis for consecrated cultural capital vis-à-vis notions of cultural literacy and standardized testing.[26] Significantly, critical whiteness studies has also contended that while whiteness may be highly visible to other racialized communities, it often remains invisible to those who share in its benefits.[27] Through a long history and massive accumulation of privileges, white people often consider themselves nonracialized, normal, and merely human. The functional invisibility of whiteness blinds those invested in it from seeing the world as it is, their social locations of privilege, and the lived experiences of others. Charles Mills has argued that such invisibility and blindness foster an *"inverted epistemology, an epistemology of ignorance, a particular pattern of localized and global cognitive dysfunctions (which are psychologically and socially functional), producing the ironic outcome that whites will in general be unable to understand the world they themselves have made."*[28] This dynamic hinders empathetic connections and coalitionist efforts for liberation. Together, these first two tenets of critical whiteness studies expose how white people both occupy the position as the racial ideal and fail to see themselves as racialized.

Critical whiteness studies actively works to unmask this system, making whiteness visible and strange.[29] But as noted earlier, whiteness is not invisible to everyone. Whiteness is entrenched in a legacy of terror and violence, often hypervisible only to its potential targets. For instance, while people of color have policed their behaviors to avoid the violences of white supremacy—lynching, the police and courts, and social geographies—those invested in whiteness are unable to see and recognize how whiteness can be associated with terror. Indeed, as Ruth Frankenberg has noted, whites often deploy discursive repertoires to script people of color as dangerous, a move that elides a very real history of race violence.[30] Critical whiteness studies also exposes how whiteness benefits from seemingly race-neutral social policies. For instance, as Gil Scott Heron's humorous and telling 1974 song/spoken word piece "Whitey on the Moon" exposes, national investments in the space program as opposed to Earth-bound poverty have a disparate economic impact on communities of color wherein wealth is redistributed to the military-industrial complex and the largely white wealthy and upper-middle class.[31] Meanwhile, the benefits never truly trickle down to the U.S. poor, disproportionately made up of people of color. Ultimately, many critical whiteness scholars have called for the abolition of whiteness as a system of racial meaning and privilege. Together, these innovations form the foundation of critical whiteness studies and in tandem with the study of aggrieved communities provide an analytic framework to foster the struggle for social justice.

Despite the vast growth in the field over the past two decades, critical whiteness studies has faltered in addressing the Chicana/o relationship to whiteness and white supremacy. In part, this stems from critical whiteness studies' reliance on the black-white binary. Growing out of the intellectual tradition of African American studies, whiteness has been largely theorized and examined as a set of logics and encoded experiences constructed against the specific histories and representations of African Americans.[32] The rigidity of this paradigm has caused a twofold problem for Chicanas/os within critical whiteness studies. First, they have been positioned as people of color without difference from African Americans. Such a move erases the historical specificity of oppression. Moreover, as Juan Perea has argued, subsuming Mexican Americans within the black pole of the dyad elides the tension between African Americans and Chicanas/os as well as other communities of color.[33] For example, as Laura Gómez has demonstrated, in nineteenth-century New Mexico, Mexican Americans owned Indigenous slaves and served on juries when such rights were withheld from Natives and African Americans.[34] Moreover, failing to recognize the differential racialization of African Americans and Chicanas/os hinders analysis of the potentials and limits of coalitionist struggle, as evidenced in the recent spate of innovative research on black-brown relations during the twentieth-century U.S. freedom struggles.[35] Nor can such a conflation account for cases of African American anti-immigrant, anti-Latina/o organizing, such as the Crispus Attucks Brigade.[36] Clearly these examples expose the limits of blanketly applying the black-white binary to all people of color.

In contrast, the black-white binary also fails when scholars all too often position Chicanas/os as off-white or near-white. Simply positioning Mexican Americans as an off-white (but soon to be wholly white) ethnic immigrant community fails in several ways.[37] Notably, not all

Mexican Americans are immigrants or even recent descendants of immigrants. Historically and culturally, they have ties to lands in the United States that predate Anglo-American presence. Scripting them as immigrants perpetuates a key white supremacist narrative that these scholars try to dismantle.[38] Moreover, as Ian Haney López has argued, the immigrant model fails because it assumes a teleology of assimilation.[39] Indeed, after over 160 years as citizens in the United States, Mexican Americans have not simply traded in their ethnic identity for the privileges of whiteness. This notion that Chicanas/os are simply off-white fundamentally ignores the "replenished ethnicity" caused by chain migration, transnational movements across generations, the shared two-thousand-mile border, the history of U.S. imperialism, and the phenotypic markedness of many Mexican Americans.[40] Thus, while critical whiteness scholarship has primarily emerged from the black-white binary, Perea, Haney López, and others have contended that such a rigid system does not account for other communities of color. One cannot simply substitute Chicanas/os, Asian Americans, or Native peoples for black in the calculus of American race relations. Rather than conceptualizing racialization as monolithic and unidirectional, proceeding from blackness to whiteness, it is imperative to recognize that whiteness is multiply constituted, often contradictory, and contingent upon its various Others. Indeed, Charles Park's work on Asian Americans and the model minority myth illustrates how whiteness is offered, withheld, and constructed through a community's positioning within consumer culture. Park and Arlene Dávila, author of *Latinos Inc.*, model how white supremacy targets Asian Americans and U.S. Latinos in fundamentally different ways than African Americans.[41] Ultimately, while these communities may share common experiences and elements of representation, they are not without difference. These aggrieved communities experience their relationship to white power in unique ways.[42] Despite this fact, critical whiteness studies has lacked a sustained interrogation of whiteness as constructed against the experiences and representations of Chicanas/os.

Arguably, Andrea Smith has offered the most innovative model for examining the multifaceted nature of white supremacy. In an attempt to rethink organizing by women of color, Smith recognizes the limitations of extrapolating the black-white binary to other communities of color.

However, she simultaneously cautions against a wholesale rejection of this binary as a paradigm. For Smith, diverse communities of struggle owe much to the efforts of African Americans and the lessons from examining oppression and power vis-à-vis the black-white binary. Indeed, Smith argues that to jettison the binary would obscure "the centrality of the slavery logic in the system of white supremacy, which is *based on a black/white binary*."[43] Rather, developing a more pliable and productive model, Smith replaces a rigid racial binary (black-white) with a set of three interlocking binaries based not solely on group identities of *race* but on oppressive *tactics*. These binaries form the pillars of white supremacy. The pillar of *slavery/capitalism* positions African Americans as property and labor, always either owned or ownable by plantations in years past or the prison-industrial complex today.[44] The pillar of *colonization/genocide* describes the relationships of Indigenous peoples to white supremacy. In this pillar, the genocide of Natives and images of the vanishing/vanished Indian underwrite the historic and continuing occupation of Native lands. Smith's final pillar, *Orientalism/war*, extends Edward Said's concept to explore how romantic, barbaric, and timeless notions of Other countries and peoples often undergird U.S. wars of empire. Notably, while Smith's binaries expose the oppressive workings of white supremacy, the racial roots of these binaries remain apparent, for these systems work and become expressed in specific ways to disparate aggrieved communities.

Smith's three-pillar model holds much potential for scholar-activists in at least three ways. First, she rightly recognizes that while diverse communities may be oppressed through a system of white supremacy, they are not oppressed in the same ways. The honest recognition of these differences is a critical step for coalition building, for the conflation of oppression may lead aggrieved communities to compete in what Smith has called the "oppression Olympics" or rank their suffering in what Chris Abani has called the "hierarchy of pain."[45] In such competitions, the only winner can be white supremacy. Second, the three-pillar model illustrates how communities of color may actively participate in the oppression of others through supporting white supremacy of a different pillar. For instance, Smith notes how Native peoples have joined the army to fight in imperialist wars structured through Orientalism. Moreover, African Americans have claimed the proverbial forty acres and a mule without recognizing that the forty acres originally belonged to Indigenous peoples.[46] While difficult, recognizing sites of complicity aides in fostering a multifront war against white supremacy. Finally, while she does not explicitly explore this dynamic, Smith's three-pillar model rests upon and exposes the linkage between cultural imaginings and the material experiences of oppression. The racial scripts of African Americans as irresponsible and criminal underpin the logics of slavery and the capitalist venture of the prison-industrial complex. Similarly the representation of always already vanishing Indians and exotic "Orientals" secures the racial logics of settler colonialism and wars of empire.

Despite the benefits of the three-pillar model, Smith's paradigm is also significant for who and what it does not account for. One must simply ask, where do Chicanas/os fit within the three pillars? Initially, because these pillars easily find root in racial binaries, one could easily argue that Chicanas/os have been elided from this model or perhaps (as Smith briefly suggests) have experienced the wars of Orientalism firsthand.[47] However, the strength of the three-pillar model is that it elucidates the *tactics* of white supremacy, not its *targets*, who may at times be coconspirators as well. That is, Smith's model emphasizes *how* white supremacy operates. Underscoring the means of racial oppression exposes the unique and multifaceted relationship Chicanas/os have historically had to whiteness and white supremacy.

Arguably, Chicanas/os have been positioned in each of the three pillars of white supremacy.[48] One may question such an assertion, arguing that Chicanas/os did not undergo the particular brutalization of chattel slavery. However, Smith's model links slavery to capitalism through the ownership and control of workers' bodies either in the private sector or in the ever-expanding reach of the prison-industrial complex.[49] Historically, Chicanas/os have experienced the force of this pillar as exploited laborers in factories, fields, and company towns. Moreover, one should not overlook the enslavement of poor, Indigenous Mexicans in the late nineteenth- and early twentieth-century regime of Porfirio Díaz, a brutal venture that grew the wealth of American investors such as William Randolph Hearst.[50] In the twentieth- and twenty-first-century United States, Chicana/o bodies occupy a disproportionate presence in the prison-industrial complex. Moreover, with the ongoing criminalization of immigration, Mexican and Central American migrants fill detention centers across the United States today. As much Chicana/o studies scholarship would suggest, Chicanas/os have also experienced the second pillar: colonization/genocide. During the nineteenth century, the Texas Revolution, the U.S.-Mexico War, the influx of squatters, and the impact of functionally corrupt legal system stripped away Mexican Americans of their lands and rights in the U.S. Southwest.[51] Beyond these formal acts of conquest, Mexico also faced many filibustering expeditions by Anglo-Americans.[52] Clearly, it must be recognized those lands belonged to Indigenous peoples prior to Mexican colonization. However, we must simultaneously recognize Chicana/o ancestry includes Indigenous peoples from both sides of the current U.S.-Mexico border.[53] The third pillar, Orientalism/war, hardly needs discussion in its relationship to Chicanas/os today. Romantic depictions of Mexico and a legacy of nativist discourse have combined to depict Mexico as a prosthetic frontier and Chicanas/os as perpetually foreign.

Placing Chicana/o history in relation to these three pillars, if imperfectly so, does not suggest that Chicanas/os have been oppressed greater than other aggrieved communities in the "oppression Olympics." Nor does this mean that Smith's three pillars are insufficient because they do not fully account for Chicanas/os. Quite the contrary: Smith's model exposes the complexity of Chicana/o relationship to white supremacy. Historically, Chicanas/os have had a unique, multifaceted, and complex relationship to whiteness: recognized as legally white yet considered socially nonwhite, claims to both immigrant and native heritages, experiencing multiple pillars of white supremacy. For these reasons and others, I propose a sustained dialogue between Chicana/o studies and critical whiteness studies to map out the reaches and particularities of whiteness on the border. But first we must account for Chicana/o studies and the whiteness problem.

The Challenge of Whiteness in Chicana/o Studies

While critical whiteness studies has faced a theoretical, paradigmatic problem in the form of the black-white binary, Chicana/o studies has encountered a set of historical, material issues that have complicated Chicana/o positioning vis-à-vis white supremacy. Until recently, these factors have worked together to hinder the examination of whiteness within Chicana/o studies. First, the wide-ranging racial heritage of Mexican Americans and phenotypic diversity has complicated Chicana/o studies interventions in the whiteness debates.[54] Historically, Mexican Americans have claimed a varied racial ancestry, including mestizo, Indigenous, African, and Spanish lineages. Moreover, they are a phenotypically diverse community. Arguably this varied physical appearance has contributed to Chicanas/os being positioned as nonwhite, off-white, and white depending upon the historical, theoretical, and political exigencies. Indeed, for a minority of the community, the acquisition of appropriate forms of capital and the often dubious claim of pure Spanish ancestry have led to strategic positioning of whiteness both in the mid-nineteenth century as well as today. Critical and observant readers will immediately note that other aggrieved communities are phenotypically diverse and that the legacy of passing in the African American community may be a parallel to the Mexican American "Spanish myth" or "fantasy heritage."[55] I do not completely disagree. However, the ability of Chicanas/os to be simultaneously positioned as and position themselves as white, off-white, and nonwhite has fomented challenges for the community in responding to white supremacy. Moreover, such phenotypic diversity has created challenges in analysis. This is evidenced in Tomás Almaguer's groundbreaking multiracial study of the history of white supremacy in nineteenth-century California. In his effort to account for the group positioning of Mexican Americans, he foregrounds them as a racial group. However, the disparities in experience are quickly apparent:

> The treaty of Guadalupe Hidalgo enabled Mexicans to obtain U.S. citizenship rights in 1849. Citizenship carried with it suffrage, which empowered Mexican elites to politically challenge Anglo control in areas of Mexican concentration. The citizenship rights Mexicans came to enjoy, though often circumvented, nevertheless protected them from the more onerous discriminatory legislation enacted against other racialized groups.
>
> The claimed European descent of the Mexican ranchero elite, the so-called *gente de razon* (literally, "people of reason"), also facilitated the assimilation of segments of the upper class into European American society. . . . In sharp contrast, the Mexican working class was generally viewed like other racialized groups. Their degraded class status, combined with their inability to claim "pure" European ancestry, contributed to Anglo perceptions that they were unassimilable and certainly unworthy of intermarrying.[56]

Note how Almaguer's analysis treats U.S. Mexicans as an ethnoracial group in the first paragraph and then quickly explains in the following paragraph that members of this community bore disparate relationships to white supremacy. This is not a limit of Almaguer's analytical think-ing, for he clearly understands that differences in physical appearance and economic ability caused darker-skinned working-class Mexican Americans to be treated differently than lighter-skinned, landed Californio elites, who were otherwise their dispossessed countrymen. Despite his repeated recognition of these disparities, one can readily see the tension in Almaguer's language. Deploying "Mexican" as a national-cum-racial category simultaneously seeks to and fails to encapsulate the vast array of experiences within the group.

A second but related factor, Mexican Americans are inheritors of at least two racial systems. In the United States, race is often conceptual-ized through a system of hypodescent wherein the category of white occupies the position of purity. Even a modicum of nonwhite ancestry makes the individual part of the nonwhite community. This racial logic is popularly referred to as the one-drop rule.[57] The U.S. racial order re-lies on a fiction of purity and rigid classification that allows little room for mixed-race peoples and interracialism. Simultaneously, Chicanas/os are the direct or indirect inheritors of the racial system of colonial New Spain and Latin America. In contrast to the United States, Mexico has long recognized racial and cultural mixture through the concept of mes-tizaje. As Martha Menchaca, Douglas Cope, and others have noted, New Spain maintained an elaborate caste system to account for race mixture in the colonial era.[58] While such a system offers a broader range of pos-sibilities for identification, it is not necessarily more egalitarian.[59] From the caste system of the colonial era to today, whiteness as lightness is still privileged in Mexico and the rest of Latin America. Indeed, beyond just inheritors of two racial systems, Chicanas/os have been historically marked by two trajectories of racial formation. As inheritors of these two systems, Chicanas/os face the challenge of white privilege within and outside of their community. That is, Chicanas/os have historically negotiated and contested the U.S. system of white supremacy. However, the Chicana/o community has also been marked by the history of light skin privilege. Complicating matters further, as suggested by the writ-ings of nineteenth-century California writer María Amparo Ruiz de

Burton, Mexican Americans entered the U.S. racial order at the same time whiteness was codified with its modern meanings.

A third complicating factor in examining whiteness in Chicana/o studies, Mexican Americans have been treated as an ethnic and a racial community. Indeed, scholars have actively debated which paradigm more accurately applies.[60] While both are socially constructed, racial categorization relies on a set of arbitrary biological, phenotypic features (skin tone, hair texture, etc.). In contrast, ethnicity is determined through cultural features (belief systems, cultural practices, traditions, etc.). Although these identity categories seem simply defined, Mexican Americans can be positioned in both. Indeed, one can trace the tension between ethnic and racial categorization in the above example of Almaguer's work.[61] Ultimately, however, this goes well beyond the effectiveness of analytical discourse. In relationship to whiteness and dominant systems of power, these paradigms and their differences are critically important. The ethnic paradigm allows for transformation through assimilation wherein Mexican Americans are off-but-soon-to-be-white. As Michael Omi and Howard Winant have suggested, there are significant drawbacks to the ethnicity model. For instance, such a paradigm undergirds calls for community "uplift" via assimilation and pulling oneself up by the proverbial bootstraps.[62] Race, as a biological category, is treated as an immutable fact rather than the social fiction it is.[63] Such a paradigm suggests that Mexican Americans are not and never will be seen as white regardless of phenotypic markers. Significantly, since the rise and fall of the U.S. civil rights movements of the 1960s and 1970s, racial essentialism has been largely repackaged as cultural difference. Mapping the effects of historical racial discrimination onto a cultural paradigm undergirds what Haney López has termed the "immigrant analogy" and its failures, for "under this conflation . . . group differences in social standing and economic success are explained as a function of group attributes or failings, not social prejudices or structural advantages and disadvantages."[64] Significantly, examining Mexican American as a racial or ethnic identity raises the question of how paradigms of whiteness, long fashioned against a racial Other, become translated for ethnically othered communities. Arguably, since Mexican Americans fit into racial and ethnic categorization imperfectly, Mexican Americans can be othered in both ways, thus suggesting that whiteness is not simply about racial differences.

Finally, during the mid-nineteenth century, Mexican Americans were legally classified as white but rendered socially nonwhite. This nonalignment between legal and social race classification has fostered unique challenges for Mexican Americans working against white supremacy. At times, being classified as legally white secured privileges unavailable to other racialized communities.[65] However, as Ignacio García and others have suggested, contrary to expectations being legally white also foreclosed access to race privileges and citizenship rights in other ways. The Mexican American legally codified equality reinstantiated de facto segregation and social injustice. For instance, in early twentieth-century Texas, Mexican Americans were often excluded from jury service, a key component of full participatory citizenship. State and local officials argued that because Mexican Americans were white they could not rely on the Equal Protection Clause of the Fourteenth Amendment, which purported to guarantee rights for African Americans. Moreover, they argued that because Mexican Americans were white they were already being judged by a jury of their peers: non-Mexican whites.[66] All this against a backdrop of racial segregation and social inequality. In contrast, African Americans legal and social race positioning did align. As unquestionably nonwhite, African Americans could deploy the Equal Protection Clause as a strategy for justice. For many years Mexican Americans, legally white, lacked the necessary supporting legal theory to contest their social discrimination. Again, this is not to suggest a heightened form of victimization or oppression. Mexican American status of "white but not equal" complicated Chicana/o strategies for justice because of their unique relationship to white supremacy.[67] Notably, legal whiteness and attempts to follow a "whiteness strategy" fostered divisions between African Americans and Mexican Americans engaged in civil rights struggles.[68] Perhaps such legal positioning and its resultant divisions is one reason for why many scholars have identified Mexican Americans as off-but-soon-to-be-white. Combined with phenotypic diversity of the community, this is quite a complicating factor.

Clearly these factors do not form an all-inclusive set that shapes Mexicans' and Mexican Americans' unique relationship to whiteness in the United States. One could also consider the impact of varying immigration generations and citizenship claims. Together, these factors obfuscate a simple analysis of Mexican American positioning vis-à-vis white supremacy. It is not enough to say that Mexican-descent peoples have had the benefits of legal whiteness when their social nonwhiteness has so evidently undercut such standing. Moreover, it is insufficient to say that Mexicans and Mexican Americans have historically been targets of white supremacy without also recognizing Mexico's own system of white supremacy. However, these factors are not merely a problem, a hindrance to the examination of white supremacy's effect on the lives of Mexican-descent peoples in the United States. Rather, they also signal an opportunity. The intersection of Chicana/o studies and critical whiteness studies is a dynamic place, a crossroads that marks myriad ways in which a community has been targeted by and negotiated white supremacy.

Despite the interplay of these complicating factors, Chicana/o studies has a long history of examining and contesting white supremacy. Indeed, the previous pages would not have been possible without such efforts. However, only a limited range of works have explicitly theorized or addressed whiteness, let alone whiteness as an ideological formation. Arguably, Chicana/o studies has engaged in several distinct strategies to deal with the challenges of white supremacy and whiteness. Notably, prior to the formalization of Chicana/o studies as a field, resistive cultural production from the early twentieth-century heroic border corridos to the cultural nationalist rhetorics of the movement years and beyond have worked to actively make legible and contest white supremacy.[69] For instance, consider how the narrator of Corky Gonzales's well-known Chicano movement poem "I Am Joaquín" resists the forces of Melting Pot assimilation. He refuses to dissolve "into the melting pot / to disappear in shame" for he ultimately proclaims, "I SHALL ENDURE! / I WILL ENDURE!"[70] Moreover, "El Plan Espiritual de Aztlán" rejected the foundational white supremacist narrative of Manifest Destiny by articulating historical precedence through claiming a Chicano-Aztec lineage.[71] These texts and others worked to raise Chicana/o cultural consciousness, yes, but as a means of undoing the psychological colonization of white supremacy located in the schools.[72] Such a reading does not suggest that core Chicana/o studies texts are part and parcel of critical whiteness studies, a truly appropriative move. Rather, such texts may be used to develop the archaeological foundations for later intersections between the two fields. Moreover, one may notice that these examples emerge from the artistic and activist work of el movimiento and not traditionally recognized academic scholarship. Here, one may suggest that Chicana/o studies grassroots origins may have been ahead of professional critics.

At another potential intersection between the fields, many Chicana/o studies scholars have sought to examine machinations of white supremacy against the marginalization of Mexican Americans. Whether concerned with material and social relations like in Neil Folely's *White Scourge*, David Montejano's *Anglos and Mexicans in the Making of Texas*, and Tomás Almaguer's *Racial Fault Lines* or turning to the realm of the symbolic such as Arnoldo de León's *They Called Them Greasers* and William Nericcio's *Tex{t}-Mex*, these works all deploy at least one common conceptual move: they treat Mexican-descent peoples as undeniably nonwhite, the Mexican Other to the white economic and social policies as well as the white imagination. Because it emerges from and seeks to examine the function of social nonwhiteness, this approach depicts white supremacy as something that one stands outside of and must resist. In this way, Mexican-descent peoples are figured as the objects of oppression. With the exception of *Tex{t}-Mex*, these studies do not engage the thornier strategies of white supremacy that rely upon romantic depictions or benevolent attitude toward Mexicans. For obvious reasons, this is a crucial paradigm for decoding the hegemony of whiteness. However, it fails to make intellectual room for more complex Mexican American negotiations of whiteness and white supremacy.

A departure from previous approaches, some scholars have forged an intersection with critical whiteness studies through analyses of the historic positioning of Mexican-descent peoples as legally white. These works do not elide the ascription of social nonwhiteness. Rather, these efforts have sought to tease out the tension therein, exploring how the legal categorization as white has simultaneously offered forth and restricted access to rights and privileges. For instance, Ian Haney López's *White by Law* notes that Mexicans were able to apply for U.S. citizenship when other socially minoritized communities were not.[73] Legal scholars such as Michael Olivas and historians such as Ignacio García have unpacked the significance of *Hernandez v. Texas*, wherein Mexican Americans challenged their exclusion from jury service, arguing that while they were white they were "a class apart."[74] Olivas, García, and others built upon and advanced earlier efforts that took as a point of departure the social nonwhiteness of Mexican-descent peoples, a crucial move away from and complement to the previous approach to whiteness within Chicana/o studies.

The final approach emerging from the intersection of Chicana/o studies and critical whiteness studies is evidenced in the scholarly works situated in Chicana/o studies that actively engage and theorize whiteness not solely as a social or legal position but also as an ideological and political category. Here, whiteness is recognized for shaping its practitioners' abilities to know and act within the world. Notably, works that deploy this approach seek to identify and uproot the ideological, symbolic, and material machinations of whiteness. A model of this can be found in Angie Chabram-Dernersesian's "On the Social Construction of Whiteness within Selected Chicana/o Discourse." Chabram-Dernersesian examines a select group of Chicano movement and post-movement texts to demonstrate how Chicana/o cultural workers have depicted whiteness on the "other side" (read: outside) of the community to make legible the history of white supremacy.[75] Her essay ultimately underscores how the internal colonial paradigm's deployment of us/them logic sought to name and hold accountable a history of racial oppression. Moreover, Chabram-Dernersesian incisively explores how the specter of whiteness as constructed on the "inside" of the Chicana/o community was used to police possible political identities.[76] In another effort to explicitly place critical whiteness studies and Chicana/o studies in dialogue, Edén Torres has explored how many contemporary Chicana/o students have become depoliticized in the post-movement years.[77] For Torres, many students who have taken advantage of the gains of el movimiento become invested in the logics that undergird whiteness. While engaging and extending the work of the first three approaches outlined here, *Whiteness on the Border* is most firmly situated within this final intersection illustrated through the work of Chabram-Dernersesian and Torres. In the vein of critical whiteness studies, this project recognizes that whiteness is more than phenotype or social categorization. Whiteness is also an ideological and discursive formulation, one that must be made legible if it is ever to be dismantled.

Over the course of its history, Chicana/o studies as a field has implicitly and explicitly worked against the ideological underpinnings of white supremacy as manifested in the Mexican Problem and other narratives of the U.S. racial project. Since the early twentieth century, and arguably before, the Mexican Problem has scripted Mexican-descent peoples as indolent, unassimilable, and disloyal.[78] Indeed, in 1949 leftist author and activist Carey McWilliams argued that "in the vast library of books and documents about ethnic and minority problems in the United States, one of the largest sections is devoted to 'The Mexican Problem.'"[79] Responding to the scholarship of Manuel Gamio, Robert Redfield, and Paul S. Taylor and its resultant social policy, many early practitioners of Chicana/o studies sought to trouble the epistemological foundations that defined Mexicans, Mexican Americans, and Mexican immigrants as a problem. *Whiteness on the Border* advances those efforts beginning with a paraphrase of the African American writer Richard Wright and an intellectual exercise: I contend that "there isn't any Mexican Problem; there is only a white problem."[80] If the Mexican Problem is recognized as an outgrowth of whiteness and white racial hegemony (i.e., white supremacy), what might be found?

Working at the intersection of Chicana/o studies and critical whiteness studies turns the critical gaze away from the Mexican Problem and toward the social order that imagined it into existence. Here, it may be useful to place my paraphrase of Wright in conversation with the work of Gloria Anzaldúa. In an underexamined moment in her widely influential *Borderlands/La Frontera*, Anzaldúa links the construction of whiteness to the functions of Mexicans in the dominant imagination. In a direct address to white readers, she states, "We need you to make public restitution: to say that, to compensate for your own sense of defectiveness, you strive for power over us, you erase our history and our experience because it makes you feel guilty—you'd rather forget your brutish acts. . . . Admit that Mexico is your double, that she exists in the shadow of this country, that we are irrevocably tied to her. Gringo, accept the doppelganger in your psyche."[81] Anzaldúa's observation brings an undercurrent of previous Chicana/o studies scholarship to the surface. Instead of focusing on the representations of Mexican-descent people and how these have contributed to the psychological colonization of Chicanas/os, Anzaldúa contends that these representations are a function of whiteness. Taking this as a point of departure, I contend that cultural imaginings of Mexico, Mexicans, and Chicanas/os function as an Other to solidify notions of whiteness as Americanness. Let us return to the examples that opened this introduction. In the case of McCarthy's *Cities of the Plain*, after the death of the West, all-American cowboy John Grady Cole must venture south of the border to enter a frontier space that will allow him to enact chivalric ideals and confront the clear enemy, the knife-wielding pachuco pimp. In Creager's song, like so many others, the narrator's whiteness and masculinity—expressions of his Americanness—find escape in Mexican women, music, and tequila. On the streets of Houston, when anti-immigrant/anti-Latina/o protestors tell a young woman to go back home, they are dumbstruck to find that she is a citizen by birth. They can only repeat their command to go back home. These examples gesture toward the triangulated relationship between whiteness, Mexicanness, and the imagining of the U.S. nation-state as a racial state. While the first two instances demonstrate how whiteness is secured, the final encounter, the young woman on the streets of Houston—whom I should acknowledge as my life and intellectual partner, Sujey Vega—clearly demonstrates that such articulations of whiteness are not without contestation. And with that, we turn to a mapping of whiteness on the border.

Mapping Whiteness on the Border

When I first began working on this book years ago, one scholar asked if the whiteness under study was in any way unique or if there was just one form of whiteness. This has been a useful question that has propelled me in the following years. And as is often the case with such dichotomous questions, the answer refuses a simple taking of sides. While one could very well argue that white supremacy and whiteness are pervasive and demonstrate a global reach, this is far from suggesting that all manifestations of white supremacy and whiteness resemble each other. As Steve Garner has suggested, treating whiteness as an analytic as well as a set of power relations opens for scrutiny social dynamics in a variety of locations marked by their own historical contexts, from the United States and England to Latin America and the Caribbean.[82] In each of these cases who and how one is considered white vary along with the potential meanings of whiteness. *Whiteness on the Border* extends Garner's observation inward, arguing that a diverse, multiracial society with its own regionally specific histories may evidence diverse forms of whiteness. However, this is not to suggest that whiteness constructed against the Mexican Other is cut out of whole cloth with nothing in common with that of the black-white binary. Rather, as Smith argues, in a multiracial society, white supremacy (and whiteness) is manifested in a myriad of ways depending upon the racialized Other as well as the historical context and political exigencies. Importantly, however, these manifestations are all part of a larger fabric or system of racial hegemony. Thus, whiteness on the border is indelibly marked by representations of, treatments of, and engagements with Mexican-descent people, but it is also simultaneously inseparable from the broader national, racial projects. Therefore, we return to the two interlocking questions that mark the form and content of whiteness on the border as well as propel the inquiry at the heart of this book: How has whiteness been forged against a Mexican Other embodied in representations of Mexico, Mexicans, and Chicanas/os? How has the Mexican American positioning within the U.S. racial order and dominant imagination enabled and limited the United States to fashion the nation-state as a racial state?

Following the 2010 census, a spate of articles appeared noting that more Latinas/os self-identified as white.[83] The media inquired as to what this could mean for Latinas/os and the future of the United States: Are Latinas/os assimilating? Was the Mexican Problem (now the Latina/o Problem) nothing but a chimera?[84] These questions of Latina/o whiteness form the complementary opposite to those that have long lamented the unassimilability of U.S. Latinas/os. Importantly, this type of article is not new. An extension of those that suggest Latinas/os are the future of the Republican Party, they are little more than what Arlene Dávila has so aptly termed "Latino spin," the myriad practices through which "Latinos are inserted into numerous debates and into contemporary institutions are in fact racially implicated and coded and, more often than not, implicated in furthering normativity."[85] And it must be recognized that many Latinas/os critiqued these articles, pointing out that Latina/o ethnoracial identification is much more complicated.[86] While understanding how and why Latinas/os forge their social identities is critical, something else lurks below the surface of these "Are Latinas/os White?" articles. Whether Latinas/os are rendered an unassimilable problem or a whitening ethnic group, the question itself, its framing, and the positioning of Latinas/os as the cultural variable occlude and reinforce whiteness as the normative to which Dávila gestures. That is, if Latinas/os are not assimilating, it is into whiteness that they do not melt. If they are becoming white, Latinas/os are then rendered as achieving the normative position. Such logic functions as an enthymeme, a silent argument reliant upon an unstated premise, whiteness is American-ness. Only by extension, Latinas/os must be measured as assimilating, whether they be immigrants of multigenerational U.S. citizens. This is the logic of whiteness on the border.

As a phrase and a conceptual paradigm, "whiteness on the border" draws together and makes use of several meanings. At the most basic level, it suggests a linkage between the U.S.-Mexico border region and imaginings of U.S. national racial identity. While it describes a region marked by its own histories and racial dynamics, the border also occupies a key position in the national imagination. Thus, the border invoked is simultaneously material and symbolic, lived and textualized. Of course, the U.S.-Mexico border is a modern creation. The Border Patrol, the wall, and other iconic images are twentieth-century innovations of the U.S. racial national project. However, as will be elucidated in the next chapter, a racial border existed in the minds of U.S. whites long before the formalization of the U.S.-Mexico boundary line. This racial border predates and charges with meaning the national border. Moreover, drawing upon border theory, I deploy this phrasing to elicit notions of construction, policing, and transgression. Despite the wide array of popular and political claims to the contrary, borders are not fixed, natural entities demarcating in clear lines an *us* from a *them*.[87] However, as Alejandro Lugo has explored, with borders come border inspections.[88] Placing this meaning of border in conversation with whiteness evokes the ways in which whiteness is constructed, policed, and transgressed beside and against the Mexican Other. Finally, the border elicits the edge, the limit. In this way, "whiteness on the border" signals the precarious lines against which whiteness exists but that might also be its end. This signification gestures toward the vulnerabilities of whiteness, those that mark its potential for abolition. Together, these disparate meanings intersect to give significance to "whiteness on the border" and mark the trajectories of inquiry throughout this book.

While its approach is not all-encompassing, *Whiteness on the Border* excavates the relationship between whiteness, Mexicanness (as embodied in Mexico, Mexicans, and Chicanas/os), and diverse claims to and imaginings of Americanness. Here, Joel Olson's theorization of whiteness and citizenship provides both a foundation and a point of departure. Olson contended that the subordination of African-descent peoples gave material advantage and symbolic meaning to whiteness as a political category of citizenship: "In the formative years of American democracy, citizenship was in a very real sense proof that one was not and could not become a slave. Given the racial character of chattel slavery in the United States, its antitheses, citizenship, was also racialized."[89] For Olson, African Americans functioned as the critical anticitizen against which white citizenship could be manifested. A similar yet distinct argument can be made for Mexican-descent peoples. Raymond Rocco and Mae Ngai have argued that despite immigration status or generation of U.S. ancestry, Chicanas/os are scripted as "perpetually foreign" and "alien citizens."[90] Robin Dale Jacobson further documents this inscription of foreignness in her analysis of anti-immigrant rhetorics. As Jacobson demonstrates, not only are immigrants racialized, but through what she terms the "association bridge" all Mexican-descent people are viewed as undocumented immigrants.[91] Taking direction from Olson, one must recognize that such rhetorical maneuvers do not simply fashion Mexicanness as Other, but simultaneously construct whiteness as unquestionably American, accruing and securing material and symbolic advantages in the process. However, a difference must also be elucidated. The proximity to Mexico and its accrued symbolic meaning reinforces the lie that Mexican-descent people are always already from a nearby elsewhere. This renders not simply Mexicans and Mexican Americans as anticitizens but also Mexico as an anti–United States.

Here, it may be useful to explore a single cultural artifact as a manifestation of whiteness on the border. Produced by D. W. Griffith and written and directed by Christy Cabanne, 1915 *Martyrs of the Alamo: The Birth of Texas* is the first filmic rendering of the infamous siege. Released a few years after the historical restoration of the Alamo began, *Martyrs* articulated the key racial-national components of whiteness on the border. One could easily say that *Martyrs* did for Texas what Griffith's *Birth of a Nation* did for the United States—it emplotted a national narrative in stark racial terms. One must wonder why *Martyrs* has received so much less attention by cultural critics when compared to *Birth*: does this suggest a blindness to the U.S. racial project beyond the black-white binary? Unsurprisingly, *Martyrs* fashions American whiteness through a binaristic contrast to the film's Mexicans. Mexicans are cruel; Americans are benevolent. The Mexican army dresses and prepares for battle with a formal pomp; the Americans—nearly all bedecked in coonskin caps—embody rugged individualism and masculinity. Reminiscent of the sexual anxieties in *Birth of a Nation*, Anglo women are subject to the harassment of Mexican soldiers. "Chivalrous" by nature, Anglo men such as the film's Silent Smith become the protectors of white womanhood. Notably, this racial-sexual dynamic continues throughout the film. After the siege, the brownfaced and thus swarthy Santa Anna takes Silent Smith's blonde love interest prisoner. When the Texas rebels defeat Santa Anna's troops at San Jacinto, they do not simply liberate the land but also secure white womanhood signified in Smith's blonde lady friend.[92]

Beyond these clear manifestations of whiteness being forged beside and against a racialized Mexican Other, a more subtle discursive maneuver is at work. The film deploys the unstable, anachronistic terms of Mexicans and Americans to structure the conflict. This is, perhaps, no surprise. One could point out that Tejanos fought alongside Anglo-Texan troops against Santa Anna, a common critique of Texas's nationalist amnesia. However, something else is also at play here. By rendering the Texas fighters as Americans, the film occludes their positions as immigrants, settlers, rebels, and Mexican citizens. National terms are inscribed upon an already oversimplified racial depiction of the conflict. But this logic goes beyond suggesting that Americans are white and Mexicans are not. Describing Texas rebels as American relocates San Antonio and the Alamo from Mexico to the United States. These Americans are no insurgent forces defying their national government and military. They are armed protectors of the United States, even when they are technically outside of the nation. This logic is underscored by Annette Marie Rodríguez's observation that the film's depiction of the siege—Mexicans storming the walls and sneaking through tunnels—becomes the precursor to more contemporary images of immigration as invasion.[93] Of course, Mexico cannot invade itself. Thus ascribing

Americanness to Texas rebels makes the Alamo—like Silent Smith's blonde love—a site of national vulnerability, a trope that we will see again. Ultimately, Griffith's iconic positioning in many historians' interrogations of white supremacy and the fact that his filmic oeuvre details encounters with both African Americans and Mexicans in the nationalist imaginings of the United States underscore that whiteness is constituted by Mexicanness as well as by blackness.

Of course, *Martyrs of the Alamo* would not be made with such earnest, straightforward racism today. Things change even as they stay the same. However, by recognizing the discursive shift of the late twentieth century, one may not find the end of or disinvestment in whiteness on the border but rather its remarkable continuity and entrenchment. Nativist cultural workers continue to draw upon the age-old tropes of Mexicans and Mexican Americans as unclean, lazy, and disloyal. Lest some think that this exists only as a fringe element, these discursive practices have become part (or stayed part) of mainstream politics. Moreover, from fiction like Cormac McCarthy's Border Trilogy to television shows like *Border Wars*, Mexico and the borderlands are still depicted as a lawless frontier in need of civilization. Indeed, the image of the sensual Mexican woman yearning for the love of an all-American (white) man (cowboy) remains a dominant trope in popular culture today.

However, as noted earlier, claims to whiteness as Americanness are not without contestation. One may read Ray González's "Ghost of John Wayne" against the racial logics at play in *Martyrs*. In González's short story, many white residents of San Antonio embrace the possibility that John Wayne's ghost haunts the Alamo's grounds, yet they hostilely reject the possibility that the ghosts of Mexican soldiers who actually died there may wander eternally as well.[94] Such an intervention troubles the notion that the site is sacred ground for one nation or one race only. Moreover, the residents' reactions to the possibility of Mexican ghosts suggest that the conflict at the Alamo is far from over—the fighting has just taken a different form. Indeed, there is a palpable, sad irony in how residents would reject the souls of actual soldiers only to embrace the ghost of a movie star.

The long-standing and pervasive practice of deploying the Mexican Other to fashion whiteness and Americanness presents significant challenges for scholars and activists working to examine and dismantle it.

As many will note, contemporary professional historical monographs rarely attempt to cover such a vast period of time. Therefore, with the exception of the following chapter, this book exclusively examines manifestations of whiteness on the border in the twentieth and twenty-first centuries because like the ghosts of Mexican soldiers in González's story, many today refuse to acknowledge, let alone counteract, anti-Mexican racism and its resulting whiteness unless it takes the form of something explicit or unless it is located in the past like that of *Martyrs*. Consider two brief examples. Would the 1990s Taco Bell Chihuahua or the popular 1960s Frito Bandito—with his refrain of "Ai, yi, yi, yi! I am the Frito Bandito. I like Fritos corn chips. I love them, I do. I want Fritos corn chips. I'll get them from you"—be looked upon favorably if they did not deploy a Mexican accent? Would anyone go to a restaurant if it were not named "Los Bandidos" but rather "The Thieves?"[95]

Whiteness on the Border is not an all-inclusive study of how whiteness has been fashioned against representations of Mexico, Mexicans, and Chicanas/os or how Chicana/o cultural workers have negotiated this terrain of whiteness. This work is a point of departure. While whiteness is an ideological and discursive formation, as noted before it often slips by unnoticed by its practitioners, rendered normative, invisible, the way things are, the way things should be. Thus, in order to work against whiteness on the border—the coterminous overlay and mapping of whiteness onto Americanness—scholars and activists must make expressions of whiteness legible. This books takes up that charge by demonstrating how deployments of the Mexican Other foster expressions of white benevolence, fear, fantasy, and desire. Notably, these are not merely emotions located within an individual's psychology. Rather, taking direction from Du Bois and Roediger, *Whiteness on the Border* looks to the symbolic, epistemic, and psychological wages of whiteness for the group. These expressions consolidate belonging and foster the "cognitive dysfunction" essential to maintaining less readily visible forms of white supremacy.[96] The question, then, emerges: where does one locate whiteness on the border and its myriad expressions?

Arguably, the power of whiteness on the border rests on its existence in a variety of social locations. Cultural workers across a range of political positions have long relied upon and deployed diverse tropes of the Mexican Other to meet their own ideological needs. Moreover, the endurance of whiteness on the border is also supported by the vast array of discursive locations from which it is regularly articulated. One can easily find the fashioning of whiteness against Mexico, Mexicans, and Chicanas/os, in film, literature, music, museums, historical texts, political speeches, and video games. The vastness of the locations and their corresponding differences in conventions and contexts suggest the flexible and diffused nature of whiteness on the border. However, the pervasiveness of this discursive constellation presents a methodological challenge. As a cultural critic, how does one read a political manifesto beside and against popular music or a film alongside the testimony found within an educational audit? These cultural manifestations are characterized by diverse genres, audiences, and conventions. Here, this book engages two strategies. First, the following chapter argues for and provides a model of reading tropologically. By focusing on tropic manifestations of white supremacy, the chapter traces both the continuity and change in the Mexican Other across a vast historical sweep. However, tropes also provide common sites of analysis where multiple texts can be opened in conversation. Second, after chapter 1, the remainder of the book turns to post-1945 articulations of whiteness as Americanness against the Mexican Other. These chapters emphasize historical and discursive contextualization as they each engage specific expressions of whiteness as Americanness.

Chapter 1 draws together a recent, growing body of scholarship that has broken critical ground in exploring the representations of Mexico, Mexicans, and Chicanas/os. Yet this is much more than a review of scholarship past. This chapter actively works against claims that white supremacy has softened in recent years as well as assertions that anti-Mexican attitudes are a relatively recent phenomenon divorced from the longue durée of the U.S. racial project. By tracing tropes of the Infernal Paradise, the Erotic, Exotic Mexicana, Mexican Lawlessness, and others across the nineteenth-century contact and conquest narratives, early twentieth-century film, and current manifestations, this chapter maps the various manifestations of the Mexican Other across time. Forging a genealogy of the Mexican Other demonstrates that while specific exigencies shape these representations, history is driven through with both continuity and change. After the genealogy, this chapter proposes that antiracist scholarship and education work against the amnesia that white supremacy requires by developing a practice of reading tropologically. The chapter then moves from a broad view to the specific forms that the Mexican Other may take. This working taxonomy of tropes of the Mexican Other explores their logics, illustrates examples across history, and theorizes their roles in constructing whiteness. With the genealogy and taxonomy established, this project turns to how these manifestations of the Mexican Other fashion specific aspects of the whiteness.

Chapter 2 examines how the Chicano nationalist discourse of Aztlán has been appropriated by anti-immigrant, anti-Latina/o activists since the late 1970s. This "nativist Aztlán" emplots fears, fantasies, and anxieties into a Chicano-identified narrative. Not only does the Aztlán-reconquista plot give narrative shape to anxieties of a cultural and political takeover in a way that appears nonracist, but it also fosters a sense of racial solidarity disguised as national solidarity. Critically, this chapter exposes how anti-immigrant discourses are bound to and shape anti-Latina/o practices as well. Building upon analyses of Patrick Buchanan's *State of Emergency*, Dave Arendt's *Reclaiming Aztlan*, and the 2008 Absolut Vodka controversy, this chapter locates the nativist Aztlán in Arizona's banning of ethnic studies in primary and secondary education.

While seeing whites as naturally just, innocent, and good has long been a component of the white racial frame, after the mid-twentieth-century racial break white Americans strove to see themselves as benevolent agents against injustice at home and abroad. Chapter 3 explores the logics of white saviorism in order to expose how seemingly antiracist or humanitarian acts may appropriate the oppression of Mexicans in order to assert whiteness and the United States as inherently good, all the while leaving the structures that allowed racial injustice to remain intact. This chapter interrogates how white saviorism operates and its dynamics are made legible through several historical and textual moments over the past seventy years. Analyses of the iconic diner scene from the novel and film *Giant* along with an examination of a historical case on which the scene may have been based illustrate the popular investment in white and American goodness vis-à-vis saviorism. Read with a critical eye, these moments expose how broad-based racial inequality was maintained as explicit and individual forms of bigotry were rejected as unjust and un-American. Turning to the 1960 film *The Magnificent Seven*, I contend that the logics of white saviorism are evidenced in and reinforce American exceptionalism and its imperialist impulses. Finally, the chapter turns to a contemporary moment wherein the state enacts and narrates a form of saviorism. Border Patrol rescue narratives cast the United States and its agents as benevolent, humanitarian actors fighting smugglers and saving migrants. The result of this savior narrative is the elision of economic and governmental policies that have fostered and exacerbated immigration and placed migrants' lives in danger. In all of these cases, representations of Mexicanness are deployed to fashion a robust benevolent whiteness that reinforces dominant narratives of American exceptionalism. Moreover, through tracing the troubling logics of white benevolence, this chapter illustrates how American exceptionalism shares many of benevolence's ideological precepts. Thus, white benevolence and American exceptionalism are triangulated against the Mexican Other, making legible how through notions of the national or individual good whiteness is made Americanness.

Chapter 4 interrogates perhaps the most challenging expression of whiteness on the border: white desire. Drawing upon the rich tradition in film, music, and literature of white Americans "loving" Mexico and Mexicanas, this chapter excavates the nationalist and racial logics at play in these acts of desire. While previous chapters establish how whites are positioned as American and above Mexicans in a racial hierarchy, chapter 4 illustrates that white desire presents a greater challenge because of the way it romances and "positively" renders the Mexican Other. However, analyzing a common dynamic found in Texas country music as well as the rhetorical work of cross-border matchmaking epitomized by "Cowboy Cupid" Ivan Thompson demonstrates that white desire is far from love. Rather, it is an expression of the U.S. racial project in sexual terms. Ultimately, this chapter draws on feminist theorizations of the politics of love to map other, antiracist engagements with Mexico, Mexicans, and Chicanas/os.

Prior to an interrogation of whiteness on the border, one must trace how Mexicanness has been imagined through the longue durée of the U.S. racial project. One must identify the disparate ways Mexicanness has been rendered in the white imagination. Here we turn to a genealogy and taxonomy of the Mexican Other.

1

What Did They Call Them after They Called Them "Greasers"?

A Genealogy and Taxonomy of the Mexican Other

> OSCAR MARTÍNEZ: Okay, Michael. Both my parents were born in
> Mexico. And, uh, they moved to the United States a year before I was
> born.
> MICHAEL SCOTT: Yeah.
> OSCAR: So I grew up in the United States.
> MICHAEL: Wow.
> OSCAR: My parents are Mexican.
> MICHAEL: Wow, that is a great story. That's the American Dream right
> there, right?
> OSCAR: Thank you.
> MICHAEL: So let me ask you, is there a term besides "Mexican" that
> you prefer? Something less offensive.
> OSCAR: Mexican isn't offensive.
> MICHAEL: Well, it has certain connotations.
> OSCAR: Like what?
> MICHAEL: Like, well, I don't know.
> OSCAR: What connotations, Michael?
> —"Diversity Day," *The Office*, season 1, episode 2

A basic precept of this critical endeavor: the figure of the Mexican Other has long been and continues to be central to the formation of whiteness on the border. For some, this may be a mundane statement—of course, there is a long tradition of Mexican stereotyping in the U.S. racial project. For others, this precept verges upon disciplinary and political heresy. As I began thinking through this project over the past few years, I spoke with family, friends, and colleagues. For some, the reaction was of obvious agreement. Others offered strenuous objections: "Really, aren't you overstating the matter. Whiteness was actually constructed against blackness. Historically, depictions of Mexican Americans have not been as central" or "Surely, attitudes about Mexicans, Mexican Americans, and Mexico have changed over the past two hundred years. You can't really lump these depictions together, can you?" Regarding the first objection, it rests on the logic of hierarchy. I would not advance the displacement of one pole of the racial dyad for another, substituting brown for black. Paraphrasing Richard Rodriguez, the heart of the U.S. racial imagination is a scary place to which no one should want to lay claim.[1] However, white supremacy has thrived through not simply a singular binary but a set of interlocking binaries that form a multidirectional network of differential racialization. This project simply seeks to identify one binary—brown-white—in contribution toward a larger antiracist scholarly effort. As for the second disciplinary response that attitudes toward Mexicans have shifted over time, the purpose of this chapter is to identify, describe, and theorize the figuration of the Mexican Other, offering a genealogy and a taxonomy that form the intellectual foundation for the critical analyses of later chapters. To do this, one may find a useful point of departure in the concluding pages of Arnoldo de León's critical study *They Called Them Greasers*.

In the conclusion of his study of Anglo-Texan attitudes toward their Mexican/Mexican American countrymen, de León finds significant changes in race relations in the twentieth century:

> Sometime in the fifteen years after World War II, attitudes toward race, "depravity," loyalty, and other aspects of prejudice underwent a visible change. . . . Legalized segregation ended, political mechanisms designed to obstruct voting toppled, and it became unpopular to be racist publically. . . . If our times are compared with the nineteenth century, Anglo Americans do not regard Mexican Americans as they did in the past. . . . Mexican Americans may no longer be suspected of being un-American, but ethnic slurs and racial epithets carry connotations that they are far from being WASPs. And even if Tejanos are no longer lynched, they are victims of psychological violence in the more subtle forms of discrimination.[2]

De León suggests that a broad-based Chicano movement and other freedom struggles as well as greater integration have led to improved relations. However, he is far from advancing the notion of a postracial utopian moment. He tempers his findings with another observation: "Still, many Anglos judge Mexican Americans *not by their character*, but by the difference they see between themselves and Tejanos."[3] How does one make meaning from de León's two-part conclusion? Are the two points inherently contradictory? Do they suggest a progress narrative where the dream of Martin Luther King that de León invokes through judging based on "character" has yet to be achieved?

It would be wise to situate de León's analysis within the framework Michael Omi and Howard Winant's concept of racial formation. Omi and Winant contended that race and racism were not fixed transhistorical forces. Race and racism are manifested out of specific historical moments and exigencies. In this way, the discourse and logics of race change over time. Thusly, according to Omi and Winant, following the civil rights struggles of the mid-twentieth century, overt racist discourse and acts have fallen from favor.[4] That is, explicit notions of white supremacy rooted in biological differences have largely given way to discourses of cultural and individual deficiencies that explain away racial inequalities. More recently, Winant has advanced the notion of the "racial break," a global realignment of the racial order wherein white supremacy has incorporated discourses of color blindness, meritocracy, and personal freedom to maintain and advance inequality.[5] Taking Omi and Winant's theorization into account, it is tempting to signify upon de León's title and ask, "What did they call them *after* they called them 'greasers'?" Or more aptly, "What do they call them now?" Embedded within these questions exists the dynamic tension between historical continuity and change.

In stating that the figure of the Mexican Other has long been and continues to be central to the formation of whiteness on the border, I am not suggesting that little has changed since the early nineteenth century. However, I am contending that scholars must not be swept away with the romance of historical change that could blind us to the longue durée of the U.S. racial project. Empire building and race making vis-à-vis white supremacy have been part of the United States since its inception, and together they form the U.S. racial project. While they have certainly changed modes of expression over the years—from settler colonialism and military conquest to economic imperialism and from biological to cultural and neoliberal legitimating discourses of white supremacy—the U.S. racial project continues today. Moreover, empire building and race making converge in whiteness on the border where whiteness is Americanness, and the nation-state is imagined as a racial state.

Reading de León in the context of the early twenty-first century, I cannot share his tempered optimism. It may well be déclassé to use racial pejoratives like "greaser," but as the epigraph from the popular television program *The Office* identifies and satirizes, those negative meanings have been attached to more neutral-sounding signifiers. That is, why use pejoratives like "greaser" when the negative connotations course through and charge "Mexican" with abundant racial meaning? In this way, it is not simply that Anglo-American racial attitudes have "softened" over time. Rather, in the post-break United States, white supremacy has disappeared into the air we breathe, making it more difficult to identify and thus more complicated to challenge. For example, when buying our first home in Maricopa County, Arizona, my partner and I noticed that several potential neighbors decorated their front yards with ceramic statues of sleeping Mexicans, eyes covered by a large sombrero and body wrapped in a serape. The neighborhood in which we purchased our first home used this iconic southwestern image of white supremacy on the paving stones for many of the houses built in the early 1980s. Today, the overtly racist trope of the lazy Mexican has been repackaged as lawn decoration and exhibitions of a southwestern aesthetic.

Despite the apparent "softening" of racial attitudes at the symbolic level, we must not overlook how Mexican-descent people remain subject to the various violent manifestations of white supremacy in the United States. In recent years, the United States has been embroiled in yet another immigration debate and its corresponding nativist backlash. States like Arizona, Indiana, and Alabama have begun instituting and enforcing their own immigration laws. In 2014, Sheriff Joe Arpaio and the Maricopa County Sheriff's Department, known for using a "volunteer posse," were found to have historically violated the constitutional rights of Latinas/os through years of racial profiling. Moreover, hate crimes against Latinas/os, particularly Mexican Americans, have

Figure 1.1. A paving stone with the sleeping Mexican motif illustrates how racialized depictions infiltrate mundane outdoor aesthetics.
Photo by author.

increased.[6] Consider the heart-rending story of David Ritcheson, a Mexican American teenager from Texas who in 2006 was beaten, tortured, and sodomized for five hours by two white high school students. After Ritcheson kissed a white girl, the assailants hurled racial slurs at him, sodomized him with PVC pipe, attempted to carve a swastika into Ritcheson's chest, and doused his body in bleach. The case made national headlines, and Ritcheson agreed to make his name public and testify before the U.S. House of Representatives. The lasting impact and trauma of the attack and being seen as "that kid" contributed to Ritcheson taking his own life a year after the event, signaling the way in which violence of the assault did not conclude in the early morning hours of April 22, 2006.[7] Should we not consider Ritcheson and many others as victims of lynching in the postracial era?[8] Doubters might suggest that I overreact—surely, these are but aberrant and abhorrent acts. My historically trained brethren may call me a "presentist." However, reading *They Called Them Greasers* in this context, I find de León's conclusion less a narrative of progress with teleological impulses toward a postracial utopia. Rather, in de León's final pages exists the dynamic tension between continuity and change, which function as the twin engines of historiography.

Importantly, the emphasis of change over continuity need not be a progressive narrative. Drawing upon Winant's theorization of the racial break and the endurance of white supremacy in the twenty-first century, Jodi Melamed offers an intellectual and political history of racial capitalism after World War II. Melamed examines literary texts to expose how writing by racially aggrieved communities can be deployed as part of official state antiracist projects that ultimately render invisible the oppressive link between race and capital. As Melamed traces the shifts from racial liberalism to liberal multiculturalism to neoliberal multiculturalism, the arc of historical change is far from progressive. Through its adaptations over the years, white supremacy has become harder to identify and contest.[9] In this way, Melamed finds common ground with Eduardo Bonilla-Silva and other scholars who have rightly noted that while white supremacy thrives today, it does so often under the radar of its beneficiaries—repackaged, it is embedded in the dominant cultural logics, making it more difficult to pinpoint and challenging to disrupt.

In order to contend that the figure of the Mexican Other has long been and continues to be central to the formation of whiteness on the border, this chapter is organized into two complementary sections. To begin, I offer a genealogy of the Mexican Other. Then, the chapter concludes with a taxonomy, a working system to classify the tropes of the Mexican Other and how they function to construct whiteness. Over the past two decades, there has been a growing body of scholarship concerning U.S. representations of Mexico, Mexicans, and Mexican Americans. Because of disciplinary conventions, however, these works have largely emerged independently from one another, potentially exacerbating the potential for the Mexican Other to be both ubiquitous and elusive.[10] By reading these works beside and against each other, this genealogy offers at least three essential outcomes. First, it traces the continuities and changes in the Mexican Other over a vast historical sweep, from the nineteenth century to the present day. Second, this genealogy identifies a lineage of scholarship that courses through and beyond Chicana/o studies. Ultimately, this growing scholarly tradition lays the foundation for the later chapters of this project and turning the critical gaze from representations of Mexican-descent people to how those representations forge manifestations of whiteness. Finally, fostering a conversation between seemingly isolated texts allows the theoretical insights of scholars like Arnoldo de León, Shelley Streeby, William Nericcio, Leo Chavez, and others to placed beside and against one another and extrapolated beyond the chronological or methodological boundaries of their studies. If the genealogy offers a rough chronological sweep of scholarship and representation, the taxonomy that follows moves tropologically. This section identifies disparate representations of Mexico, Mexicans, and Chicanas/os in order to briefly explore how they have functioned vis-à-vis whiteness across time. From the early nineteenth century to the present day, the Mexican Other has been figured through tropes of the Infernal Paradise; the Violent, Savage Mexican; the Lawless Mexican; the Erotic, Exotic Mexicana; the Nonindustrious Mexican; the Mexican Invasion; and others. Beyond simply identifying trends of white supremacy, I contend that reading tropologically provides a necessary strategy for considering and working against the resilience of these racial hauntings. That is, recognizing the continuity and change between contemporary depictions of the Mexican Other and their nineteenth- and twentieth-century forebears is foundational to building antiracist strategies.

A Genealogy of the Mexican Other; or, Constructing a Burkean Parlor

The existing scholarship on the Mexican Other has yet to be placed in a full, dynamic conversation. Many of these works derive from distinct disciplinary traditions—from literary studies and history to film studies

and anthropology—but they can all be positioned within the scholarly
traditions of Chicana/o studies and American studies. Perhaps inadvertently cleaving the fields from one another, many of these works locate
the origins of the Mexican Other in the material conditions and political
exigencies of the time under examination. In other words, these scholarly works emphasize the depictions of Mexican-descent people within
specific historical moments and thus implicitly reinforce an emphasis
on change over time. U.S. settlement and conquest, capitalist expansion,
and the development of the print industry, railroads, and photography
gave shape and substance to renderings of Mexican-descent peoples.
Consider William Nericcio's innovative *Tex{t}-Mex*. Nericcio opens his
examination by historicizing the image of the Mexican in the U.S. imagination.[11] For Nericcio, the years of the Mexican Revolution (1910–20)
were critical. During that time not only did the United States occupy
Mexico and engage in an eleven-month punitive expedition in a quest
for Pancho Villa, but also the popularization of photography and the
postcard led to the mass transborder circulation of images of Mexico
and Mexicans.[12] For Nericcio, this ocular currency sets the stage for later
Hollywood figurations of the Mexican. Nericcio's focus on the visual and
historical confluence structures his argument. But what happens when
the critical gaze moves from these images to their word-image predeces-
sors? In *American Sensations*, Shelley Streeby locates the origins of the
Hollywood Mexican not in postcards and the Mexican Revolution but
in U.S. expansion and the sensational literature of the mid-nineteenth
century.[13] Implicit in Streeby's assertion is the recognition that images
are not simply consumed by the eye, but images rendered in verbal form
are etched within the mind's eye. Reading Nericcio alongside Streeby
gestures toward two critical observations. First, tropes of the Mexican
Other do not cohere neatly to specific genres or media of representation. Rather, as tropes, they circulate through a variety of forms: visual,
written, spoken, and enthymetically unsaid. Importantly, this does not
diminish works like Nericcio's. Instead it suggests that his theorizations
can be expanded as they are resituated beyond the visual. Second, reading Nericcio, Streeby, and others in this tradition together suggests an
advantage in reading representations of the Mexican Other not simply
within their discrete historical contexts but as deployments of a vast
symbolic reservoir.

Signifying upon the 1980s historiographic intervention of Thomas Bender, I am suggesting that such a disciplinary emphasis on the parts obfuscates our understanding of the whole.[14] That is, placing importance on genres or time periods may well obscure a more totalizing analysis of manifestations of the Mexican Other and its organizing function for white supremacy. Thus, the following pages offer a loose stitching together of scholarship on the Mexican Other. To forge a historical synthesis, one must construct a Burkean parlor. According to Kenneth Burke, the parlor is an apt model for entering a discourse. Imagine that you step into a parlor where an engaging conversation is taking place. You must first listen and take note of the positions being staked out prior to entering the discourse yourself.[15] Because of the way the scholarship on the Mexican Other has developed, the Burkean parlor does not exist as such. Imagine entering a home with a few people gathered in the parlor. In other rooms, however, individuals are engaged in divergent yet related conversations. They must be called down to the parlor, introduced to each other, and asked to join the conversation. From that conversation the genealogy of the Mexican Other may emerge.

Critically, however, reading these works beside and against one another provides more than a conversation or a semichronological sketching of whiteness on the border. By illustrating the long history of anti-Mexican racialization, the following pages demonstrate the ideological and discursive nature of whiteness on the border and its dependency on the Mexican Other. This genealogy moves scholars and activists toward a poststructuralist recognition of white supremacy and U.S. nationalism. Returning to the above discussion of Nericcio and Streeby, tropes of the Mexican Other form a vast symbolic reservoir circulating in a variety of discursive forms. Instead of treating them solely as deployments of autonomous individuals or bound to discrete, historically bracketed times, this genealogy suggests that these figurations are carriers of ideology, interpellating and constituting their subjects with each iteration. In other words, while popular discourse contains and gives shape to the stories people tell about themselves and others, in complementary fashion these stories also forge and reproduce ideology across time and place.

In stitching together a body of scholarship on the Mexican Other, de León's *They Called Them Greasers* is a critical point of departure, for it both delves into some of the earliest Anglo-American contact narratives and is one of the first scholarly explorations of the Mexican image in the white mind.[16] Through an analysis of newspaper accounts and other discursive sites, de León maps the various Anglo attitudes toward Tejanos throughout the nineteenth century. De León's investigation begins with the large-scale Anglo immigration that came with Mexican independence and when Moses Austin was granted colonization rights in 1821. From there, de León traces Anglo depictions of Mexicans across a turbulent century that included two wars, mass Anglo migration to previously Mexican-settled areas, and years of racial violence and insurgency in South Texas. De León identifies at least four tropes that organized Anglo attitudes and underwrote Anglo actions. Mexicans were scripted as indolent, morally defective, un-American, and savagely violent.[17] Foundational to forging a long view of anti-Mexican racialization, one must recognize that these tropes have yet to dissipate. Indeed, not only are they readily present in contemporary discourses, but they have also surfaced in the scholarship of others.

Importantly, de León's analysis also positions the construction of the Mexican Other as part of a tradition of white supremacy. As he notes early on, if most whites had no previous contact with Mexicans, what made them so abhorrent?[18] In part, de León answers this question by exposing how the Mexican Other was not fashioned ex nihilo. Rather, Anglos drew upon a long ethnoracial discursive tradition, from "a pseudo-scientific lore acquired from generations of interaction with blacks and Indians" to notions of Mexicanness extrapolated from the Black Legend.[19] Yet while "'niggers,' 'redskins,' and 'greasers' intimately intermingled in the Anglo-Texan mind," these racial figments were not synonymous and interchangeable.[20] For example, while African Americans were depicted as violent, sexual threats, Mexicans were seen as brutal and savage in acts of war and conflict. De León suggests that these symbolic differences explain the disparate manifestations of Anglo lynchings of African Americans and Mexicans.[21] Importantly, these racializing discourses fashioned white identity. Repeatedly, de León contends that "Anglos saw Mexicans as mirror opposites of themselves" and that they should avoid becoming like Mexicans.[22] Notably, de León's book was written prior to the academic popularization of critical theory and over a decade before the scholarly emergence of critical whiteness studies. That being said, his linkage of anti-Mexican attitudes to previous racializations suggests the ways in which discourse functions as a carrier of ideology. Moreover, de León's tropes of the Mexican Other simultaneously gesture toward unstated tropic embodiments of whiteness. That is, if Mexicans are lazy, disloyal, savage, and immoral, then whites "as mirror opposites" are hardworking, loyal, civilized, and moral beings—the ideal citizen-subjects. These racial discourses not only provided the logic underwriting settlement of Mexican lands, but also functioned to justify Anglos remaining distinct from Mexicans and positioning themselves atop a racial hierarchy.[23] Such attitudes about whiteness structured the material history of nineteenth-century Texas, but in stitching together the historiography on the Mexican Other, de León's work is just the beginning.

Shelley Streeby's *American Sensations* broadens the examination of the Mexican Other beyond Texas to the U.S. national empire-building and race-making project. Deploying methods of literary criticism, Streeby's study turns to nineteenth-century sensational fiction—characterized by suspenseful themes of murder, seduction, and other forms of intrigue—to trace discourses and anxieties of expansion, race, and national identity through the depiction of Mexicans, Mexico, and the U.S.-Mexico War.[24] Despite the apparent disciplinary differences that set Streeby's work apart from de León's, it is critical to note that the tropes de León identified circulate through Streeby's tome.[25] Some sensational fiction depicted Mexicans as nonindustrious, thriftless, or lazy as a means for justifying and normalizing U.S. expansion and white supremacy.[26] Mexicans, and Mexican men in particular, were ascribed attributes of savagery vis-à-vis the Black Legend.[27] Moreover, the racialization of national incorporation was gendered as Mexican men were described as unfit and Mexican women were potentially assimilable as the erotic exotic.[28] In addition to the four tropes identified by de León, Streeby notes that Mexico was often rendered as a site of chaos and disunity. Depicting Mexico as a "false nation" bolstered claims to the imagined organic unity of the United States.[29] Furthermore, representations of Mexico's mixed-race and Indigenous population fostered a complex dynamic in the U.S. imagination, both working to justify expansion and augmenting anxieties about the potential for a nonwhite population to corrode or invade the United States.[30]

Such a sketch runs the risk of homogenizing the diverse and often contradictory iterations of the Mexican Other that Streeby richly uncovers. However, what is imperative about Streeby's work for this project is how she unveils the linkage between racialization, imperialism, and U.S. nationalist identities. For instance, seemingly "positive" depictions of Mexicans were used to support U.S. imperial expansion whereas "negative" representations were associated with those who did not wish to engage in a conquest of Mexico.[31] Moreover, the depiction of Mexicans was not simply used to justify or critique U.S. expansion. Renderings of Mexicans, Mexico, and the U.S.-Mexico War were key in consolidating whiteness within the United States. Positioned against an external and potentially internal Mexican Other, Irish and other off-white U.S. ethnics could be brought into the fold of the racial, national, imperial project.[32] Through Streeby, one can trace the roots of anti-Mexican whiteness as Americanness back to nineteenth-century national and imperial discourses.

In this genealogy of the Mexican Other, Jason Ruiz's *Americans in the Treasure House* demonstrates how ideology and discursive strategies shift depending upon the political exigencies. Ruiz examines depictions of Mexico and Mexicans by U.S. travelers during the Porfiriato (1876–1911), which for certain tropes of the Mexican Other may be seen as a period of exception. During the reign of Mexican president Porfirio Díaz, Mexico was marked by political and economic stability, and the nation underwent significant technological modernization. These local factors along with the opening of the Mexican Central Railway in 1884 increased Anglo-American travel into Mexico. These travelers produced a rich body of narrative and photographic renderings of Mexico and its inhabitants, depicting Mexico as a site of potential investment and empire building. Examining a time after U.S. "domestic" borders were established, Ruiz's project forms a continuation of and a departure from Streeby's. While both illustrate how representations of Mexico and Mexicans evidence the contemporaneous logics of race and empire, the shape of the U.S. imperial project had changed through the Porfiriato. By the late nineteenth century, the United States was less concerned with the expansion of its official borders on the continent and more concerned with the territorial expansion of its markets.[33] As a result, many of the tropes abundant in de León's and Streeby's work were temporarily suppressed as Mexico and its inhabitants were cast as a viable target for market expansion.

During the Porfiriato, U.S. travelers largely represented Mexico as a "sister republic," rich with natural resources but in need of U.S. intervention in the forms of investment and modernized labor practices in order to reach its potential.[34] The discourse of the sister republic, of course, did not signal a fraternal bond of coequal nation-states joined in the project of democracy. Rather, this gendered discourse suggested a clearly unequal power relationship wherein the United States would profit by raising up and protecting its "little sister" republic.[35] Perhaps unsurprisingly, some of the tropes at play in the analyses of de León and Streeby, while subordinated, also organized this era of the U.S. empire-building, race-making project. For example, during this time Mexican men were rendered not necessarily as lazy but as potentially hardworking laborers who merely lacked a Protestant work ethic and modern technologies. Such depictions evoked the potential of U.S. investment when coupled with Anglo-American or mestizo colonial guidance.[36] This trope and its undergirding logic are clearly reminiscent of de León's discussion of Tejanos as indolent, but in this case Indigenous Mexicans were depicted as laboring bodies unable to achieve efficiency on their own.[37] Moreover, Ruiz explores the way in which Mexican women were fashioned as erotic and hyperfertile, rendering them as ideal mothers or sites of sexual temptation and disease.[38] Here, one may clearly hear the echoes of Streeby's sensational literature.

At first glance the depictions of Mexico and Mexicans during the Porfiriato seem to lack the ugliest aspects of the Mexican Other. Ruiz, however, works against dividing these representations along lines of the more and less malignant. Rather, these tropic alterations mark a shift in the U.S. empire-building, race-making project. That is, during the critical years of de León's and Streeby's studies, the United States was actively expanding its borders through military conquest and settler colonialism.[39] Tropes of savagery and moral degeneracy rhetorically and ideologically structured this expansion. Indeed, Charles Mills has contended that this is one of the key ways in which white supremacy is linked to the colonial project. Mills argues that desirable lands must be unpeopled either by erasing the original inhabitants (e.g., the vanishing Indian trope) or by calling into question the very humanity and personhood of those inhabitants.[40] During the Porfiriato, however, military expansion into Mexico was not the strategy du jure. Thus, Ruiz's study does not find the anxieties of racial, national incorporation described by Streeby, for the United States and its citizens traveling in Mexico were concerned more with market incorporation and economic imperialism. This is evidenced in two ways. First, as Ruiz notes, travelers were concerned not with whether Mexicans would make suitable citizens—they would not— but with whether they could be viable laborers.[41] Mills's discussion of personhood as it relates to white supremacy exposes that U.S. depictions during the Porfiriato cast Mexicans not as subpersons outside of the social contract and unable to participate in governance but as semipersons who could contribute labor in the modernization of Mexico.[42] Second, U.S. writers mediated the "problem of Indian difference" by imagining mestizos, typified through Porfirio Díaz, as a viable managerial class and modern, technological laboring subjects. In this way, the white United States could invest capital and provide technological guidance as off-white mestizos extracted labor and managed Mexico's massive Indigenous population. Indeed, applying Mills, one may see this rendering of mestizos as casting them not as viable citizens within the United States but as persons who could become signatories of Mexico's social contract.

The Porfiriato as an era of exception is particularly useful to theorizing a genealogy of anti-Mexican racialization, for it exposes that seemingly "positive" depictions of Mexico and Mexican-descent people may well support white supremacy and the U.S. national project. Indeed, such renderings may be more effective because their supremacist impulses are so difficult to make legible, an aspect that will be explored in later chapters. This era of exception came to a close as Mexico's economic and political stability faltered toward the end of the Porfiriato. With the conclusion of debt slavery and brutal exercising of state power, U.S. writers again turned to other tropes within the vast symbolic reservoir of the Mexican Other. Once U.S. economic investments were less secure and military incursions were required to maintain the U.S. imperial-racial project, the image of the greaser returned to prominence. In historical confluence with the emergence of film technologies, the Mexican greaser now appeared not just in travel literature and popular fiction but on the silver screen. Here, one may recall *Martyrs of the Alamo* (1915) examined in the introduction to this book. Moreover, as troops occupied Veracruz in 1914, the city and its inhabitants were described in less than modernizable ways. While tropical Veracruz had long been looked down upon by U.S. travelers and functioned as a barometer of Mexico's potential in the U.S. racial-imperial imaginings, with U.S. occupation troops were cast as vulnerable to venereal disease, and the erotic, morally degenerate tropes that de León first examined came back to the fore as the rhetorical and political exigencies of the moment shifted.[43]

As the Mexican Other emerged in travel writing and sensational literature of the nineteenth century, in the twentieth century it spread and took root in Hollywood cinema and other forms of popular culture. In this regard, William Nericcio's *Tex{t}-Mex* is essential to forging a genealogy of the Mexican Other. Focusing on twentieth-century visual depictions of Mexicans, particularly within Hollywood's golden era (approximately 1930–60), Nericcio frames his theoretical examination with a large historical claim: the Hollywood Mexican can be traced back, in part, to the U.S. occupation of Veracruz and the postcards that circulated in the 1910s United States that depicted Mexico and the revolution.[44] From here, Nericcio theorizes that stereotypes are discursive and cognitive bloodstains, "the socially conserved oral and textual remnants of communities in conflict."[45] Through Nericcio, the discourse that emerged from and justified the use of military force lingers today, haunting the U.S. racial imagination as external enemies (i.e., Mexicans) have become internal Others (i.e., Mexican Americans). While this move locates a visual origin of the Mexican Other, it simultaneously evidences the impulse in this scholarly tradition to root the origins of the symbolic in specific material conditions: revolution begets postcards begets the Hollywood Mexican. Of course, a broader temporal field view illustrates that such depictions have long been in existence. For example, read against de León, the origins of the Hollywood Mexican could be located not just in the discourse surrounding Anglo settlement of Texas but also in preexisting racial discourses. Recognizing such is critical to making wider use of Nericcio's theoretical interventions.

While this genealogy resists a fixed origin of the Mexican Other, Nericcio's use of postcolonial and poststructuralist theory to expose the force and function of discourse in world creation is foundational to conceptualizing whiteness on the border. For Nericcio, stereotypes of the Mexican found in advertisements and other cultural texts "work because they are familiar, and they are familiar because the logic that sustains them is reinforced by their very existence."[46] Through Nericcio, these tropes are recognized as "influenzal," marking the way language and images circulate as contagions in society.[47] This is critical because it resists the concept of the autonomous individual subject who can wield language as he wishes. Rather, in the poststructuralist move, it is the language—and images and thus ideology—that makes the subject. This theoretical intervention cannot be understated, for it suggests how white supremacist tropes survive and thrive after the racial break in an era when explicit white supremacy is largely rejected. Drawing on a discussion of Adolph Hitler in his exploration of Hollywood animators, Nericcio contends that "animators as well as their spectators act, 'obeying a law they do not . . . know, but which [they can] recite in [their] dreams' . . . these words offer us a better view and clearer access to the enabling ether called ideology."[48] In this poststructuralist view, people do not simply wield negative images of Mexicans for a given, immediate purpose. That is, people do not merely use racial discourse. Rather, as Joe Feagin has suggested, there is a "hidden curriculum" that teaches white ideology through social interactions and media.[49] Thus, racial discourse, as bloodstains of conflict, uses and constructs people as ideology interpellates subjects. Here, Nericcio lays the groundwork for an exploration of how these tropes circulate, evolve, and thrive into the twenty-first century.

In this genealogy, Nericcio's work is significant also in its reminder that whiteness on the border does not go without response. Nericcio postulates the concept of Xicanosmosis whereby Chicana/o cultural workers like Gilbert Hernandez and Nericcio himself actively work to undermine the long history of white supremacist symbolization, producing images that subvert the Mexican Other and infiltrate the eyes and minds of readers and viewers. This move creates a shift in the scholarship on the Mexican Other, asking for a continued engagement on the part of Chicana/o cultural workers and their allies. Beyond seeking a scholarly analysis, Nericcio calls for artist-activists, armed with ink, digital animation software, and other cultural weapons, to revolt against the logics, language, and codes of white supremacy. Practicing what he preaches, Nericcio has become an interesting model for the Chicano public intellectual. While his *Tex{t}-Mex* clearly identifies and analyzes this history of anti-Mexican white supremacy in U.S. popular culture, his blog and his art exhibits demonstrate the culture-jamming potential of Xicanosmosis.[50]

One of the earliest studies in this body of scholarship, Daniel Cooper Alarcón's *The Aztec Palimpsest*, forms a useful complement to Nericcio's work as it largely focuses on twentieth-century representations of Mexico in the U.S. imagination. Influenced by Edward Said's concept of Orientalism, whereby colonialism is made possible and legible through discourse, Alarcón explores how Mexico has been fashioned as an Infernal Paradise. Drawing on Malcolm Lowry, Alarcón identifies four components of the Infernal Paradise trope: Mexico is depicted as a meeting place between the Old and New Worlds, Mexico and its inhabitants are rendered as colorful and fascinated by death, Mexico is fashioned as timeless or ahistorical and thus becomes the symbolic background for a spiritual quest, and finally the authors assume "mythic proportions."[51]

Beyond being an early entrant into this Burkean parlor, Alarcón offers three critical contributions to future examinations of the Mexican Other. First, in identifying and examining the deployment of this trope, Alarcón works transhistorically. The manifestation of the Infernal Paradise seems less dependent upon change over time and more fashioned through the continuity and changes in discursive exigencies of the moment. For example, by linking the discursive strategies of a nineteenth-century text like Richard Henry Dana's *Two Years before the Mast* to twentieth-century tourism, Alarcón suggests both the pervasiveness of racial tropes and their role in the longue durée of the U.S. imperial and race-making project. Second, Alarcón demonstrates that representations of Mexico and Mexicans are not solely the discursive and ideological ground of Anglo-America. Through readings of the works of Rudolfo Anaya, Richard Rodriguez, Sandra Cisneros, and others, Alarcón contends that the Infernal Paradise trope has also been used by Mexican Americans to fashion a U.S.-positioned identity.[52] Such a move is imperative to recognizing that Mexican Americans do not stand outside of whiteness on the border. For example, consider how Oscar Zeta Acosta's representations of Mexico and Mexican women rely upon and reinforce white supremacy and heteropatriarchy.[53] As a third contribution to this scholarly tradition, Alarcón gestures toward the way these representations of Mexico and Mexicans accrue meaning through their relationship to space. While Alarcón is concerned with Mexico in the modern imagination, he suggests that depictions of its inhabitants undergird this figuration of Mexico. That is, whether in the nineteenth or twentieth century, Mexico as Infernal Paradise is dependent upon its denizens being fashioned as backward, exotic, savage, erotic, and so on. As such, these renderings of Mexicans dialectically charge a timeless Mexico with meaning in order to justify a range of U.S. imperial and racial projects from military conquest to tourism.

Published fourteen years after de León's study and several years prior to the other works discussed in this genealogy, *The Aztec Palimpsest* broke significant ground. Reading Alarcón through the context of those who have followed, however, allows new questions to be raised and critical insights to be gleaned. Notably, Alarcón does not turn his attention to representations of Mexican Americans, for they are simply beyond his critical field view. In the United States, however, representations of Mexican Americans are intricately bound to depictions of Mexico and Mexicans. In the U.S. racial imagination, the border between Mexicans, Mexican Americans, and Mexico (and arguably Latin America) is porous. Consider how Mae Ngai and Raymond Rocco have explored the ways in which Mexican Americans are cast as "alien citizens" and "perpetually foreign." Moreover, through her interviews of anti-immigrant activists, Robin Dale Jacobson has demonstrated the slippage between categories such as Latino, immigrant, and criminal in the popular imagination.[54] The categories of Mexico, Mexican, and Mexican American as well as their symbolic attributes are often partially, but certainly not completely, interchangeable. Furthermore, with his location of the Infernal Paradise in Mexico and its inhabitants, Alarcón inadvertently raises other questions central to whiteness on the border: What happens when Mexico vis-à-vis its citizens or their descendants resides in the United States? Does this give shape and substance to the U.S. domestic racial project that de León, Streeby, and Nericcio investigated? Arguably, this results not merely with the exotification of domestic subjects, but also with what Leo Chavez has termed the Latino Threat Narrative.

At first glance, Chavez's *Latino Threat* may seem to have little in common with works like Nericcio's and Alarcón's. Clearly this project, at the intersection of anthropology and immigration studies, does not self-consciously emerge from previous examinations of Mexico as an

Infernal Paradise, the eroticization of Hollywood Latinas, or sensational literary depictions of ruthless Mexicans. Chavez's work, however, can be made to speak back to scholarship on the Mexican Other, indeed forging a critical juncture in the intellectual project that I am sketching. An extension of and departure from his *Covering Immigration*, Chavez's *Latino Threat* offers a discourse analysis surrounding Latino immigration and national incorporation. Chavez contends that while other immigrant groups have been recipients of variously positive and negative views within the United States, Mexicans and Latinos more broadly have been the subject of the most consistently alarming discourse. Through this narrative, U.S. Latinas/os and Latina/o immigrants are scripted as hyperfertile, disease carrying, criminal, and disloyal. Here, one cannot help but hear the echoes of de León's initial four tropes of the Mexican Other. Historically speaking, while other immigrant communities have been welcomed and shunned depending upon economic and political historical contexts, Chavez demonstrates a form of Mexican, or Latino, exceptionalism wherein Mexican immigrants in times of plenty as well as in times of hardship are cast as threats to and drains upon the United States. In *The Latino Threat*, Chavez argues that a threat narrative draws upon and organizes underlying assumptions about Mexican and Latina/o immigrants and U.S. Latinas/os.[55] For Chavez, "The Latino Threat Narrative is pervasive even when not explicitly mentioned. It is the cultural dark matter filling space with taken-for-granted 'truths' in debates over immigration on radio and TV talk shows, in newspaper editorials, and on Internet blogs."[56] The world-ordering power of the narrative is central in that it provides meaning to social experiences even as ideological precepts are left unstated. Much of Chavez's project is dedicated to identifying, analyzing, and disproving these "taken-for-granted 'truths.'"

Placing Chavez's work in conversation with scholarship on the Mexican Other both adds to that body of critical inquiry and elucidates aspects of Chavez that may otherwise go underdeveloped. First, Chavez highlights the historical continuity in U.S. attitudes toward Mexican and Latina/o immigration. This underscores and reinforces a healthy skepticism about emphasizing historical change over continuity. While many things have changed over the past two hundred years, attitudes—a mix of both pejorative and romantic—about Mexico, Mexicans, and Chicanas/os have endured. Indeed, they have pervaded through reconfigurations of age-old tropes. Second, Chavez implicitly forges a connection between the logic of the Infernal Paradise and the Latino Threat Narrative. While Ruiz and Alarcón demonstrated how Mexico and Mexicans were rendered as tied to the past and shorn from the narrative of history, Chavez notes a similar dynamic on this side of the border: "It was as if Mexican Americans and other Latinos existed in an ahistorical space apart from the life that took place all around them. They were cast as 'alien-citizens,' perpetual foreigners with divided allegiances despite being U.S. citizens by birth, even after many generations. Such notions have become an acceptable part of the public discourse even among otherwise learned scholars."[57] In this discussion of recent nativists, Chavez suggests that an Orientalist logic of timelessness also underwrites claims that Mexican Americans cannot be seen as modern subjects to the nation. Beyond depicting Mexicans as simply tied to a premodern past, as seen in Ruiz's and Alarcón's scholarship, nativists also depict Mexican Americans as wedded to national allegiances that their nineteenth-century ancestors might not have held.[58]

Finally, reading Chavez against scholars like de León and Nericcio also opens subordinated aspects of his argument. For example, Chavez contends that the Latino Threat normalizes hierarchies between citizens and noncitizens, and like others who work on immigration, he locates rises in nativism with shifts in immigration policy.[59] However, as Chavez recognizes, the Latino Threat is not solely concerned with immigrants. Rather, it renders "perpetually foreign" Mexican Americans who may tie their ancestry in current U.S. lands back to the nineteenth century and beyond. They are again figured as subpersons unable to enter the social contract and unfit for U.S. democracy. Because the Latino Threat incorporates both Mexican immigrants and Mexican Americans as the perpetually foreign Other, the narrative does not simply normalize hierarchies between citizen and noncitizen. Rather, it also normalizes a hierarchy between whites and nonwhites, and the categories of citizen and alien are written onto those racial categories. That is, through the Latino Threat Narrative, to be nonwhite is to be a noncitizen, or potentially an anticitizen. In this way, the cultural work of the Mexican Other aligns with the broad history of the U.S. racial project.[60] Thus, while nativist anxieties may have flared around 1965's Immigration and Nationality

Act or 1986's Immigration Reform and Control Act, they should not be seen as discrete from white fears and retrenchment following gains of the various U.S. civil rights movements and the rise of Reagan conservatism. Read in this way, one may extrapolate Chavez to make an analogous argument to that of Streeby. That is, while Streeby contended that scholars should challenge the bifurcation of foreign and domestic wars and that the U.S. racial project was shaped by both, Chavez also shows that "foreign" and "domestic" subjects are brought together in the fashioning of the United States as a racialized nation-state.

Clearly this genealogy does not provide a comprehensive interrogation of all scholarship on the Mexican Other. One could certainly incorporate key insights from Américo Paredes, Rosaura Sánchez, Ramón Gutíerrez, Otto Santa Ana, Natalia Molina, or many other scholars in the field of Chicana/o studies. That being said, this brief sketch evidences both a large, growing body of scholarship as well as the long endurance of the Mexican Other. Renderings of Mexico, Mexicans, and Chicanas/os underwrote Anglo-American settler colonialism in the early nineteenth century, economic imperialism during the Porfiriato, as well as tourism and nativism in recent years. Importantly, however, constructing this scholarly dialogue does much more than survey what has gone before. This genealogy also opens critical interventions for scholars and activists seeking to understand and contest white supremacy and its anti-Mexican, anti-Latino manifestations in the present.

Echoing interventions of poststructuralist theory, this long view of the Mexican Other suggests that these tropes do not simply emerge ex nihilo from discrete historical moments, nor are such renderings deployed by autonomous individual subjects. While the Mexican Other was certainly shaped and disseminated by Hollywood images, travel narratives, and dime fiction, many of these discursive strategies can be traced back to and, according to de León, prior to contact with Mexicans and the colonization of Texas. Such a perspective fundamentally challenges the notion that anti-Latino manifestations of white supremacy are somehow new or linked to a rise in the U.S. Latino population. Rather, the Mexican Other has long been used to fashion whiteness on the border. Perhaps more importantly, however, this long view evinces that tropes of the Mexican Other interpellate their subjects. Instead of simply positing that individuals have historically used problematic renderings of Mexico, Mexicans, and Chicanas/os, one may also articulate a complementary equation: as carriers of ideology, these tropes circulate discursively, interpellating and constituting their political subjects. As such, the origins and political effects of the Mexican Other slip and slide below the consciousness of those engaged in the discourse. As noted before, Nericcio's allusion to Hitler's propaganda machine is prescient: those engaging the discourses of the Mexican Other are "'obeying a law they do not . . . know, but which [they can] recite in [their] dreams.'"[61] Recognizing the poststructural implications of this long view also suggests that just as these tropes continue to circulate, so do their ideological underpinnings. In other words, because tropes that were once used to perform the discursive and ideological work of white supremacy and empire still appear in various modified forms, they should be recognized as evolved expressions of white supremacy and empire.

This long view of the Mexican Other also challenges the idea that these tropes are just remnants or holdovers from a less enlightened U.S. racial past. Rather, they perform very real cultural work in the present. Through an evocative and theoretically rich turn of phrase, Nericcio describes tropes of the Mexican Other as "bloodstains" born in previous military conquests and occupations of Mexico. Here, he is far from suggesting that these figurations have no ill effect today. Indeed, they emerged from the past and live on in the present. Antonio Gramsci offers another model for understanding the cultural work performed by these tropes, one that elucidates an ongoing war. According to Gramsci, war of maneuver describes overt military conflict, while war of position names the formal and informal social pedagogies that make hegemony possible.[62] These may range from curricular inequalities and inadequate access to social services to voter suppression and denial of citizenship rights. Thus, contemporary deployments of the Mexican Other may be seen not simply as vestiges of previous military conflict but as the manifestation of war by other means.[63] Through this frame, Lorna Dee Cervantes's "Poem for the Young White Man Who Asked Me How I, an Intelligent, Well-Read Person, Could Believe in the War between Races" makes the war of position visible. Cervantes's narrator speaks of the

> . . . snipers in the schools . . .
> (I know you don't believe this.

You think this is nothing
but faddish exaggeration. But they
are not shooting at you.)

I'm marked by the color of my skin.
The bullets are discrete and designed to kill slowly.
They are aiming at my children.[64]

Reading Cervantes's poem, it is difficult not to consider tropes of the Mexican Other as the bullets that "bury deeper than logic" and cause her psychic wounds:

. . . my stumbling mind, my
"excuse me" tongue, and this
nagging preoccupation
with the feeling of not being good enough.[65]

Importantly, recognizing the continued manifestations of the Mexican Other as part of the war of position suggests two insights. First, these tropes are not only "bloodstains," but also symbolic bullets causing psychological and material harm. Second, in a war of position, particularly in the hegemony of the post–civil rights United States, Cervantes exposes the possibility for a war of position to be waged even as and perhaps because one party in the war is able to deny the conflict even exists.

Finally, this long view of the Mexican Other demonstrates the need to read tropologically. In the 1980s, Henry Louis Gates Jr. and Houston Baker offered groundbreaking models or reading tropologically as they argued for the existence of and interrogated the cultural work of a long-enduring African American discursive, artistic, and literary tradition. According to Gates, tropes are characterized by repetition and difference across successive iterations.[66] Such a formulation allowed Gates to make visible previously unrecognized linkages in African and African American literature and culture. Likewise, for critics of white supremacy and its endurance, reading tropologically makes legible both continuity and change (i.e., Gates's repetition and difference) over time, for reading tropologically allows cultural critics to examine multiple iterations across disparate contexts against each other simultaneously. Here, an example may prove useful. In recent years, college campuses have seen the growth of racial costuming and parties where white-identified students dress like and perform their ideas of racial Others.[67] From black gangbangers to pregnant teenage cholas, these are images pulled from both Hollywood screens and the most troubling parts of the U.S. racial imagination. What has been stunning is how many white and white-identified individuals argue that these instances are not racist in nature. No ill will was intended, they assure me when we discuss this in class. They claim that we must take these incidents within their contexts of post–civil rights U.S. postracialism and irony. In essence, they contend that only the history occurring during their lifetimes matters.[68] Here, as in my classes, I counter that we must maintain a long view of history and read tropologically. Recognizing that recent racial costuming is but a repetition with a difference from minstrelsy, dime novel depictions, characters from greaser films, and sadly much, much more, allows cultural critics—including our students—to mine the similarities between eras of explicit white supremacy and purported postracial color blindness. Reading tropologically actively contests the American amnesia that contemporary white supremacy relies upon, calling attention to and for accountability for patterns of behavior and discursive practices that have long been central to the U.S. racial project even as the concept of race has changed over the years.

Ultimately, reading tropologically anchors these iterations in a broader context, beside and against their not-too-different forebears. This genealogy and long view of the Mexican Other need not flatten out difference, arguing for historical continuity over change. Certainly change has occurred—it just does not always bear the upward lilt of progress. Consider the epigraph to this chapter drawn from the television comedy *The Office* and the brutal attack of David Ritcheson discussed earlier—such a strange and deeply uncomfortable pairing. Prior to the racial break it was unquestionable that racist attitudes shaped racial violence. Today, in the post-break United States, those attitudes persist even as they might not be expressed in mixed company or even acknowledged in the consciousness of an individual. In other words, while it may violate social norms to say or think "greaser," "spic," or "wetback," there is truth to Michael Scott's words: "is there a term besides 'Mexican' that you prefer? Something less offensive . . . it has certain connotations." Lest Oscar's question go unanswered—"What connotations, Michael?"—in the post-break era "Mexican" still bears the connotations that legitimate and normalize disparate incarceration rates, educational inequality, and brutal assaults like the one endured by Ritcheson. Yet if reading tropologically is a critical strategy for making legible and contesting white supremacy, tropes of the Mexican Other must be identified in their various historical incarnations. Thus, we turn from a genealogy, with its emphasis on historical breadth, to a working taxonomy that seeks to unpack the cultural work performed by various formations of the Mexican Other.

A Taxonomy of the Mexican Other

At the outset of this book, I described whiteness on the border as emerging from and fashioned by a broad, ever sprawling discursive constellation found in a variety of forms from Hollywood cinema and political statements to music and news media. The genealogy has clearly demonstrated that these discursive practices are long enduring and rooted in U.S. traditions of white supremacy, nation-building, and empire. Indeed, as noted previously and explicated in the pages to follow, deployments of the Mexican Other have consistently rendered Mexican-descent people as subpersons unfit for U.S. national or white racial incorporation as well as legitimating military and economic conquest of Mexican lands. In order to examine how whiteness is formed across genre and historical period, a working taxonomy is required. A system of classification, a taxonomy allows for order to be identified and mined where initially disorder seemed to reign.[69] But what is meant by a *working* taxonomy? To begin, I recognize that the sketch offered here is continually evolving and thus necessarily incomplete. That being said, explicating a system of classification provides a roadmap for future analysis. Furthermore, "working" implies and thus recognizes that this system is an imposed order of things. Importantly, the tropes explored here are not discrete atomized entities. Rather, they overlap and interpenetrate—indeed, they are often interdependent. I am aware that some may be troubled by the potential for significant overlap. For example, where exactly is the line to be drawn between deployments of the Infernal Paradise and iterations of the Erotic, Exotic Mexicana or the

Savage, Violent Mexican? Arguably a line should not be drawn cleaving one from the others. In a discursive network, multiple lines should be drawn illustrating the connections between seemingly distinct nodes. For example, eroticized figurations of Mexicanas are often foundational to rendering Mexico as an escapist paradise or an infernal hellscape. While the phrasing of a working taxonomy may initially appear to evidence scholarly hedging, a lack of confidence in one's argument, in actuality it provides the room for play and flexibility necessitated by the overlapping and interpenetrating nature of this discourse. What follows is a broad-ranging outline of the tropes and logics of the Mexican Other.

Infernal Paradise

Arguably the *ur*-trope of the Mexican Other, the Infernal Paradise is characterized by the contradictory impulse to render Mexico as a place of both heavenly splendor and hellish horror. Echoing Said's formulation of Orientalism, the Infernal Paradise fashions Mexico as timeless or outside the historical arc of progress.[70] This notion of timelessness undergirds and is reinforced by articulations of Mexico's natural beauty, ancient civilization, and potential for and failure to achieve modernity. Like others in this taxonomy, examples of the Infernal Paradise abound transhistorically. In the early to mid-nineteenth century, Richard Henry Dana described then Mexican California as a wealth of beauty and natural resources left underdeveloped because of the population.[71] Alarcón has suggested that this is rooted in the Infernal Paradise tradition not just because Dana describes the potential riches of Mexican California but because he also warns that California may have deleterious effects on U.S. whites, stripping away their enterprising spirit.[72] Moreover, Ramón Gutiérrez's analysis of William G. Ritch's U.S. booster literature describing the recently conquered New Mexico also elicits this trope through references to both natural resources and the lack of modernization.[73] The Infernal Paradise also appears in many U.S. films and literature. For example, in *The Treasure of the Sierra Madre* (1948), Mexico is both the paradisiacal site of potential riches via the titular treasure and the site of chaotic violence epitomized by the none-too-bright bandidos who "don't need no stinkin' badges." Yet the infernal aspect is not limited to Mexicans. Rather, in this twentieth-century version of the Pardoner's Tale, life

Figure 1.2. In *The Treasure of the Sierra Madre* Humphrey Bogart plays Dobbs, an American whose search for treasure in Mexico drives him to betray his countrymen and ultimately leads to his demise at the hands of Mexicanos. *The Treasure of the Sierra Madre*, Warner Brothers Studios.

in Mexico and attainment of treasure foster the greed and mistrust in Humphrey Bogart's Dobbs, ultimately leading to his death. Perhaps the true horror of Mexico in this trope is not the lawlessness and savagery of Mexicans, but Mexico's ability to draw out such characteristics in U.S. whites. In recent years the Infernal Paradise has also emerged in country music. Consider songs like Robert Earl Keen's "Sonora's Death Row," where a mescal-induced hallucination leads a man to mistakenly murder his friend. In Toby Keith's "Stays in Mexico," a married insurance salesman from South Dakota has an affair with an Arizona elementary school teacher when they meet on vacation, only for Keith to croon, "Don't bite off more than you can chew / There's things down here the Devil himself wouldn't do / Just remember when you let it all go / What happens down in Mexico, stays in Mexico."[74]

The Infernal Paradise trope serves the needs of white supremacy, U.S. nationalism, and empire in a variety of ways. The examples of Dana's California and Ritch's New Mexico illustrate how this trope may be deployed to legitimate colonization. When military and economic expansion are not in order, the Infernal Paradise also forms an imagined frontier space. That is, after U.S. expansion and settlement westward, U.S. cultural producers have looked south of the border to reimagine the frontier.[75] Not only does Mexico as Infernal Paradise become an imagined space for U.S. subjects to test and forge their own (white masculine) identities, but it also becomes an impermanent, or uninhabitable, space. That is, U.S. whites may go to Mexico to seek paradise, but through finding hell, they must return. The implicit return is obviously to the United States—an anti-Mexico—characterized by progress and order.[76] By extension, U.S. whites are thus modern subjects—unfit for the chaos *over there*, they would do well to participate in the predictably modern and ordered world of the United States. Finally, I would like to postulate another implication or effect of the Infernal Paradise trope. These tales of romanticized yet failed migration may well displace or occlude stories of Mexican immigration. That is, the Infernal Paradise also functions as an inversion of the American Dream. Instead of the American Dream trope where immigrants from Mexico and elsewhere find a U.S. paradise, the Infernal Paradise shows Anglo-Americans traveling south in search of heaven ultimately find hell. Such a pairing reinforces the hegemonic iteration of the United States as land of opportunity and elides the stories of many immigrants who arrive in the United States to find nightmarish conditions and a "cage of gold."[77]

The Violent, Savage Mexican

While the trope of Mexican violence and savagery supports the hellish component of the Infernal Paradise, it also charges Mexican-descent people with particular meaning. Evidencing the dynamics Mills located as central to Enlightenment philosophy, depicting Mexicans and Mexican Americans as particularly skilled and capable of savage violence and atrocities positions them as subpersons incapable of rational thought, civilized society, and democratic participation. As Mills rightly notes, constructing this subperson—this savage Other—was a critical component in consolidating the concept of the autonomous rational individual subject and fashioning European man as the model for universal humanity. Importantly, Mexicans are doubly cursed with supposedly savage heritages. While some have located the roots of Mexican violence in the Black Legend, others have contended that the origins of their subpersonhood derives from Aztec ancestry. On special occasions purveyors of white supremacist discourses have deployed mestizaje as the reason behind this exceptionally Mexican savagery.[78]

This trope, like the others, has been remarkably durable. While de León and Streeby cite iterations of this trope from throughout much of the nineteenth century, the notion of Mexican savagery fell from view during the Porfiriato. As Ruiz suggests, such an image of Mexicans would not have cultivated financial investments south of the border. Importantly, however, whites are not the only victims of Mexican violence. When Mexican violence threatens "docile" Mexican subjects, the trope may be used to justify intervention. One could contend that the trope of Mexican savagery was certainly present in and framed interpretations of the anti-Porfiriato tracts of John Kenneth Turner, who sought to expose the horrors of debt slavery south of the border.[79] After the Porfiriato, the trope resurfaced with a vengeance in the greaser films and postcards of the 1910s and 1920s. Importantly, the trope does not distinguish between Mexicans and Mexican Americans, for juridical citizenship does not matter in the imagination of white supremacy. For example, it is the pachuco youth who perpetrate the sexual violence against the white woman in Orson Welles's *Touch of Evil*.[80] Moreover, when thousands of U.S. servicemen and other white allies brutalized Mexican American communities during the 1943 Zoot Suit Riots, E. Duran Ayres, a representative from the Los Angeles Sherriff's Office, contended that pachuco delinquency was a result of savage Aztec ancestry.[81] Nor has this investment in the Mexican savage dissipated in recent years. One can find similarly masochistic subperson cholos in the nearly unwatchable *End of Watch* (2012), malignant foils to the postracial brown and white dynamic duo played by Michael Peña and Jake Gyllenhaal. Finally, one may consider the way in which this trope has framed and given meaning to the narco violence in Mexico. This is not to dismiss the very real and horrific violence that has wrought havoc to the country. Rather, this trope is both reinforced by such violence and likely conditions U.S. whites to see narco violence as natural, a mere extension/continuation of what has gone on for years. Moreover, such renderings elide violence north of the border as well as U.S. complicity through lax gun laws.

This trope is so enduring perhaps because it serves so many functions. First, it has been used to justify and obscure U.S. white violence. In a move reminiscent of Ruth Frankenberg's discussion of white projection, casting Mexicans as violent can be used to legitimate U.S. white violence in the forms of conquest, lynching, border enforcement, and police brutality.[82] Moreover, Mexican violence can be marshaled for nativist arguments in which this attribute of subpersonhood makes one unfit for democratic participation within the nation. Mexican violence may also foster support for white innocence and white benevolence, as potential victims of Mexican savagery. This undergirds and is reinforced by notions of white moral purity. That is, whites must be protected from Mexican violence by any means necessary whether that be an erased conquest, an often forgotten race war, or nativist immigration restrictions.

The Lawless Mexican

A close relative of the Violent, Savage Mexican trope, the figure of the Lawless Mexican—or Mexican Lawlessness and Mexican-Chicano Criminality—is embodied in bandidos, corrupt federales, "illegal" immigrants, and Chicano gangs. This trope functions to render Mexicans as always already criminal and unable to forge or maintain a rule-governed democratic order. Like the Savage, Violent trope, depictions of lawlessness position Mexicans as subpersons, a continuation of the white supremacist logic Mills located in Enlightenment thought. This trope may also be marshaled to serve the needs of U.S. nativism, for renderings of lawless Mexicans undergird claims that Mexicans are unfit potential subjects of democracy within the United States. Importantly, this trope also reinforces the Infernal Paradise, for it is not simply that Mexico as a land is lawless and thus infernal. Rather, its people and their disregard for rule and order cultivate the chaos that is Mexico in the U.S. imagination.

With the exception of the Porfiriato, this trope has demonstrated remarkable endurance in its varied manifestations over the years. Indeed, one may even argue that the cultural work of this trope was present though its explicit articulation was muted during Diaz's rule, for much of the project to render Mexico a viable site of investment responded

implicitly to the anxieties of this trope. Perhaps one of the earliest figurations of this trope, in the nineteenth century Mexican Lawlessness
figured in tales of banditry in U.S. papers, dime novels, and professional
histories. Even during the Porfiriato, on the U.S. side of the border Mexicans were easy-made suspects of horse thievery and other forms of mal-
feasance.[83] This image obviously carried over to Hollywood Westerns.[84]
But Mexican Lawlessness is figured not just via banditry and thievery.
A key manifestation has been police corruption and the seemingly ever-
present *mordida* (bribe) in depictions of Mexico.

As intimated earlier, the trope of Mexican Lawlessness contributes to
the U.S. racial and national projects in part by constituting brown bodies as unfit for self governance *over there*. And thus, as subpersons, they
must be contained or controlled. Mexican chaos south of the border
must not cross. Moreover, this trope implicitly reinforces key aspects
of American exceptionalism—and whites' central positioning as ideal
citizen subjects. By reading Mexico and Mexicans as lawless subpersons
inhabiting a nondemocratic space, the United States is enthymetically
positioned as pure and upright amid a sea of corruption. The potential
of Anglo-American corruption and the history of antidemocratic U.S.
actions are pushed from view as the gaze turns toward the imaginary
south of the border.

The Erotic, Exotic Mexicana

Sometimes demure, sometimes licentious, the Erotic, Exotic Mexicana joins long-standing figurations of Catholic hyperfertility to the
racialized logic of an erotic Other. Charged with innocence, potential
sexuality, and hyperfertility, this trope yokes together the multitude of
figurations of Mexicanas as desirable, sexual objects of the white American gaze. The Erotic, Exotic Mexicana, however, constitutes more than
the desirability of brown bodies. In some ways akin to the masculine
Latin Lover, this gendered formulation functions differently, for these
imagined Mexicanas initiate or return the desire, *wanting* or *needing*
white men. Importantly, not all iterations are "positive" in endorsing
Mexican women as suitable partners for Anglo men, for some also spell
out the danger of transracial desire. All iterations, though, are charged
with a critical erotic potential that marks the Mexicana as somehow

different, exotic, a type not available within Anglo-America. Examples of this trope abound from travel literature of the conquest and the Porfiriato to Hollywood iterations of the Latin Spitfire like that found in *Duel in the Sun* or the cross-border dalliances described in the lyrics of the Zac Brown Band, George Strait, Robert Earl Keen, and numerous others in the country music tradition. Notably, when Mexicanas are not tied to white men in the popular imagination today, their sexuality is often framed as a social drain through hyperfertility such as in the discourses of anchor babies and welfare dependency.

This trope does not simply fashion Mexicanas as subpersons unfit for democracy as the violent and lawless tropes do. Indeed, sometimes these figurations may be deployed to render Mexicanas as fit for joining the white American family.[85] Thus, it should be unsurprising that this trope was maintained in the travel discourse of the Porfiriato when others were subdued in order to fashion Mexico as a viable site of investment.[86] Ultimately, the importance of this trope emerges from the way these Mexicanas are charged with the desire or potential desire for Anglo-Americans. As such, the Erotic, Exotic Mexicana organizes a logic of consent, exceptionalism, and supremacy. As de León suggested, characterizing Mexicanas as desiring Anglo-Americans worked to both bolster the supremacy of white masculinity and mediate potential tensions arising around transracial desire.[87] However, such renderings also legitimate conquest under the rhetoric of "they want us here." Importantly, these tropic manifestations often position Anglo-Americans as the desired choice of Mexicanas above and beyond Mexican males. Such a move seeks to naturalize U.S. whites as exceptional and superior. One must recognize how these dynamics of desire may function as synecdoches wherein the U.S. nation-state is imagined to also be exceptional and supreme.

The Nonindustrious Mexican

Over the years, Mexican-descent people have been cast as lazy even as the United States has depended upon Mexican labor at home and abroad. How does one account for the contradiction within these imagined lazy, laboring Mexicans? The trope of the Nonindustrious Mexican mediates this internal tension, for within this trope Mexicans are rendered as indolent, sleepy, and slothful, or when they are working,

Figure 1.3. The Salty Senorita of Scottsdale, Arizona, tropes upon the Erotic, Exotic Mexicana in an effort to sell tasty margaritas, comida Mexicana, and dominant racial scripts. Photo by author.

they are positioned as needing a differently racialized managerial class to bring them into modernity or ensure that a task is completed with satisfactory results. In other words, whether taking a siesta or laboring continually, Mexicans are often scripted as lacking entrepreneurial energies and a self-reliant, Waspy work ethic. Ironically, this trope readily elides the industrious nature of Mexicans who historically settled the frontier region, worked as braceros, or crossed the desert to make new lives. These tasks and others require a level of industriousness, but alas the racial logics of white supremacy should not be evaluated solely by their proximity to reality. The trope of the Nonindustrious Mexican can be found across the past two hundred years. Consider the narrative that emerged from the Battle of San Jacinto, concluding Texas's War for Independence. Sam Houston and his army of Texas troops charged the Mexican army during their afternoon siesta. As taught to each Texas middle school student, such a narrative juxtaposes the lazy Mexican to the industrious white American.[88] Moreover, as Ramón Gutiérrez noted, Mexican failures at industry underwrote the logics of Manifest Destiny as Anglo-Americans were called to settle and modernize New Mexico. Even during the Porfiriato, when Mexican labor was being framed as an asset to investment, U.S. discourses articulated the need for modern (read: U.S. and white) techniques to be introduced and managed by an off-white mestizo class. And as noted before, this trope remains in the post-break era from Speedy Gonzales and his sleepy friends to the afore-mentioned southwestern aesthetic of Mexicans sleeping on cactuses (how ridiculously uncomfortable!). One must even consider that this trope implicitly undergirds claims that Mexican immigrants are a drain on social services like welfare, for which they are ineligible.

Clearly, this trope functions to support the U.S. racial and imperial projects in a variety of ways. Notably, per Gutiérrez and Ruiz, the concept of the Nonindustrious Mexican supports both Anglo-American westward expansion as well as the sharing of economic and technological aid in order to lift up nonindustrious (but potentially industrious) Mexicans during the Porfiriato. This trope implicitly, and sometimes explicitly, reinforces the positioning of whites as ideal industrious workers. Importantly, the nonindustrious yet laboring Mexican has been used to argue both for and against immigration in recent years. As nonindustrious laborers, Mexicans have been seen by business interests as ideal for manual labor without the potential for upward mobility or the needs of middle-class aspirant whites, ostensibly rendering them perfectly exploitable. Likewise, nativists have contended that Mexican immigrants, because they lack an entrepreneurial sprit, will forge the base of a growing working underclass and become a drain on social services.

The Perpetual Foreigner

Central to the discourse of the Mexican Problem, this trope engages the ways in which Mexican-descent people are cast as disloyal, unassimilable, and thus unfit as U.S. subjects. Critically, perhaps more than previous tropes, the concept of the perpetually foreign Mexican conflates Mexican immigrants and Mexican Americans whose families have been in what are now U.S. lands for generations. Whether immigrants or birthright citizens, this trope figures all as Spanish speakers with

Figure 1.4. Sign for the Lazy 8 Motel in Tempe, Arizona, uses the trope of the Nonindustrious Mexican to advertise a good night's rest. Photo by author.

political loyalties and cultural attachments to Mexico, and a disinterest in becoming "true Americans." In other words, the notion of perpetual foreignness renders Mexicans and Mexican Americans as simultaneously internal to and a distinct Other within the U.S. racial imagination. Historically, this trope has manifested in a variety of forms. De León first examines the trope of Mexican (American) disloyalty as manifested when Mexican Americans subscribed to the values of American democracy but not the practices that failed to live up to those values. For de León, "the Tejano's lack of patriotism was more of a figment of the white mind than a reality. The many critical comments Anglos made on the issue throughout the nineteenth century were logical extensions of their view that Mexicanos who were racially and culturally different could not have patriotic feelings similar to their own."[89] In the early twentieth century, social scientists described this as the Mexican Problem. Notably, Mexican scholars like Manuel Gamio and Octavio Paz also entered the fray and joined the racializing discourse.[90] Today, it is common for politicians, pundits, the white population at large, and often the Latina/o entertainment and marketing industries to assume that people of Mexican descent speak Spanish, are immigrants, and maintain direct ties to Mexico. By extension, the previously discussed tropes are all at the ready, available for ascription to Mexicans and Mexican Americans alike.

Clearly the trope of the perpetually foreign Mexican links the U.S. racial and national projects. That is, as Mexicans are figured as nonwhite, they are also imagined to be not quite full citizens. This is particularly important in understanding the dynamic tension between social and legal categories of whiteness. While Mexicans were categorized as white and thus eligible for U.S. citizenship through the application of the Treaty of Guadalupe Hidalgo, ascribing a status of perpetually foreign and thus socially nonwhite has historically and continues to undergird the withholding of *full* citizenship. Importantly, the Perpetual Foreigner trope does not simply withhold whiteness and Americanness from Mexican decent people. Rather, it also works to consolidate and normalize U.S. whiteness. Streeby noted nineteenth-century "representations suggest that European immigrants, specifically the Irish, were being admitted into the national and racial 'community' at the expense of those, such as Indians and Mexican, from whom territory was being taken away."[91] In terms of recent immigration, Sujey Vega has demonstrated how claims of Mexican refusal to assimilate often rely upon and reinforce the erasure of complex European immigration histories, where claims that "my ancestors came here, chose to learn English, and give up their old ways" are often romantic tales that underscore contemporary white belonging more than reflections of historical accuracy.[92] Indeed, one is tempted to apply Vega's analysis to the Mexican Problem discourse of the early twentieth century. It does not seem a difficult leap to consider those claims of failed assimilation as a means not just for erasing the contemporaneous racialization of Mexicans but also for occluding the different and unnatural consolidation of whiteness among European Americans in the nineteenth and twentieth centuries.

The Mexican Invasion

Whether framed as a potential or currently ongoing invasion, this trope figures Mexican-descent people as racially and culturally distinct. Thus, their national incorporation into the assumedly white United States will not happen smoothly. Notably, this is a fear not of military invasion per se but of cultural and biological influence and takeover. Critically, this Mexican invasion is rooted in many of the tropes discussed earlier. That which is contained *over there* in the Infernal Paradise will spread across the border, contaminating the United States. Constructed as either biologically or culturally inferior, Mexicans will bring lawlessness and violence across the border. Due to their lack of industriousness, they will be social drains. Echoing an aspect of the Erotic, Exotic Mexicana, the invasion will take place not just through cultural influence but through the hyperfertility of Mexican women. While this trope has clearly changed and grown over time, early examples can be found in nativist arguments against the Mexican-American War. According to Streeby, those who questioned the benevolence of the U.S. imperial project often did so through fear of Irish-Mexican alliances and the potential for a "Catholic empire that shadowed the United States."[93] Moreover, anti-imperialists contended that the United States should respect the international boundary "because immigration and the mixing of peoples" that imperialism could spur would be dangerous to the United States.[94] In the early twentieth century, the trope of Mexican invasion can be found in texts like *Martyrs of the Alamo* discussed in the introduction, wherein invasion is imagined in a particularly military formulation. The trope of Mexican invasion may also be found circulating beneath the surface of early twentieth-century discussions of the Mexican Problem: "What is the United States to do with this present, growing mass of unassimilating and unassimilable Mexicans?" Despite these early manifestations of the trope, the Mexican Invasion has certainly become more prevalent in the post-break era. With the rise of civil rights gains, immigration reforms, and a growing U.S. Latino population, reconquista fears have found new prevalence in the past few decades. Today, in their most fringe iteration, old anxieties of Mexicans bringing Nazism across the border have been repackaged with Mexicans and Chicanas/os functioning as a fifth column for al-Qaeda or other Islamist extremist groups.

The Mexican invasion trope organizes key logics of U.S. nationalism. First and foremost, this trope figures the United States as without question a white nation. Without the underlying assumption of the United

States as always already white, the potential for large-scale Mexican migration loses its threatening potential. In twentieth-century articulations, this trope also linked and conflated U.S. Latinos and Mexican immigrants. That is, failure of Mexican Americans to achieve social whiteness (despite a system of white supremacy that makes this impossible) becomes an argument against Mexican immigration. Likewise, the "replenished ethnicity" forged by Mexican immigrants forms a useful alibi for racializing Mexican Americans as unassimilable, different, and perpetually foreign.[95] Perhaps most importantly, the trope of Mexican invasion undergirds two other aspects of the U.S. racial, national project. First, the potential for Mexican invasion casts whites as under siege and thus embodiments of innocence and belonging. Indeed, this dynamic tension between articulating an invasive Mexico and forgetting a history of U.S. invasions can be found in texts like *Martyrs of the Alamo* to polemics like those of Samuel Huntington and Patrick Buchanan from the early twenty-first century. Moreover, in a second, related attribute, the threat of Mexican invasion also elides a very real history of U.S. military and economic imperialism.

* * *

This working taxonomy is necessarily incomplete, and sadly the examples offered here merely scratch the surface. A longer interrogation could have addressed stereotypes about Mexican competence, fatalism, or a vast array of ascriptions that figure Mexican-descent people as subpersons unfit for the racial democracy of the United States. What is essential about the taxonomy, however, is that each of these disparate and interconnected entries illustrates the continuity between nineteenth- and early twentieth-century manifestations of anti-Mexican racialization and recent iterations. Contemporary racism is hardly hidden from view if one knows where and chooses to look: the Infernal Paradise of Cormac McCarthy's border trilogy; the Erotic, Exotic Mexicana of the Salty Señorita, a restaurant in Old Town Scottsdale, Arizona; Mexican violence undergirding white innocence and heroism in the 2012 film *Savages*; assertions of nonindustriousness in the claims that "lazy" Mexicans "steal our jobs"; political screeds by Samuel Huntington, Patrick Buchanan, Donald Trump, and others lamenting the browning of America. The list goes on. Stretching back two hundred years and into our future, the discursive and ideological constellation of whiteness on the border is a long-enduring, prevalent, and dynamic component of the U.S. racial project.

Through the Looking Glass; or, Making Tropes of Whiteness Visible and Strange

This chapter has worked to identify, explore, and interrogate the endurance and dynamics of readily available tropes of the Mexican Other. In varying forms across the nineteenth, twentieth, and early twenty-first centuries, these figurations have organized the logics of the U.S. racial project, including white supremacy and imperialism. In each case, the Mexican Other was a "hallucination," a spectacular and spectral projection that met the needs of whiteness and Americanness, or whiteness as Americanness.[96] Whether explicitly racist, nostalgic, or purportedly ironic and postracial, all of these tropic deployments rely upon and reinforce the fantasy that the United States has always been and must remain a white nation.[97] However, as antiracist scholars and activists have argued, one of the central tenants of whiteness is its invisibility—positioned as an unmarked category, whiteness has long been scripted as the natural and universal. As such, whiteness works through inference and enthymeme, yet it is ever present in the tropes. Consider how white masculinity is made desirable via the Erotic, Exotic Mexicana or how white lawfulness is implicitly shorn up through depictions of Mexican Lawlessness. In these tropic iterations, however, whiteness engages in a sleight of hand, distracting its participants to look *over there*, see the Mexican Other, and pay no attention to the logics of the U.S. racial project.

But whiteness isn't invisible to all. As Steve Garner, Ruth Frankenberg, and others have noted, there is a long history of whiteness being hypervisible to people of color. Antiracist scholars and activists have engaged a project of making whiteness visible to all. George Yancy has called for people to point out insidious practices of whiteness—"Look, a White!" he says. Richard Dyer has argued for efforts to "make whiteness strange"—dislodging whiteness from its normative position is crucial for social transformation. Such a move is particularly critical in the post-break era when many have been seduced by notions of color blindness, postracialism, and the romance of progress. In the post-break era, white supremacy operates carte blanche in the United States as it falls below the radar of many of its practitioners.[98] Thus, the following chapters move through the looking glass in an effort to identify tropes of whiteness on the border. Making them strange and interrogating their logics and the cultural work that they perform are foundational moves for justice struggles in the contemporary era.

2

"They Are Coming to Conquer Us!"

The Nativist Aztlán, and the Fears and Fantasies of Whiteness

This is myth and fabricated nonsense.
—Patrick J. Buchanan, *State of Emergency*

Anxieties about a potential or ongoing Mexican invasion, framed around the national incorporation of Mexican-descent people, have long pervaded the U.S. racial imagination. In the lead-up to and during the U.S.-Mexican War, nativists warned that national expansion would dramatically increase the nonwhite population: what would become of the U.S. national and racial character? With the large-scale migration spurred by the Mexican Revolution, the creation of U.S. Mexican enclaves, and competing nationalization campaigns, early twentieth-century social scientists, politicians, and nativists were concerned with the Mexican Problem.[1] A complement to the white supremacist discourse of the Negro Problem, the Mexican Problem expressed concern over the increasing U.S. Mexican population, their presumed resistance to assimilation, and the potential social ills that were said to come with them. In recent decades, articulations of a Mexican invasion have gone beyond merely expressing fears of increased immigration and unassimilability. Rather, contemporary nativists have also incorporated a central narrative of the 1960s and 1970s Chicano movement. While the story of Aztlán allowed Chicanas/os to claim Indigenous ancestry and historical precedence in the U.S. Southwest, this *nativist* Aztlán organizes the logics of fear and belonging that are key components in forging the U.S. nation-state as a racial state.

Here, an example is telling. On May 23, 2006, the CNN program *Lou Dobbs Tonight* displayed a map of Aztlán to frame immigration with Mexican governmental aggression and "radical Latino" politics. In a brief segment, after detailing the growth in Utah's undocumented population, correspondent Casey Wian characterized then Mexican President Vicente Fox's U.S. visit as a "Mexican military incursion" and suggested that the trip could be called Fox's "Aztlán tour, since the three states he'll visit—Utah, Washington, and California—are all part of some radical groups' vision of the mythical indigenous homeland." In swift fashion, Dobbs's broadcast linked the Mexican government and Chicano nationalism to the ongoing immigration debate. Importantly, the connective tissue of Wian's argument went unquestioned: that the Mexican government and "radical" Latinas/os are pushing for immigration reform as a means of taking over the U.S. Southwest. Moreover, deploying the discourse of "military incursion" and "reconquest" simultaneously worked to justify and elide the long, ongoing process of militarizing the U.S.-Mexico border. Walls, electronic sensors, drones, volunteer militias become naturalized responses to the perceived threat.

As the Dobbs example suggests, the immigration debate has been marked by a return to Aztlán. Beginning in the late 1960s, Chicano nationalists articulated their presence in the Southwest as an ancestral homecoming. Embracing the concept of Indigenous identity and claiming lineage to the Aztecs, Chicanas/os asserted a historical primacy and contested their positioning as "perpetually foreign." Today, in an era when nativists consistently defend themselves against charges of racism, this reemergence and refashioning of Aztlán by the political right signifies a coded strategy for racial attack. Thus, the nativist fascination with Aztlán raises significant questions: How did a narrative foundation of the Chicano movement become a tool of contemporary nativism? More specifically, if Aztlán was used to contest white supremacist narratives of U.S. nationalism, then how has it been transformed to reinforce those selfsame narratives by forging a basis for white grievances? To address these questions, this chapter contends that nativist deployments of Aztlán emerge out of the political exigencies of an era marked by heightened globalization and multicultural gains. In the appropriation of a foundational Chicano trope, nativists have strategically fashioned a safe form for articulating and emplotting white nationalism, the expression of white supremacy through a model of ethnic nationalism wherein the nation and full citizen subjects are imagined as white, both phenotypically and ideologically. Indeed, white supremacist narratives that Aztlán was used to contest have been repackaged in the legitimat-

Figure 2.1. During the segment, *Lou Dobbs Tonight* displayed this map to illustrate and give credence to the Aztlán-reconquista narrative. The map is sourced from the Council of Conservative Citizens, a far-right U.S. political organization known for its white supremacist leanings. *Lou Dobbs Tonight*, CNN.

ing cloak of Chicano discourse. This chapter explores the rise and reign of the Aztlán scare, examining its circulation in political discourse as manifestations of the fears, fantasies, and anxieties of whiteness on the border. Ultimately, this interrogation of the nativist Aztlán provides the analytic tools needed to develop a response.

Aztlán: Then and Now

While the mythohistorical narrative of Aztlán has a rich and complicated history, it achieved its modern significance when it became a foundational narrative of the Chicano movement in 1969. During the movement, imagining and claiming the U.S. Southwest as Aztlán became a powerful, unifying force among Chicanas/os in the struggle against white supremacy and U.S. hegemony. Through the poetry of Alurista and "El Plan Espiritual de Aztlán," the narrative of the Aztec homeland was mapped onto the geographic territories colonized by and ceded to the United States under the Treaty of Guadalupe Hidalgo. Prior to the invocation of Aztlán in 1969, claims to land were largely made by New Mexico's Alianza Federal de Mercedes under the leadership of Reies López Tijerina. Unlike the Spanish land grants that undergirded Alianza claims, the Aztlán narrative allowed all Chicanas/os to assert belonging in the U.S. Southwest.[2] This deployment of Aztlán provided a territorial imagination to the cultural nationalism that worked to unify disparate movement interests. Despite its unifying function, Aztlán was not charged with a singular meaning during the movement years. While the various visions of Aztlán seem to indicate a lack of cohesion, Rafael Pérez-Torres has offered the compelling argument that Aztlán is a shifting or empty signifier, filled with multiple, competing meanings.[3] For some, actualizing Aztlán was a process of political empowerment, including gaining control of local and regional institutions. For others, Aztlán's power stemmed from its ability to name the cultural, spiritual, and psychological aspirations of Chicanas/os. Even as these political and cultural meanings appear disparate, they came together, at least temporarily, through Aztlán.[4] Importantly, movimiento articulations of Aztlán, such as "El Plan Espiritual de Aztlán," united the sometimes revolutionary rhetoric of cultural nationalism with largely reformist goals. That is, while claims to Aztlán were abundant, the material goals of most activists were reformist in nature. Rather than establishing a sovereign territory, Chicanas/os actively worked for governmental institutions that would serve their communities, education that would be culturally relevant, and other forms of uplift.

Aztlán also performed critical discursive and ideological work for el movimiento. Beyond the unification of a regionally and strategically diverse collection of struggles, Aztlán contested central anti-Mexican, white supremacist narratives. Through claiming Indigenous heritage, Chicanas/os refuted the very concept of Melting Pot assimilation. Indeed, locating indigeneity at the center of the movement imagination, Chicanas/os contended that cultural retention was an asset and not a Mexican Problem. Moreover, in rescripting the U.S. Southwest as Aztlán, Chicanas/os asserted historical primacy and challenged the notion that they were perpetually foreign, disrupting the powerful narrative of Manifest Destiny.[5]

While Aztlán has been deployed and reformulated by Chicanas/os since the movement, from the late 1970s onward some on the political right have charged Aztlán to be a plot for a cultural and geopolitical takeover of the U.S. Southwest, often termed "la reconquista."[6] Although this manifestation of Aztlán has been around for almost forty years, it gains significant traction when immigration reform takes political center stage. As early as the 1980s, nativists wielded Aztlán as a means for articulating fears of Latina/o immigration to the Southwest and the loss of power that it may portend. For instance, in 1986, the same year that the Immigration Reform and Control Act was signed into law, Colorado Governor Richard Lamm stated that cultural separatism would tear the United States apart by the year 2000 and that the Southwest would secede; the new nation of Aztlán would then likely cause another civil war.[7] Nearly ten years later, Aztlán reemerged in the political discourse of the right as California, and indeed the nation, debated Proposition 187 and other immigrant-targeting legislation. During the mid-1990s, the Aztlán-reconquista narrative repeatedly emerged in editorials and letters to the editor of conservative papers like the Washington Times. For example, in 1996 Bob Djurdjevic of Phoenix, Arizona, wrote the Times to warn that "the United States is being invaded by Mexico. The intent is to retake the American Southwest and rename it Aztlan. Those who resist are called racist and subject to attack. This is a clear act of aggression and those who aid in this endeavor are guilty of sedition."[8] During the early twenty-first century, Aztlán has gained dramatic currency on the right. Technological advances of the Internet have propelled nativist fears of Aztlán well beyond the pages of conservative newspapers. Now, websites, blogs, and video-sharing sites have augmented the ability to disseminate the Aztlán-reconquista narrative.[9] Along with technological advances, the 2000 census and the September 11, 2001, attacks fomented anxiety over immigration wherein Diana West, Joseph Farah, and others drew parallels between Chicano civil rights activists and struggles of the Muslim world, from Palestine to al-Qaeda. As Jorge Mariscal has argued, these rhetorical moves expose less a logical connection between communities of struggle and more a "fear of a brown planet."[10] Significantly, the use of Aztlán as reconquista grew tremendously with the 2006 immigration debates and protests.

Previous scholars have categorized and examined a wide array of anti-immigrant rhetorical strategies: depicting immigrants as animals, natural disasters, and parasites, claiming white economic victimhood and balanced budget conservatism, and articulating fears of an immigrant invasion and cultural takeover.[11] One can easily find traces and structures of these tropes in articulations of the nativist Aztlán. However, Aztlán stands apart from these efforts because it is a clear and direct appropriation of Chicano movement discourse. To this point, there has been little critical analysis on the Aztlán scare. In *The Latino Threat*, Leo Chavez explores deployments of the nativist Aztlán as part of a broader threat narrative. Chavez contends that Latinas/os are positioned as a threat through a set of false and often unchallenged assumptions that Latinas/os are linguistically and culturally unassimilable, an economic drain, and carriers of disease and that they reproduce at levels that are a danger to the nation. The Aztlán-reconquista trope draws these disparate threads into one threat narrative, for it emplotts these grievances into an organized and unifying conspiracy.[12] While Chavez is correct in asserting that these manifestations of Aztlán are clearly part of a broader nativist project, I contend that scholars and activists must inquire how Aztlán was transformed from a counternarrative of el movimiento to one that can be utilized to maintain white nationalism through stoking and giving narrative structure to fears, fantasies, and anxieties of whiteness. This nativist Aztlán provides a rich opportunity for study, for while Lou Dobbs, Patrick Buchanan, and others decry a coming reconquista, this rhetorical strategy masks and reinforces the white supremacy that Aztlán has been used to contest. Ultimately, critical analysis of this phenomenon is required if scholars and activists are to develop cogent and coherent responses.

First, however, this moment must be placed in dialogue with the U.S. legacy of nativism and anti-immigrant hysteria. As Juan Perea has so astutely articulated, "We have been through all of this before."[13] Throughout U.S. history, many groups have been targets of xenophobia. In his work, John Higham identified three forms of U.S. nativism, contending that immigrant communities were constituted by and targeted through religion, race, and political ideology.[14] For example, throughout the nineteenth century, Catholics were subject to religious nativism. The antilabor Immigration Act of 1903, which called for the exclusion of "anarchists," and the Red Scares of the twentieth century exemplify nativism against political dissidents. The Chinese, Irish, and Japanese have all been targeted by exclusion acts that evidence racial nativism.[15] It must be noted, however, that these three classic forms of nativism do not work in isolation. For example, the predominantly Catholic Irish were targeted through both race and religion. Indeed, recognizing the intersection of seemingly distinct nativist strategies exposes machinations of contemporary anti-immigrant efforts. Since the 1990s, the primarily anti-Mexican, and more broadly anti-Latina/o, efforts have been described as a "new nativism," which has found legislative form in California's 1994 Proposition 187, U.S. Congressman Jim Sensenbrenner's 2004 HR 4437, and Arizona's 2010 SB 1070 as well as corresponding conservative media and political campaigns.[16] As René Galindo and Jami Vigil have argued, contemporary nativism "involves an intersection of racism and defensive nationalism."[17] Placing Galindo and Vigil's assessment in dialogue with the understanding that nativism takes many forms, one may contend that these new anti-immigrant efforts function at the intersection of racial and political nativism, targeting an ethnoracial community through scripting them as a political and economic threat.[18] Examining the nativist Aztlán exposes how racial and political nativism function together in the current anti-immigrant era.

Operating at the intersection of racial and political nativism, current anti-immigrant efforts emerge, in part, in response to the crisis of globalization and the evisceration of the social wage. Indeed, scholars have traced the origins of this nativist resurgence: demographic shifts resulting from the changing of the national origins quota in the Immigration and Nationality Act of 1965, the end of the Cold War, the fashioning of an imagined internal enemy instead of an external one, local and national economic declines, the rise of balanced budget conservatism, and, since September 11, 2001, the substitution of Latinas/os for the perceived brown menace of Middle Eastern enemies.[19] Here, it is critical to recognize that the nativist Aztlán conceals the contradictions and effects of capitalism, globalization, and neoliberalism. As Lisa Lowe and David Noble have argued, U.S. capitalism depends upon the fantasy of a bounded and pure nation while it simultaneously requires a boundless market and the influx of labor.[20] With the inability to question free-market logics and the need to imagine a static, stable nation, Aztlán provides an explanatory narrative, transforming immigrant labor fleeing home because of the devastating effects of NAFTA and other trade policies into an invading army bent on national and racial conquest. Moreover, the nativist Aztlán positions immigrants and U.S. Latinas/os as scapegoats for ever diminishing economic and social wages caused by neoliberalism and balanced budget conservatism: "They are coming to take our jobs as well as the rights and privileges of (white) citizenship." However, it is important to note that the nativist Aztlán does not merely respond to the pressures of globalization and free-market capitalism.

The nativist Aztlán and the new nativism more broadly emerge out of the political exigencies of the post–civil rights, multicultural era. If nativism is a continuous stream in the American consciousness with corresponding ebbs and flows, the sociopolitical tumult of the 1960s has caused a change of course. As David Roediger and others have argued, the civil rights movement and the multicultural turn have created a challenge to the political right wherein discussions of race cannot clearly be articulated in "an openly racist voice."[21] In this era, race-neutral and liberal discourse (i.e., opportunity, assimilation, etc.) is marshaled against target communities.[22] Prior to the Chicano movement of the 1960s and 1970s, anti-Mexican racism and nativism often deployed three interrelated narratives: the Melting Pot, positing that to become fully American immigrants must assimilate through melting away their home culture; the Mexican Problem, arguing that Mexicans were a failed immigrant community because they kept immigrating and did not melt away into Anglo-America; and Manifest Destiny, naturalizing the conquest of the continental United States and erasing the historical legacies of Mexican and Native populations. While these narratives certainly circulate in nativist and popular discourses today, they are muted in their overtly racist manifestations. Thus, I would also contend that the political right has learned from the 1960s. Today, racial attacks must be sanitized and framed in race-neutral language. Moreover, as Kevin Johnson has suggested, immigrant communities often serve as proxies for those that share similar characteristics.[23] Therefore, it should be no surprise that Chicano narratives are redeployed against Mexican immigrants, for in many ways Chicanas/os were also always the targets of such white supremacist efforts. Through appropriating Aztlán, nativists have fashioned a narrative screen upon which they can project anxieties and fantasies central to the maintenance of whiteness as it is bound to national identity. The nativist Aztlán supplements earlier white supremacist narratives of the Melting Pot, the Mexican Problem, and Manifest Destiny, repackaging old fears in a new legitimating story, revitalizing them for the multicultural era, and providing the tools by which nativist ideology and discourse can spread.

While it is essential to tease out the workings of disparate nativist strands, scholars must also recognize that the core dynamics of nativism are bound to expressions of white supremacy and American exceptionalism. Regardless of the targeted population, the core dynamics of nativism are largely the same: the nation is imagined as static, pure, and innocent through the emphasis of an external-cum-internal threat. These dynamics have been marshaled against disparate communities and in ways that are not directly tied to anti-immigrant movements. For instance, one can easily find these dynamics at play in the discourse of frontier security that was used to justify conquest of Native lands.[24] Moreover, U.S. politicians have long deployed the specter of communism and threats to the U.S. body and way of life to undergird military interventions in Asia and Latin America.[25] In both cases, we see that nativism shares elements with other expressions of nationalism and imperial desires.[26] Thus, placing the dynamics of nativism in this context suggests that upticks in U.S. nativism are not outliers marking the political extremes but rather expressions of the dominant U.S. politico-racial logics.

Placed in this context, the nativist Aztlán is not merely a political tactic. Rather, it is grounded in and marked by the maintenance and reinforcement of whiteness. The Aztlán-reconquista narrative exposes the deployment of white victimhood as a means of forging racial solidarity. In other words, the articulation of a brown menace is another manifestation of the assertion of white nationalism. Examined in such a way, nativist visions of Aztlán are less an oddity of the conspiratorial fringe and more part and parcel of the logic of racial hegemony. This relationship between whiteness and the Aztlán-reconquista narrative becomes particularly troubling when one considers that Chicano deployments of Aztlán were in many ways injunctions to dismantle white supremacy. How, then, can this narrative be used at cross-purposes? And what might these reformulations of a central Chicano narrative illustrate about contemporary manifestations of white nationalism? These questions become a strategy for approaching this discursive return to Aztlán. These deployments repackage nativism and white supremacy anew in an era of rapid globalization and multiculturalism, giving legitimacy and narrative structure to old fears. Moving forward, this chapter explores four discursive moments of this return to Aztlán: the writings of Patrick Buchanan, Dave Arendt's novelization of the Aztlán Plot, the 2008 Absolut Vodka controversy, and the presence of reconquista fantasies in Arizona's recent debate over Mexican American studies in public primary and secondary education. While emerging from disparate discursive sites, these cases illustrate the way in which this nativist Aztlán has spread from the fringes into the mainstream and how racial anxieties can be transformed into fantasies of whiteness on the border, fantasies that target both Chicanas/os and Mexican immigrants with very material consequences.

Pat Buchanan's Aztlán

Nativist deployments of Aztlán are notoriously difficult to pin down. They often emerge from narrow and ephemeral means of communication: editorials, letters to the editor, blogs, and components of larger conservative, anti-immigrant, and sometimes explicitly white supremacist websites. While useful in disseminating fear, these locations limit the development of a fully articulated argument. Thus, the writings of Patrick J. Buchanan become central to any study of a nativist Aztlán. Buchanan's work offers perhaps the most articulate and sustained attempt to fashion a nativist Aztlán. Notably, Buchanan's role as a public intellectual and cultural worker of the political right spans the modern history of Aztlán, from the Chicano movement years when he served as an advisor to Richard Nixon to the contemporary immigration debate. Buchanan is likely best known for his presidential campaigns in 1992, 1996, and 2000 in which he ran on decidedly anti-immigrant and anti-globalization platforms. Indeed, Buchanan's political campaigns actively expressed fears of the changing complexion of America and served as precursors to his recent articulations of Aztlán hysteria.[27] By 2006, Buchanan had repositioned himself as a cable news commentator and—specifically through the publication of *Death of the West* (2002) and *State of Emergency* (2006)—an immigration expert. Arguably, his continuing presence on cable news makes his engagement of the Aztlán-reconquista narrative that much more intriguing and significant.

Buchanan most thoroughly addresses Aztlán in his *State of Emergency*, a polemic written in response to the ongoing immigration debate, the Sensenbrenner Bill (HR 4437), and the immigration marches of spring 2006, giving his audience a narrative structure to express their anxieties. *State of Emergency* actively contests Chicano nationalist discourse and refashions Aztlán not as an Indigenous homeland but as a Mexican-Chicano plot. Like many before him, Buchanan draws upon "El Plan Espiritual de Aztlán" and the political rhetoric of a few Chicano intellectuals to cast MEChA (Movimiento Estudiantil Chicano de Aztlán) and Chicano activists as a Chicano version of the Aryan Nation and argue that Mexico, its citizens, and their descendents are willing to act upon their "historic claims upon American lands."[28] What stands out about Buchanan's treatment of Aztlán is his effort to address the Chicano narrative head-on:

> Aztlan is the mythical land out of which the Aztec people came, a millennium ago, before they began the trek south to establish their empire. In history, Aztlan is in northwestern Mexico. In Chicano lore, it is the land from Oregon to California to Texas, stolen by the Americans.
>
> This is myth and fabricated nonsense.[29]

Here, Buchanan's treatment of Aztlán is quite strategic. Not only does he seek to refute Chicano claims to a homeland in the U.S. Southwest, but by writing this Aztlán off as "fabricated nonsense," he seeks to strip it of its meaning. Doing so allows Buchanan to charge Aztlán with new meaning in his next chapter: "The Aztlan Plot." No longer is Aztlán an ancestral homeland, a conceptual site of Chicano unification, or an ongoing plan for community uplift. Rather, Aztlán is a conspiratorial plot undertaken by the Mexican government, Chicano activists, and Mexican immigrants, seeking the dissolution of national sovereignty and the downfall of the United States. In the words of Buchanan,

> This then is the Aztlan Strategy: endless migration from Mexico north, the Hispanicization of the American Southwest, and dual citizenship for all Mexican-Americans. The goals: Erase the border. Grow the influence, through Mexican-Americans, over how America disposes of her wealth and power. Gradually circumscribe the sovereignty of the United

States. Lastly, economic and political merger of the nations in a binational union. And in the nuptial agreement, a commitment to share the wealth and power.

Stated bluntly, the Aztlan Strategy entails the end of the United States as a sovereign, self-sufficient, independent republic, the passing away of the American nation. *They are coming to conquer us.*[30]

Notably, Buchanan's Aztlán is cast as a threat, both external and internal. For while the Mexican government and Mexican immigrants conspire to retake the U.S. Southwest, they are aided by the post-1960s "racial chauvinism" of "Hispanic militants."[31] By fashioning Aztlán as a plot for a cultural and geopolitical reconquista, Buchanan charges all Chicano articulations of Aztlán as a threat to the United States, a threat to whiteness. Indeed, his description of the "nuptial agreement" and his evocation of Mexican Americans as disloyal and hyperfertile gesture toward a threat not just to America or whiteness but to whiteness as Americanness. Moreover, such a totalizing rescripting of Aztlán into a Mexican-Chicano plot has the potential to transform even the most innocuous deployments of Aztlán for his readers. A community center or a student organization bearing Aztlán in the name become "proof" of a larger conspiracy.

Significantly, while Aztlán allowed Chicano cultural workers to forge a usable past, Buchanan's construction of an Aztlán Plot and its embodiment of white anxieties is also bound to a strategic narrating of history. As several scholars have explored, the construction of whiteness is dependent upon and secured through a process of forgetting—both strategic and collective—akin to amnesia. Indeed, many scholars have linked such elisions to the formation of racial hegemony.[32] For instance, in *The Racial Contract*, Charles W. Mills argues that the discursive erasure of Native peoples was needed to legitimate imperial expansion.[33] In a complementary forgetting, Renato Rosaldo's theory of "imperialist nostalgia" suggests that imperial powers celebrate Indigenous communities only after they have been sufficiently destroyed.[34] Thus, it becomes unsurprising that before he establishes the Aztlán Plot proper, Buchanan walks a historical tightrope, simultaneously imploring his readers to remember and forget the past. At several points, Buchanan enjoins his readers to "understand the history Mexicans are taught never to forget."[35] That history, of course, is that Mexico has "historical claims to U.S. lands" and for that reason Mexico has "A Grudge Against the Gringo."[36] In other words, Buchanan clearly recognizes the potential of Aztlán to counter the concept of Manifest Destiny.

Writing in a post-movement era, Buchanan faces the challenge of addressing Aztlán and asserting the claims of Manifest Destiny. Strategically, Buchanan simultaneously narrates and delegitimizes Mexico's historical grievances. He does this in several ways. First, he recognizes that the United States did take half of Mexico's territory, but he also repeatedly notes Mexico's ineffective rule and the "unsettled" nature of those lands. This notion of a vast, empty frontier may of course be surprising to the Mexican and Native peoples living for centuries in those territories. However, Buchanan's argument embodies the racial logics Mills has associated with white settler states, wherein colonized spaces are rhetorically emptied so that they can be "peopled" and can legitimate the contemporary white power structure.[37] Second, Buchanan repeatedly fashions a historical relationship between the nations wherein the United States is the big brother/protector of its little neighbor to the south. Most notably, this emerges through his discussions of the Monroe Doctrine and the Good Neighbor Policy.[38] Here, Buchanan's logic clearly echoes the countersubversion strategies that Michael Rogin has contended are so central to American exceptionalism and imperialist tendencies.[39] The United States is imagined as pure and just against the backdrop of a corrupt and demonized Latin America. In doing so, Buchanan elides U.S. imperialist tendencies, rescripting them to support a narrative in which the United States acts heroically and Mexico has long failed to appreciate U.S. support. In this way, the Aztlán-reconquista narrative supplements Manifest Destiny, for not only does Buchanan reassert the legitimacy of U.S. imperial endeavors, but he simultaneously fashions the United States as victim. This national victimhood functions as an extension of claims to white victimhood, further exposing the linkages between racial and political nativism that form a core of white nationalism.

Throughout Buchanan's injunctions to strategically remember and forget, there are disruptions in the narrative, disruptions that signal white anxieties. Buchanan recounts almost two hundred years of Mexican-U.S. relations to establish a context for his fears of a recon-

quista. But one must simply ask the question: doesn't one need a conquest before there can be a *re*conquest? Buchanan avoids such a simple,
frank discussion, yet the anxiety is palpable in his writing. This is particularly evidenced in his discussion of the lead-up to the Texas War
for Independence. Buchanan argues that Texas secession was inevitable
because the Anglo-American immigrants who settled in Texas did not
assimilate.[40] Buchanan treads lightly on this topic. Clearly, he wants to
underscore a historical parallel. However, he does not wish to acknowledge that this was an active conquest of Texas or that Mexico's assimila-
tionist immigration policies did not work. Despite these ruptures in the
narrative, Buchanan's injunction to remember-to-forget establishes the
foundation of white victimhood. Indeed, Buchanan's fear of a coming
reconquista is eerily reminiscent of the strategic appropriation of pain
described by Patricia Williams. In her influential *Alchemy of Race and
Rights*, Williams explores the ways in which the oppressor deflects blame
onto the oppressed and claims victimization as a means for continuing the hegemonic status quo.[41] While Manifest Destiny may have been
the narrative foundation of U.S. imperialism, Buchanan's Aztlán is the
strategic narrative deployment to maintain power through the articulation of fear and victimhood. Moreover, Buchanan spends page after
page explicating the grievances of white America as a means of deflect-
ing attention from the historical legacy of pain forged through imperial
expansion and the consolidation of white privilege.

For Buchanan, the Aztlán Plot places the United States and its so-
cioracial order in jeopardy. This is perhaps best demonstrated when
he explains how the reconquista will occur. The takeover of the U.S.
Southwest will not be achieved "militarily, but ethnically, linguistically,
and culturally, through transfer of millions of Mexicans into the United
States and Migration of 'Anglos' out of the lands Mexico lost in 1848."[42]
White flight on a scale never seen before will create huge demographic,
electoral, and thus power shifts. Here, Buchanan's Aztlán Plot hinges on
his conceptualization of the United States through a paradigm of ethnic or cultural nationalism. Buchanan contends that the United States
is not held together by a common creed, a model of civic nationalism,
but a common culture.[43] Thus, it is not by happenstance that U.S.-born
Latinas/os—politicians, college students, community activists—are
scripted together with immigrants as an internal threat to the nation-

state. Doing so implicitly reinforces the conflation of white and American. Such efforts are echoed by calls to establish English as the official language and to defund communities of color in terms of social services and education.

Arguably, Buchanan and others of the nativist right are able to appropriate the Aztlán narrative and Chicano nationalist discourse so easily because both deployments of Aztlán rely upon a model of ethnic nationalism. This is not to suggest that the discursive separatism of el movimiento is complicit with white supremacy. Rather, they rely on the same logical structure of imagining a nation through ethnoracial affiliation. While Chicano nationalism asserted a right to belong in the U.S. Southwest, such rhetoric fed into long-standing fears of nonassimilation and conquest.

In this way, Buchanan's Aztlán Plot remakes the Melting Pot and Mexican Problem anew. He warns that the potential, or in his words ongoing, dissolution of U.S. national sovereignty is to be achieved through cultural disunification. In other words, in the multicultural era, Chicanas/os are failing to melt away into white America. Drawing upon Samuel Huntington and others, Buchanan argues that cultural disunity leads to a weakened nation.[44] Moreover, he extends this argument by questioning the feasibility of racial integration: "Not only do Mexicans come from a different culture, they are, 85 percent of them, mestizo, or Amerindian. History teaches that separate races take even longer to integrate. Our 60 million citizens of German descent are fully assimilated, but millions of African, Latin American, and Caribbean descent are not."[45] Significantly, Buchanan never declares the United States to be a white nation in such simple terms. To do so explicitly would violate the discursive conventions of the post-break, multicultural era. Marking the power and pliability of whiteness, he couches his argument through a concern for the nation, a nation that he conceives as culturally (i.e., racially) unified.[46] In doing so, Buchanan inscribes the anxieties of the Melting Pot and the Mexican Problem onto the rise of Chicano identity politics and its foundational narrative of Aztlán. Here, the Aztlán-reconquista narrative forges a basis for white solidarity. As George Lipsitz has argued about nativist discourse more generally, "this manifestation of privilege masquerading as powerlessness does not really need to convince the electorate at large in order to succeed; its true aim is to build a sense of besieged solidarity within its own group."[47] In the case of the nativist Aztlán, few need actually believe that a takeover of the Southwest will actually occur, for a major dividend of whiteness is simply belonging, specifically in an era when it is unpopular to explicitly assert whiteness as the grounds for membership in the club or national imagination. Finally, in tandem with these other aspects, the articulation of Aztlán as reconquista emplotts a narrative of white victimization. As many have previously noted anti-immigrant and anti-multicultural discourses often pitch white Americans as a community under siege.

In his construction of a nativist Aztlán, Buchanan works to defend and deploy white solidarity through the guise of white victimhood. Fashioning whites as an aggrieved community is, of course, nothing new. Indeed, it is a rather entrenched strategy common to both the political right and white supremacist groups. What is new is the appropriation of Chicano discourse to lend legitimacy to nativist anxieties. Indeed, making his work even more stunning is the way in which he appropriates the discourses of inequality and grievance to protect white privilege. The undercurrent of Buchanan's argument, however, is telling. Through the dual threats of his Aztlán Plot, Buchanan maps white identity and privilege onto the geopolitical territory of the United States. Thus, whiteness becomes the unnamed, unmarked category that structures Buchanan's arguments and fears. During el movimiento, Aztlán empowered Chicanas/os to fight against Melting Pot assimilation, the Mexican Problem, and Manifest Destiny. But in the hands of Buchanan, Aztlán is fashioned to redeploy those old stories. As a screen for the projection of white anxieties, Aztlán is transformed from a narrative foundation for a community of struggle to a narrative that reinforces racial hegemony and white nationalism. But the nativist Aztlán is not simply bound to fears of a brown invasion, it simultaneously allows for the articulation of white fantasies.

Suspense Thrillers and the Fantasies of White Anxiety

While Buchanan's work offers a sustained articulation of the Aztlán-reconquista narrative, another cultural artifact imagines those nativist fears and anxieties into existence. Dave Arendt's novel *Reclaiming Aztlan* (2007) places the reconquista narrative at the center of the suspense-thriller genre.[48] Significantly, this novel illustrates the ways in which the vision of a nativist Aztlán travels, moving from brief, ephemeral articulations on editorial pages and websites to the keystone chapters of Buchanan's recent work to a 360-plus-page novel that seeks to blend white anxieties and entertainment. Prior to the novel, Arendt had worked as a police officer in Chula Vista, California, and testified in narcotics cases. On the book's back cover, Arendt uses this work history to claim authority on border issues. Together, this claim to authority and the novel have given Arendt access to speaking engagements. For instance, in June 2007 Arendt was the keynote speaker for Arizona's Flagstaff Republican Women. The organization's newsletter advertised the event, describing the novel as "a fiction [sic] thriller which addresses the stark realities of illegal immigration."[49] Moreover, the newsletter noted that "Dave is deeply concerned about the future of our United States and would like to share why and what we need to do about it. We are not being told the facts about this very real problem. It's not too late—yet."[50] Here, the ominous tone of the talk is clear. Arendt was invited to disseminate fear through the Aztlán-reconquista narrative, with the novel serving as vehicle and platform for anti-immigrant organizing.[51] While *Reclaiming Aztlan* certainly helped spread the Aztlán-as-reconquista narrative, the significance of its analysis is not rooted in the novel's influence. *Reclaiming Aztlan* does not have the widespread readership of Buchanan's best sellers. Rather, Arendt's book further demonstrates the influence of Buchanan and the ways in which the nativist Aztlán has traversed disparate discursive forms: from editorials and blogs to historical-political treatises and fiction. Perhaps most importantly, however, *Reclaiming Aztlan* exposes how the Aztlán-as-reconquista narrative can be deployed to repackage racial anxieties into white fantasies.

The novel tells the story of Pat Bahaar, a Department of Homeland Security border agent, and his efforts to stop a plot by Sergio Juarez-Zuniga, Mexico's Deputy Director of Internal Security, to retake the U.S. Southwest. Bahaar is, of course, the only hope to stop the Aztlán Plot. While Bahaar embodies the nation's hopes in its time of need, the Aztlán Plot is fostered and actualized by his nemesis, Juarez-Zuniga. During his college years, Juarez-Zuniga came to Los Angeles to play soccer for UCLA. There, he became involved with the Chicano student organization MEChA, and the seeds of his reconquista dreams were sewn.[52] Years later Juarez-Zuniga has all of the pieces of his plan in place. As Deputy Director of Internal Security, he convinces the United States that Mexico will stop illegal immigration and border crime. To help repatriate immigrants back to Mexico, Juarez-Zuniga establishes diplomatic centers in the U.S. border states. These locations are secretly connected to Mexico via a network of underground tunnels. Instead of moving Mexicans south, these centers are used to smuggle immigrants, from Mexico and elsewhere, as well as shipments of drugs north. Once in the diplomatic centers, the immigrants are given driver's licenses for a variety of states. After they settle in the new communities, Juarez-Zuniga uses these immigrants to commit large-scale voter fraud. Ultimately, a Latina/o political party (functioning as a stand-in for the 1960s and 1970s La Raza Unida Party) is swept into power across the Southwest. The leader of this party is Hugo Martin, an old friend of Juarez-Zuniga from his MEChA days.[53] Notably, Martin, MEChA, and the Latina/o political party work in tandem to reinforce the unassimilability of U.S. Latinas/os in nativism's white nationalist imagination. Despite this convoluted scenario, Juarez-Zuniga's plot (or is it Arendt's?) strikes all the cords of Buchanan's anxieties: voter fraud, drug trafficking, Middle Eastern immigrants, loss of political power, dissolution of national sovereignty. In contrast to Buchanan's works, however, *Reclaiming Aztlan* transforms speculative fears into political fantasies, giving flesh and form to the foretold worries of earlier nativist cultural workers. Moreover, when reading with a long view of history, articulated anxieties of voter fraud and drug trafficking become recognizable as repetitions of the Lawless Mexican and Infernal Paradise tropes discussed earlier.

Central to the nativist Aztlán's positioning in the politics of the multicultural era, the novel does not suggest that immigration itself is bad, just some forms of immigration and immigrants. Indeed, this deployment of a good immigrant/bad immigrant narrative echoes much contemporary anti-immigrant discourse wherein "our ancestors came here legally" has become a common strategy of rejecting immigration through a guise of acceptance. This discursive strategy is built upon the concepts of Melting Pot assimilation and the Mexican Problem wherein good immigrants are able to culturally and racially melt away. Those who do not are defined as a social problem or a cultural and political threat. Arendt repeatedly makes note of the immigrant ancestors of his main characters and mentions a few minor immigrant characters. Here, Arendt deploys the common "truth-denying truism" that this is a nation of immigrants and in the past newcomers actively divested themselves of the old country in order to more quickly assimilate.[54] This strategy elides two aspects of U.S. immigration history. Assimilation was rarely as quick and voluntary as it is remembered to be. Moreover, U.S. immigration laws have long disparately impacted different racial and ethnic groups. As Ian Haney López and others have noted, race-based immigration policy has shaped the demographic makeup of the United States as well as the nation's racial imagination.[55] Indeed, those who claim that their ancestors came legally do so by ignoring that such a legal status was bound to their ancestors' standing as white. Through relying on such narratives, Arendt fashions positive immigration as that in which individuals can embrace capitalism and pull themselves up by their proverbial bootstraps.[56] Not surprisingly, almost all of Arendt's positive models of immigration are white.[57] This good immigration/bad immigration dynamic allows the novel to vilify Mexican immigrants as unassimilable and reinforce the notion that Mexican-descent peoples will be perpetual foreigners. Moreover, this rhetorical move simultaneously maintains the American mythos that the United States is a welcoming nation of immigrants where all things are possible, a narrative that upholds benevolence and grit while masking the history that U.S. immigration policy has long shaped national racial demographics. The logics of this strategy allow nativists to deploy a racially encoded agenda under the guise of race neutrality or nonracism, packaging old hates in a way that they may pass inspection and gain traction in the contemporary era. Moreover, such a move provides the necessary guise of factuality to the "very real problem" observed by the Flagstaff Republican Women.

Perhaps the novel's most interesting theorization of the U.S.-Mexico border emerges as Arendt draws on a comparison of Mexicans and Chicanas/os to Palestinians.[58] For years, scholars and activists have articulated a connection between these communities of struggle, focusing on the disputed nature of international boundaries as well as the material and psychological impact of deterritorialization and living in occupied territory.[59] In contrast, Arendt uses the Palestinian conflict to echo nativist concerns of Aztlán. The novel suggests that the Palestinian Authority had no interest in peace because "peace with Israel would require them to become self sufficient, and why do that when others doled out billions to them."[60] This description of self-serving corruption echoes the long tradition of casting Mexico and Mexicans as lawless and reverberates with the specific way in which the text describes Mexico's choice in turning a blind eye toward drugs, corruption, and immigration. Moreover, Arendt contends that the Palestinians "never owned the land and yet laid claim to it."[61] Arguably, this connection between the Palestinian territories and the U.S. Southwest allows for Arendt to implicitly draw upon the concept of Manifest Destiny. For Arendt, both the United States and Israel have long-standing and divine claims to the land. Through such a formulation, the politics of blind support for Israel's borders, sovereignty, and security is mapped out through the discourse of nativism, and vice versa.

As Arendt yokes Mexican immigration together with the conflicts in the Middle East, he ultimately relies upon a paradigm of ethnic nationalism and deploys a Huntingtonian model of the Clash of Civilizations. Arendt, like Buchanan and other nativist cultural workers, scripts a global conflict between Western civilization—embodied in whiteness—and *Other* cultures. Thus, it becomes unsurprising and sadly unironic when Arendt remarks that the "Attacks of the World Trade Centers on 9–11–2001 had *changed the complexion* of domestic safety."[62] The conflicts in the Middle East and the immigration debate are not linked through concerns for "domestic safety." Rather, they are bound together because they function as a means to express white anxieties of a collapsing social order, one they feel is collapsing through the pressures of globalization and multiculturalism.

While the novel enacts the fears and anxieties of contemporary nativism, it simultaneously fashions Bahaar as a fantasized national hero whose white masculinity is the only answer to the threat of a brown menace. Bahaar's embodiment of white masculinity is evidenced most clearly through his interactions with Juarez-Zuniga. Indeed, this contest of masculinities emerges at their first meeting where upon Juarez-Zuniga aggressively squeezes Bahaar as they shake hands. Bahaar considers this behavior "macho" and returns "an equal amount of pressure on Sergio's *soft hand*."[63] The two men continue to increase the strength of their grips until "suddenly Sergio's grip relaxed, a sign of defeat."[64] In this exchange, despite his soft hands, Juarez-Zuniga is the clear aggressor who is quickly "outmanned" by his American nemesis through brute force.[65] Describing the aggression as "macho," Arendt frames this contest as not between men but between culturally inscribed masculinities. And it is clear that Bahaar's embodiment of whiteness bears the potential to crush Juarez-Zuniga.

Arendt extends this contest of nationalized, racialized masculinities through perhaps the oldest trope in the book. Upon seeing a photograph of Bahaar's wife Diane, Juarez-Zuniga immediately becomes captivated by her beauty, marked by her "tall and slender" figure and "golden hair."[66] Juarez-Zuniga then decides that he must conquer not only the United States but also Diane. Indeed, after he decides that he must have Diane, Juarez-Zuniga says to himself "and that will be your fate, Pat Bahaar. I'll take your country, your wife and your life."[67] Indeed, this moment reads like the nineteenth-century sensationalist fiction that Streeby has described. As the embodiment of national hopes, Bahaar must then protect his wife and his land, his home and his nation. Significantly, the novel's climax further inscribes Bahaar as the protector of the nation and white womanhood. After the Aztlán plan has initially succeeded through an electoral takeover, Juarez-Zuniga sends operatives to kill Bahaar and kidnap Diane. The home invasion parallels the national invasion. And while Bahaar is able to save Diane, kill the intruders, and escape, his home is destroyed and he must live in hiding, solidifying the metaphor of home invasion as national invasion—a trope often used by nativists against those they cast as intruders.

In many ways, *Reclaiming Aztlan* gives shape to the nightmare of Patrick Buchanan and other nativist cultural workers. The novel does not solely foretell of a potential threat but enacts it for readers, transforming a far-fetched conspiracy into a textualized reality. Yet like Buchanan, Arendt also gestures to the future to disseminate fears of a reconquista and the threat it holds to the U.S. racial project. After the national and home invasions, Bahaar and Diane escape to Idaho and assume new identities. Here, one must wonder if the location was chosen purposefully: Idaho being one of the whitest regions of the country, beyond the geographic territories ceded in 1848, and home to many white supremacist fringe groups. In the final pages, Juarez-Zuniga's men find out the new location and identities of Bahaar and Diane, and whiteness is again at risk.

While *Reclaiming Aztlan* certainly strives to be a political thriller, this conclusion clearly evokes a dystopia more commonly found in science fiction.[68] One may suggest that science fiction's convention of imagining the future to comment upon and intervene within the present is at play here. Recall the way in which the Flagstaff Republican Women framed Arendt's appearance: Arendt was "deeply concerned about the future of our United States. . . . *It's not too late—yet.*"[69] Arendt leaves readers with a fear that a reconquista may be just the first step. Even as Bahaar's hero positioning allows him to embody white nationalist fantasies against the fears of a brown menace, the ending returns to the anxieties of whiteness and deploys potential victimhood as a call to arms.

The work of Buchanan and Arendt illustrates how the foundational narrative of the Chicano movement has been adopted and adapted by the nativist right. Giving age-old anxieties a gloss of legitimacy and new life, Aztlán is a screen for the projection of fears and fantasies, providing a narrative structure to the renewed articulation of the Melting Pot, the Mexican Problem, and Manifest Destiny. But the significance of this return to Aztlán is found not just in the ability to repackage white anxieties and fantasies. Rather, the power of the Aztlán scare is also located in its ability to frame the immigration debate even at the most benign of moments, providing form to the anxieties of whiteness at the smallest provocations.

Absolut Aztlán

Following the articulation of a nativist Aztlán by Buchanan, Arendt, and others, the fears of a nativist Aztlán reached a popular culture zenith with the Absolut Vodka controversy of 2008. Early in the year, Absolut ran a series of advertisements with the slogan "In an Absolut World." In the United States, the campaign juxtaposed this slogan with images of a woman holding a martini beside a pregnant man in one iteration and a politician with a Pinocchio nose at a podium in another. In Mexico, this campaign took the shape of a map depicting the nation's territories prior to Texas secession and U.S. conquest of the Southwest. The image was emblazoned with the campaign slogan "In an Absolut World" and a bottle of vodka. Designed by the Mexico City–based Teran/TBWA, the advertisement was placed in the Mexican celebrity magazine *Quién* and on billboards, running for two months prior to gaining attention in the United States. In the first few days of April, the ad gained attention north of the border and fomented controversy in the conservative blogosphere. Conservative cultural workers Michelle Malkin, Matt Drudge, and others posted the image, arguing that Absolut was undermining and attacking the sovereignty of U.S. borders. Followers echoed concerns that Absolut was supporting a reconquista vis-à-vis illegal immigration, and joined in the calls for a national boycott of the foreign owned vodka.[70] On April 5, 2008, Absolut caved, retracting the ad and contending that the advertisement was designed for a Mexican audience and its specific sensibilities. Despite the retraction, the controversy became the focal point of conservative commentators in the next few days. On April 7 and 8, Lou Dobbs, Glenn Beck, and others further disseminated the story, magnifying the connections to threats to sovereignty and repeating calls for a nationwide boycott. Seizing the moment, and making a strange instance utterly bizarre, U.S.-owned Skyy Vodka entered the fray, announcing their unquestioned support for the 160-year-old Treaty of Guadalupe Hidalgo, hoping to capitalize (in the many senses of the word) on the situation.[71]

The Absolut ad and the resulting controversy expose the amnesiac foundations of whiteness. According to Absolut's official apology, the ad was supposed to speak to Mexican sensibilities, depicting a more ideal time in the nation's history: the time between independence from colonial Spain and the conquest of U.S. expansion.[72] While the ad is framed as a depiction of an idyllic past, the push back was almost always articulated through the present. A common concern was that of an ongoing effort to dismantle the sovereignty of the U.S. borders. For instance, a post on "The Uncooperative Blogger" stated that "this is just unbelievably offensive and I am just sick of companies that make money in the U.S. and support this kind of illegal alien/Mexican threat to our sovereignty. Time for a Boycott!"[73] Alan Carl of the blog "Donklephant" argued, "You simply [don't] make jokes about national borders. People get touchy about borders, they fight wars over borders."[74] Here, the irony of amnesia is striking, for it was the United States in the nineteenth century that made light of and violated the sovereignty of its neighbor's borders. Indeed, it may be that the ad received such vitriolic attention specifically because it was an injunction to remember against the long-sustained and structured efforts to forget. The Absolut ad challenges white supremacist narratives of Manifest Destiny and the Mexican Problem, reminding the U.S. audience that this land was not always American but the object of imperial expansion. This anxiety of whiteness at the intersection of remembering and forgetting echoes the historical negotiations of Pat Buchanan. In both cases, nativist cultural workers articulate their concerns about the present beside and against the ghosts of the past.

This manifestation of the nativist Aztlán is fascinating in part because of the way in which the advertisement was redirected as a dog whistle, striking the right tone to foment fear and loathing while simultaneously remaining inaudible to many. Notably, the advertisement did not explicitly invoke Aztlán or a reconquest. Unlike the work of Buchanan, Arendt, and others, the ad did not forge a narrative. Rather, it tapped into this preexisting narrative and its corresponding anxieties of whiteness, establishing the grounds for the controversy. Conservative cultural workers deployed the advertisement to stoke nativist fears and boost their ratings. Perhaps the most telling example comes from the April 7, 2008, broadcast of *Lou Dobbs Tonight*. Dobbs used the scandalized Absolut story as a teaser at the end of the preceding show and the beginning of his own. During the story itself, Dobbs and correspondent Casey Wian used the ad to legitimize nativist fears of a coming reconquista:

> WIAN: Yeah, Lou, Absolut Vodka is now apologizing for that ad that shows Mexican territory extending into the United States as far north as the Washington State border. We'll have details coming up.
> DOBBS: Look forward to it and Casey, I thought that was just a little fringe element in this country. . . . You mean there's some kind of like national interest in this subject in Mexico itself?
> WIAN: A lot of folks have been saying that this is a fantasy and there's no such ideas, . . . among many Mexicans, but it's there.

And later:

> DOBBS: And would you like to just share with our audience how many times this broadcast, you and I and other journalists associated with us here have been criticized for even suggesting the idea that [re-

conquista] was even a marginal concept at the fringe of the left-wing radical nut jobs who are excited about this issue?

WIAN: I couldn't come close to counting the number of times we have been criticized but it's often and this idea, though, despite the protestations of people like the Southern Poverty Law Center, is alive and well on both sides of the border, Lou.[75]

The same hour on CNN *Headline News*, Glenn Beck also deployed the ad as evidence of the coming reconquista, declaring, "This movement is real. It's called reconquista. Its goal is alive and well, and it is absolute insanity."[76] Strategically, Beck used the controversy as a lead-in to an argument against San Francisco's status as a sanctuary city, further connecting the vodka ad and the immigration threat. Clearly Dobbs, Wian, and Beck used the Absolut controversy to evidence the mainstream nature of the reconquista. This advertising campaign was no mere happenstance nor an expression of ironic Mexican humor. Rather, to these nativist cultural workers, this "proved" that something more nefarious was afoot, only if one is to take Dobbs, Wian, and Beck at face value. However, it is also critical to note that these broadcasts aired after Absolut retracted and apologized for the image. As such, one must ask what the purpose of a nationwide boycott would be. Since Absolut had already capitulated, the calls for a boycott and establishing the reconquista conspiracy as mainstream functioned to foster the besieged solidarity of white nationalism where the mask of victimhood pays the psychological dividends of belonging.

Like previous instances, the Absolut controversy allowed nativist cultural workers to position themselves as victims while simultaneously reinforcing their ability to wield power. Positioning the United States and whites as victims of Mexican aggression works on several levels. Articulations of victimhood conceal the privileges of whiteness in the system of U.S. racial hegemony. Moreover, these claims fashion a basis for white solidarity. Perhaps most important for this case, asserting victimhood works to attain white privilege on a global scale. While the ad was created for and published in Mexico, many saw it as two-faced, arguing that advertising regardless of location should not contest U.S. (white) sensibilities. The underlying argument is that global marketing should only support a U.S. hegemonic worldview that is structured by and buttresses the power and privileges of whiteness. Should any campaign challenge this order, it will be swiftly met with calls for national boycotts and claims of victimhood. Significantly, the protestations against Absolut expose a conflict between markets and the power to map capitalism. While nativists wish to fortify geopolitical borders to halt the movement of people, through boycotts and media campaigns they accept the global flow of capital if it is directed and restricted to reinforce racial hegemony. Thus, the transnational nature of the Absolut controversy exposes the potentially global reach of whiteness.

Notably, cries of white victimhood and striking moments of historical amnesia mark the backlash against Absolut in ways reminiscent of the discursive strategies of Pat Buchanan, Dave Arendt, and other earlier manifestations of a nativist Aztlán.[77] Arguably, however, the significance of the Absolut Vodka controversy is not simply that there is yet another example of nativists inscribing white supremacy onto a central narrative of Chicano thought. The example of Absolut Aztlán demonstrates how nativists have successfully reframed the Aztlán narrative. While Buchanan, Arendt, and others have painstakingly appropriated Aztlán and emplotted a coming reconquista and corresponding white anxieties and fantasies onto it, this example illustrates that the right has developed a discursive framework capable of countering the counternarrative. In other words, this phenomenon has reached a stage wherein humorous and innocuous references to the historic U.S.-Mexican border, let alone Chicano articulations of Aztlán, immediately trigger the nativist reconquista hysteria.

The Absolut controversy also illustrates that white anxieties are activated by not just the crossing of borders but the questioning of them. While Buchanan and Arendt articulated a fear of an immigrant invasion that threatens to change the racial and cultural makeup of the United States, the Absolut controversy demonstrates fears of a threat to the ideological makeup of the United States, an ideology of white nationalism that requires a careful amnesia regarding how U.S. borders and the nation's racial composition came to be as well as an international prohibition against calling into question the dominant narratives of the U.S. racial project. Thus, it should not be surprising that the fears and fantasies of the nativist Aztlán also emerged in Arizona's recent debate over the role of ethnic studies in primary and secondary education.

Teaching Aztlán; or, The Transitive Property of Hate

Previously, this chapter demonstrated how the nativist Aztlán has expressed the fear of a challenge to the U.S. racial order as well as how this narrative has been deployed against Mexican immigrants. However, the value of Aztlán to white supremacy is not simply that it offers narrative form to racial anxieties or that it fosters white solidarity—although it does both. Rather, Aztlán also targets Chicanas/os as part of this broad reconquista plot. Recall that Kevin Johnson has contended that immigrant communities serve as stand-ins for those who share similar characteristics.[78] While Chicanas/os have more legal protections and are thus more difficult to expel and oppress than Mexican immigrants, the nativist Aztlán scripts Chicanas/os as perpetually foreign, disloyal, and unfit for white democracy.[79] That is, because this narrative renders Chicanas/os as in league with Mexican immigrants and the Mexican government, it calls into question their social and juridical belonging. Here, it is clear that nativism and white supremacy are not discrete ideological systems, for just as nativism may take a racist shape, so may racism deploy the logics and discursive strategies of nativism.

Drawing upon racial and political nativism, these manifestations of Aztlán have been used against not only immigrants but also Mexican Americans more broadly. Former Los Angeles Mayor Antonio Villaraigosa, former California Lieutenant Governor Cruz Bustamante, and other politicians have withstood organized campaigns seeking to discredit and disqualify them for elected office because of their affiliation with the student organization MEChA. Formed at the height of the Chicano movement, MEChA is known for its efforts to foster Chicano consciousness and grow Chicano influence in educational institutions. Today's nativist campaigns depict MEChA as a radical organization by emphasizing the rhetorical flourishes of "El Plan Espiritual de Aztlán" and thus claiming that the organization is working toward a secessionist movement.[80] Moreover, these depictions of MEChA also yoke the student group together with the anti-Semitic fringe group La Voz de Aztlán, which is well known for its web presence and its repeated calls for a reconquest of the Southwest.[81] Strategically, this works on several levels. Evincing a new turn in racial nativism, these efforts frame MEChA as a radical, race-based, and racist organization. Note the post-break, multicultural rhetorical shift: Mechistas are a threat not because they will racially degrade the United States, but because they are "racist." This tactic allows contemporary nativists to invert racial power dynamics and claim the moral high ground. Deploying the nativist Aztlán in this way forces the politicians to either reject MEChA or pay the political price. Should the politicians refuse to denounce MEChA, they will appear radical. If they do renounce MEChA, the conservative cultural workers also gain, delegitimizing a key organization that has long worked for educational attainment and curricular reform.

Unsurprisingly, similar efforts have also been deployed against Mexican American student and community activists. For instance, MEChA chapters on several California university campuses have been targeted for initiatives to remove funding.[82] These strategic uses of Aztlán, despite their varied purposes, share a common strategy. They draw attention to radical and sometimes revolutionary rhetoric of the 1960s as a means of articulating cultural anxieties about fairly reformist goals. In other words, they seek to discredit and defund efforts such as culturally relevant programming on school campuses through decrying MEChA as a threat to American society, echoing earlier efforts of political nativism from the Alien and Sedition Acts of 1798 to the Red Scares of the 1900s. MEChA, Chicanas/os, and Mexican immigrants are not portrayed as a racial threat but are recast as a cultural and political danger to American society. Moreover, this strategy is instructive because the Aztlán-reconquista narrative provides a means for attacking not only Mexican immigrants but also Mexican American politicians and activists who seek to improve the conditions of Mexican-descent communities and thereby challenge white supremacy. As Julio Cammarota has suggested, attacks on MEChA and their reliance on the reconquista narrative often place multiculturalism directly in their sights.[83] Here, one need consider only how Arizona's SB 1070 and HB 2281 target immigrants and Mexican Americans in disparate, yet complementary ways.

In April 2010, U.S. and international media turned their attention to Arizona and the passing of SB 1070, a bill that required local police to ascertain the citizenship status of everyone suspected of being undocumented and turn them over to Immigration and Customs Enforcement if they could not provide appropriate documentation. Governor Jan Brewer signed HB 2281 into law three weeks after its more famous legislative kin. Developed by then Arizona state superintendent and later Attorney General Tom Horne and former state representative and later state superintendent John Huppenthal, HB 2281 outlawed courses that promoted the overthrow of the U.S. government, instilled racial resentment, were designed for students of a particular ethnic group, or advocated ethnic solidarity. While written to broadly target any racially oriented and potentially seditious courses, HB 2281 was used to specifically target the Mexican American studies (MAS) courses of Tucson Unified School District (TUSD) that Horne and Huppenthal had long railed against. When Huppenthal declared the courses in violation of the law, the TUSD Governing Board initially supported the MAS program. However, amid a series of lawsuits and the pressure of losing significant levels of state funding, the board acquiesced: courses were suspended, books were boxed up and shipped out, curriculum was banned, and teachers and administrative support staff were relocated or fired. Much of the scholarly and activist response has rightly recognized HB 2281 as an attack on communities of color, arguing that the ban is an attempt to forge neoliberal consumer-citizens and reproduce dominant ideologies of color blindness, individualism, and American exceptionalism.[84]

At first glance, the language of HB 2281 could seem innocuous or paranoid. However, while ethnic studies may offer critical perspectives on U.S. and world history, as a field it hardly advances the overthrow of the U.S. government or the development of racial resentment.[85] This bill, particularly its prohibition against teaching and advocating governmental insurrection, is rendered logical when one considers that the rhetoric of the nativist Aztlán underwrote this legislative act. As such, HB 2281 and its articulated fear of racial resentment and insurrection should be read not solely as state educational policy but as a dog whistle of nativism and white supremacy.

The nativist roots of HB 2281 are exposed in the Cambium Audit, a curricular review of the TUSD MAS program called for by Huppenthal. While the report largely clears MAS of any wrongdoing, the appendix details the concerns of one community member who lays claim to starting the investigation into MAS:

This person was initially concerned over statements made to her by Mexican people entering the United States for whom she was translating Spanish to English. According to her, they spoke of plans to enter the U.S. illegally, "take back their land, and throw the gringos out." She became concerned, along with others that this mind-set was being taught to students within the instructional setting of the classroom. She, along with a political activism group with whom she is involved, contacted Tom Horne, then State Superintendent of Schools for Arizona, for assistance in viewing textbooks used within the MASD [Mexican American Studies Department] program. After a comprehensive review of these materials, this person created a packet of her findings and began researching the program more extensively, which she has continued to do over the past several years, presenting her results to Mr. Horne and other interested parties. She continued this research because she was, in her own words, "horrified about the hate and revolution that they are teaching in our schools."

This individual is concerned about the instruction of the concept of Aztlan. Aztlan is the mythical place where the Aztecs supposedly settled many years ago. It is unclear as to exactly where this place would have been located if it indeed existed. There is some controversy over Aztlan itself that is contributing to the controversy regarding the MASD classes. This has been a difficult abstraction for the audit team to research. According to this interviewed community member, Aztlan is the name of the movement that Mexican people are using to take over the U.S. Therefore, she does not believe that it is appropriate for it to be taught in our schools.[86]

The Cambium Audit calls into question the legitimacy of this individual's concerns, for her reconquista description of Aztlán does not align with that described by teachers and students as "a mythical place that represents peace and harmony for all races."[87] However, a few critical elements of her interview stand out. She claims personal knowledge of immigrants plotting an overthrow of the United States (one must wonder if they laughed maniacally when they disclosed their dastardly plot). She and other believers in the nativist Aztlán initiated contact with Horne. And finally, even though she had never spoken with students or witnessed any MAS classes, "she has heard stories about Mexican American students deciding they are being victimized once they have taken the MAS classes. It is her belief that the MAS students are very angry and 'have a bad attitude' because, 'All they [MAS teachers] do is teach them to hate a particular ethnic group and to hate all white people.'"[88] Indeed, one cannot help but recognize the fears elucidated by Buchanan and emplotted by Arendt as they are manifested in the summary of this individual's interview. The nativist roots of HB 2281, however, go beyond illustrating yet another articulation of anti-Mexican reconquista anxieties and fantasies.

This moment also demonstrates what one may call the transitive property of white supremacy whereby anti-Latina/o legislation is organized by anti-immigrant hysteria just as anti-immigrant acts are fostered by a disdain for and indirectly target Mexican Americans. While this individual is anonymous in the Cambium Audit, Laura Leighton recounts an almost identical story in the anti-immigrant documentary *Southern Exposure*. Leighton is a member of Arizonans for Immigration Control and an outspoken anti-immigration activist. The documentary illustrates how the nativist Arizonans for Immigration Control were at the forefront of organizing against MAS classes and Mexican American students. Clearly, the Cambium Audit suggests and *Southern Exposure* demonstrates that MAS was targeted in part because community members and politicians saw the development of a specific, radical political consciousness among Chicana/o students as an extension of and magnifying the impact of Mexican immigration. Importantly, however, SB 1070 illustrates a complementary dynamic. While SB 1070 clearly targeted Latina/o immigrants, U.S. Latinas/os were also targets of police and civilian suspicion, inappropriately detained, and thus rendered perpetually foreign. Again, the logics and tactics of white supremacy and nativism are not discrete but mutually constituting elements of the U.S. racial project. Whether Mexican immigrants or seventh-generation Mexican Americans, Mexican-descent peoples, through the deployment of the nativist Aztlán, are always foreign and subversive in a land they can claim as their own.

Ultimately, the way in which the nativist Aztlán can be wielded against U.S. Latinas/os, particularly in schools, evidences the ideological aspect of whiteness. Charles Mills has described whiteness as a "cognitive gated community" where evidence of pervasive racial injustice is denied entry into the white mind.[89] The evocative language of a "cognitive gated community" is particularly useful when discussing anti-

Latina/o, anti-immigrant policies. Just as HR 4437, SB 1070, and calls for greater border militarization have augmented the policing of brown bodies on the border and throughout the United States, HB 2281 sought to regulate nonwhite minds.[90] Reminiscent of the Absolut Aztlán controversy where conservatives recoiled at the questioning of U.S. borders and the histories that brought them into being, Horne, Huppenthal, and those who rallied against MAS tried to stand in as the border guards regulating the cognitive gated community of Arizona schools. Further illustrating the cognitive gated community of whiteness, in 2014 State Superintendent Huppenthal came under fire for anonymously posting on the Internet; among his commentary was a desire to see all Spanish-language media banned in Arizona. Here, again, the logic and discourse of political nativism supports white supremacy. While Mexican-descent people may be perpetually foreign, for anti-MAS advocates like the community member above, the schools must turn them into white-minded U.S. subjects.

Beyond the Nativist Aztlán

For some, it may be tempting to write off the nativist Aztlán as a conspiratorial fringe element: Pat Buchanan, Lou Dobbs, Glenn Beck, and their ilk are nuts, and they have lost standing in the culture industry since the 2006 immigration protests. To such objections, my response is fourfold. First, Buchanan, Dobbs, and Beck have achieved and maintain a readership and media presence far beyond that of the vast majority of serious, legitimate scholars, signaling the potential impact of their work.[91] Second, the nativist Aztlán has been circulating in conservative circles since the late 1970s, so its seeming recession from mainstream media since the immigration debate of 2006–8 does not suggest that this narrative has disappeared altogether. Third, regardless of the paranoid, conspiratorial trappings of the Aztlán-reconquista plot, this narrative has been a mobilizing force in anti-immigrant, anti-Latina/o legislative efforts. Finally, and perhaps most important, the nativist Aztlán crystallizes the anxieties of the less vocal, less conspiratorial everyday whites, the loose collection of assumptions that Chavez described as the Latino Threat narrative. The nativist Aztlán conflates Mexicans and Mexican Americans, rendering them unassimilable and perpetually foreign. The nativist Aztlán emplotts immigrants as flaunting the rule of law, taking the easy way, and becoming drains on social services. In this narrative frame, Mexicans and Mexican Americans (because what's the difference?) do not *choose* to assimilate like the Germans and Irish before them. They bring crime and other social ills. And thus, the complexion of America is changing.

Whether found in the nativist Aztlán or the everyday discourse of whites, these beliefs make legible the coterminous nation of Americanness and whiteness. As with whiteness, America and Americans are imagined as pure, innocent, benevolent, and thus vulnerable. Fears, fantasies, and anxieties converge to forge racial and ideological solidarity, militarize the border, and shape curriculum to produce white-minded subjects of the U.S. racial state. Recognizing this, how do antiracist scholars and activists work against these fears, fantasies, and anxieties of whiteness on the border?

Despite the ascendancy of the nativist Aztlán on the political right, the Aztlán narrative has been largely absent from the discourse of pro-immigration advocates. As many have noted, white shirts and U.S. flags have become the predominant symbols of the immigration rights marches of 2006 onward. For Beth Baker-Cristales, these rhetorically strategic choices deploy "a largely defensive and reactive vocabulary and iconography meant to affirm that immigrants are *not* criminals and *not* terrorists."[92] Baker-Cristales argues that in proving Latinas/os were not criminals or terrorists, the protests failed to construct alternative models of citizenship or develop strong counters to dominant U.S. narratives.[93] While Baker-Cristales may be absolutely correct in her analysis of defensive symbolization, the rise and reign of a nativist Aztlán provides a powerful cautionary tale. Radical as well as reformist counternarratives can and will be appropriated. Current and future struggles for social justice require multiple, flexible, and ever evolving narrative and symbolic strategies because "yesterday's solutions can become today's problems."[94] Indeed, neither white shirts and U.S. flags nor articulations of Aztlán will sustain struggle without the danger of co-optation—neither the politics of respectability not the rhetoric of cultural nationalism alone may be an adequate response to the flexible and supple nature of contemporary white supremacy.[95] In the past few years, immigration activists, largely through youth leadership, have taken another tack. Embracing a stance of "undocumented and unafraid," they have charged citizenship with its active, participatory potential without relying on cultural symbolization. Might "undocumented and unafraid" offer another route, a model for civic activism that eschews or subverts the white racial frame? One may be cautiously hopeful. It is certainly a powerful and inspiring political stance. However, it may well play into the frame of Latina/o invasion and white vulnerability. But one must remember that whiteness on the border is not just about fear. Indeed, its most tenacious aspects may well be white benevolence and white desire, attributes that mask oppression in the name of heroism and love.

3

With Friends Like These

The Supremacist Logic of Saviorism

In the summer of 2014, more than sixty thousand unaccompanied minors made their way from home countries in Latin America to the Texas-Mexico border. The vast majority came from El Salvador, Honduras, and Guatemala.[1] U.S. Customs and Border Protection was overwhelmed, and the humanitarian crisis quickly became a media firestorm. Republicans used the situation to criticize President Obama's immigration policies, and nativists across the United States protested the relocation of migrants in detention centers outside of Texas. On the July 25 episode of *Real Time*, comedian and political commentator Bill Maher used the controversy to lampoon Republicans and anti-immigrant activists. Maher and his staff rewrote the Dr. Seuss classic *Oh, the Places You'll Go!* into a parody of nativism: *Oh, the Places You'll Go! . . . and Get Kicked Out Of!* With the lights turned down, as if reading a child to bed, Maher delivered his mock Seussian tale that began,

> Howdy there, partner.
> Today is your day.
> You've made it to Brownsville;
> Now please go away.
> You had dreams of Miami.
> You had dreams of Chicago.
> One day you thought,
> "I'll wash dishes at Spago."

As Maher read, mocked up images from the book appeared on screen. Throughout a young brown-skinned boy wearing the stereotypical sombrero and serape was depicted as the subject and imagined audience for Maher's Seussian reading. In the next few days the clip circulated through social media. Typifying much of the liberal response, Carolina Moreno from the mainstream progressive *Huffington Post* lauded the skit and embraced the critique of the political right.[2]

Importantly, not everyone was pleased with Maher's rhetorical strategy and comedic prowess. The Latino-focused political and cultural criticism website *Latino Rebels* responded to Maher's mocking of anti-immigrant racism with "No mames!," roughly translated as "stop fucking with me." Of course, *Latino Rebels* did not take offense on behalf of the political right. Rather, the site objected to Maher's reliance upon and reinforcement of Latino stereotypes for the sake of a joke. Maher's skit conflated Central American migrants with Mexicans through the long-enduring image of the Mexican wearing a sombrero and serape. One of Maher's biggest punch lines was when he asserted that these children come to the United States dreaming of becoming dishwashers in high-end eateries. *Latino Rebels* recognized that some would suggest that they missed the point of comedy and that they "should calm down a bit and chill."[3] What makes *Latino Rebels'* critique so insightful, however, is not simply their objection to racist stereotypes, but rather their objection to the use of racist stereotypes as they are wrapped within and deployed to serve a purportedly liberal political agenda. For *Latino Rebels*, Maher's skit positioned him as the great "White Savior" who could defend immigrants from racist Republicans while simultaneously relying upon and reinforcing anti-Mexican, anti-Latino white supremacist scripts.

Latino Rebels' critique of Maher's skit makes an essential move as it exposes how anti-Latino racism can be mobilized to bolster central logics of whiteness. Maher's skit evidences the politics and rhetorical position of white goodness and white saviorism. Maher's deployment of anti-Mexican stereotypes did not seek to elicit hatred and outright disdain for immigrants. Rather, the skit sought to foster feelings of white progressive righteousness against backward bigots on the political right. As such, the skit is less about immigrants and immigration, for it transforms the experiences of migrants facing a humanitarian crisis into a joke to strike out against conservative callousness and hypocrisy. In the end, Maher and his audience shared a communal laugh as they imagined themselves the good whites, the benevolent ones who would fight those villainous bigots on behalf the immigrant children Maher had simultaneously transformed into a long-enduring image of anti-Mexican

Figure 3.1. Bill Maher deploys Mexican stereotypes in order to attack nativist Republicans and claim the mantle of White Savior. *Real Time with Bill Maher*, HBO.

racism. In this way, Maher's skit epitomizes the supremacist logics of white saviorism.

Of course this position of white goodness and saviorism is nothing new. As others have noted, whiteness has been charged with innocence, virtue, purity, goodness, and benevolence since the emergence of colonialism and the racial project. This can be seen in how Europeans aligned whiteness with Christianity through a moral duality of good and evil during the Crusades.[4] Moreover, the Enlightenment project fashioned the belief that Europeans were civilized, self-governing, and rational, an ideological move that undergirded the colonization of the Americas as Others were scripted as savages in order to expropriate Native land or enslave African and Native peoples.[5] In these cases, white goodness justifies and rationalizes inhumanity. That is, no one wants to consider themselves complicit or participating in evil acts, so a discourse of goodness has long inoculated whites as it projects evil and its attributes onto the recipients of white supremacy. Importantly, white saviorism is a particular manifestation of white goodness. While white goodness relies on a savage Other and a binary relationship, it is formed through a rejection of the Other. White saviorism, however, is not so simple. White saviorism reinforces the goodness of whites by arguing that whites must lift up the Other from their state of savagery. Here one may think of nineteenth-century colonial discourses epitomized in Rudyard Kipling's "White Man's Burden," the civilizing missions of Christian colonization of the Americas, or the work of Americanization programs in the early twentieth century as a means for dealing with the "Mexican Problem" in the United States.[6] In these cases, white saviorism seeks to rescue communities of color from themselves and their nonwhiteness. As such, goodness and saviorism are intertwined and mutually reinforcing. Goodness—scripted as internal and innate—provides the underlying logic for saviorism, which is outwardly expressed and provides the unquestionable proof of white goodness.

Notably, what I am describing as saviorism can and has been called by other names over the years: benevolence, humanitarianism, messianism, philanthropy, charity, paternalism, righteousness.[7] Discrete, overlapping, and sometimes interchangeable, these terms name a rhetorical and political posture of goodness that may ultimately reinforce inequality. While specific manifestations may differ, white saviorism expresses a common dynamic. A white person stands up for an aggrieved, racialized person against a present danger or injustice. The act of saviorism simultaneously maintains and conceals other, broader forms of injustice. The righteous act reinforces the association between whiteness and goodness. Finally, although this step is often unstated, the aggrieved subject is compelled to owe a debt of gratitude to the white savior, again reinforcing the racial order.

Yet white saviorism also intersects with and takes a national form through American exceptionalism where white goodness is evidenced through rescuing aggrieved peoples from oppressors. Indeed, consider how rhetoric of Mexican governmental oppression of the Mexican people was used to justify the U.S.-Mexican War.[8] Moreover, Bill Maher's contemporary deployment of white saviorism takes a national form as it is expressed through and relies upon the American Dream trope and hollow belief in the United States' long acceptance of immigrants via the Huddled Masses myth.[9] Here, the discourses of white saviorism and American exceptionalism converge. The national project echoes the logic and language of the racial project. This chapter turns to these assertions of white goodness and white saviorism, exploring how purportedly positive attitudes and actions toward Mexico, Mexicans, and

Mexican Americans support white supremacy, American exceptionalism, and the imagining of the nation-state as a racial state.

While white goodness and white saviorism are long-enduring manifestations of white supremacy, they take on a greater significance during and after the racial break. With the growing rejection of explicit forms of white supremacy, whiteness has appropriated and incorporated some concerns for people of color as a means for maintaining core elements of its racial symbology. That is, rather than simply forging white goodness against a savage other, U.S. whiteness has increasingly imagined itself as a protective force of racialized communities at home and abroad. In other words, a discourse of "we are not them" has become less explicit and a rhetoric of "we must protect them" has gained currency.[10] In part, this results from the U.S. desire to imagine itself as a pure and exceptional ideal with the rise of fascism, communism, and other specters of global power in the twentieth and twenty-first centuries. Here, white saviorism is bound to and is the racial manifestation of American exceptionalism that often finds expression in U.S. imperialism.

Through a range of historical and textual moments, this chapter demonstrates how seemingly positive acts work to elide and reinforce inequality as part of the national-racial project. The diner scene from the novel and film *Giant* as well as the case of Macario García illustrate central dynamics of white saviorism as well as a popular investment in associating whiteness and Americanness with goodness, equality, and justice at the cusp of the racial break. From there, I examine the national and racial logics of saviorism at play in the film *The Magnificent Seven*. The film evidences how white saviorism forges a national-racial fantasy where the white United States would repeatedly rescue third world others from the spectral forces of evil. Finally, the chapter uncovers the dynamics of U.S. white saviorism in Border Patrol rescue narratives, which are structured by the nation's official discourse of humanitarianism, hiding the impact of neoliberal economic policies and the militarization of the border. Deployed to "protect" Mexico, Mexicans, and Mexican Americans, these fantasies of white saviorism bolster the racial logics of U.S. nationalism. They imagine the United States as a white nation, good and benevolent to aggrieved communities at home and capable of intervening on behalf of Others abroad. Importantly, in these symbolic manifestations, whiteness on the border simultaneously seeks to obscure systemic forms of white supremacy and U.S. imperialism as it strips away the agency of those who have historically fought for survival and justice.

No Mexicans Allowed; or, Serving Up White Saviorism in Three Takes

One of the most iconic scenes in U.S. cinema, the penultimate scene of George Stevens's 1956 film *Giant* evidences the seductive and suprema-cist aspects of white saviorism. Bick Benedict (Rock Hudson) walks into a West Texas roadside diner with his family. Seemingly standing up for the rights of the oppressed and for justice in a new social order, he con-fronts Sarge, the diner's owner, about the refusal to serve an unnamed Mexican American family.[11] Previously in the film, Bick was paternalis-tic and exploitive of his Mexican workers, a contrast to his wife Leslie's racial progressivism. The two titanic men fight an epic battle; punches are thrown and tables are turned as "The Yellow Rose of Texas" and its military beat score the scene. Ultimately, Bick falls at the hands of Sarge, but he has undergone a transformation of racial consciousness—no lon-ger an out-and-out racist who exploits his Mexican American workers, Bick Benedict embodies white saviorism.[12]

Despite its iconic standing, this celluloid moment of 1956 is neither the first nor the last incarnation of this scene. In Edna Ferber's 1952 novel *Giant*, Bick and the unnamed Mexican American family are entirely ab-sent from the scene. Rather, the owner of the diner orders members of the wealthy Benedict family to leave because of their phenotypically Mexican features. Since the 1990s, Chicano authors like Tino Villanueva, Luis Alberto Urrea, and Alex Espinoza have all reimagined this iconic scene in efforts to trouble the logic of saviorism and make the dynamics of whiteness legible.[13] Influenced by these Chicano revisions, I contend that reading the film's version of the scene against the novel's as well as against a historical case on which it may be based illustrates both why white saviorism may be popularly celebrated and how it retains core aspects of white supremacy.

Giant follows the relationship of Leslie and Bick Benedict over their brief courtship and years of marriage. They are a seemingly mismatched pair, Leslie from the eastern United States, Bick from Texas, where he runs his family's massive cattle business, Reata Ranch. The evolution of their relationship over the years is mirrored by the shifting social order around them. Ranching, a time-honored way of life, is losing ground to the booming oil industry, and as such established families like the Benedicts are forced to adapt and make way for the nouveau riche, as embodied in Bick's one-time employee and continual nemesis Jett Rink. The shifting social order is also evidenced through Leslie and Bick's children. Their daughter Luz marries a man who chooses to run a small plot of land over the Benedict's large Reata. More significant to this analysis, their son Jordan rejects the family business to become a doctor, marries Juana, a Mexican American woman, and practices medicine for the local Tejano community.

Perhaps unsurprisingly, when scholars have interrogated the racial politics of Ferber's novel and the film iteration of *Giant*, much of the critical energy has focused on the texts' treatment of anti-Mexican discrimination. As the documentary *Children of Giant* described it, *Giant* was a revisionist Western that explored greed, gender roles, and race relations in ways that were "daring and controversial" at the time.[14] Some critics have contended that Ferber's experience as a Jewish woman growing up in the Midwest facing anti-Semitism forged her ability to create strong female characters that could blur the distinction of cultural insider and outsider to fashion a forceful social critique.[15] Certainly, as scholars have noted, the novel offered a forceful condemnation of anti–Mexican American racism in Texas.[16] While many agree that the novel was ahead of its time, the film's racial politics have received a varied response. Monique James Baxter argued that the film introduced America to the potential of antiracist struggle, contending that "*Giant's* most important accomplishment was that it awakened a generation of Americans to the realization that they need not accept discrimination as a fact of life."[17] In contrast, Don Graham and others have noted the dramatic shift from the novel to the film, wherein Ferber's forceful critique was watered down and undermined.[18] Within Chicana/o studies, scholars have also debated the potential and limitations of the film's race politics. In his analysis of the mestizo body in American cultural production, Rafael Pérez-Torres contends that while the film does present "previously absent affirmative images of Mexicans," it denies Mexicans agency and continues their subordination in the racial hierarchy.[19] In sharp distinction, José E. Limón has argued that the film must be historicized, and in doing so was a radical intervention for its time.[20]

While *Giant*'s racial meaning is clearly a site of contention, a gap in this critical conversation should be immediately apparent. Even as much of this scholarship has focused on the racial-cultural work of these texts, little attention has been paid to how these texts, and the iconic scene in particular, create meaning within a system of whiteness.[21] I contend that whiteness functions as an invisible center of meaning for these texts. Although much previous scholarship has positioned *Giant* as either racially problematic or enlightened, turning critical attention to whiteness exposes how seemingly enlightened works actively perpetuate racial hierarchies. Here, we must turn to Ferber's novel and the original diner scene.

Take 1: Ferber's Giant, the Novel

Today, Ferber's original incarnation has been dramatically overshadowed by its filmic adaptation, but in 1952, at the time of its release, the novel was a tremendous success that sparked strong reaction both lauding and decrying the work. In her research travels prior to writing *Giant*, Ferber met Dr. Hector P. García, a physician serving the Tejano community and civil rights activist. With García as her guide, Ferber toured the Mexican American communities he served. Ferber spoke with García's Mexican American patients and learned about race relations in Texas.[22] Like much of her earlier writing, *Giant* fashioned a forceful social critique through popular fiction. While reviewers heaped praise on the novel across the United States, the response from white Texans was not so kind. Ferber received letters calling for her to be lynched or shot.[23] While many white Texans decried the novel's inaccuracies, the novel's condemnation of anti-Mexican racism propelled the firestorm. Significantly, these reactions can be grounded in the novel's thematic climax, the diner scene.

Ferber's original diner scene differs markedly from its iconic revision in the film. While the scene occurs in the penultimate chapter, chronologically it takes place prior to the novel's first four chapters, when the Benedict family travels to and attends the grand opening of Jett Rink's airport.[24] On the way to another ranch, Leslie, her daughter Luz, her daughter-in-law Juana, and her grandson Jordy decide to stop at a new diner to quell young Jordy's appetite. Leslie, Juana, and Jordy enter the diner and are promptly confronted by the proprietor, who tells them, "We don't serve Mexicans here."[25] At first Leslie is confused, then indignant. She responds, "You can't be talking to me!"[26] When Luz enters the diner, she confronts this injustice by yelling at and threatening the proprietor. During the encounter, the owner shoves the youngest Benedict, the child Jordy. Ultimately, as Luz is about to invoke the family name, Leslie halts her, saying, "No! No, Luz! No name. Come."[27] Without further confrontation, the four Benedicts leave, stunned and infuriated. On the drive home, Leslie gets Juana and Luz to promise not to tell anyone about the incident, at least not until after the opening of Jett Rink's airport.[28]

The diner encounter permeates Leslie's discussion of racial injustice afterward. In the final chapter, Leslie returns to the Benedict ranch, withholding the incident from Bick. Lamenting the fall of ranching and the rise of the oil industry, Bick complains that his son works "with the greasers in Vientecito" and that his grandson "looks like a real cholo."[29] Still affected by the diner incident earlier in the day, Leslie responds, "Darling, don't say things like that! They're terrible. They're wrong. You don't know how wrong. You'll be sorry."[30] She then gestures toward the future with the belief that the previous generations of Benedicts had been failures but "our Jordon and our Luz . . . after a hundred years it looks as if the Benedict family is going to be a real success at last."[31] Here, Leslie seems to recognize a new, potentially more egalitarian social order on the horizon. Significantly, she does not view the wealth and privilege of the Benedicts in years past as a marker of success. In the next few days, the Benedict family will travel to Jett Rink's celebration. Juana will again be refused service, this time at Jett Rink's hotel hair salon. When Jordan confronts him, Jett kicks Jordan in the groin, emasculating the young Benedict.[32] As Bick steps forward to fight Jett on behalf of his son and the family name, Leslie holds him back. At this, the novel's chronological conclusion, Leslie asserts that racial injustice has consequences for all as she repeats her comments from a few days prior: "You see. It's caught up with you, it's caught up with us. It always does."[33]

As the thematic climax, the diner scene builds upon the novel's exploration of racial injustice and white saviorism. Throughout the text,

Leslie learns of and confronts Bick about the unjust land acquisition, the impoverished and squalid living conditions of the ranch's Mexican workers, the rights of migrants, and the political corruption of controlling the Mexican vote, to name but a few issues. Even as these concerns lead to repeated conflicts between Leslie and Bick, the confrontations are too often left unresolved—Bick continues on his way and Leslie works behind the scenes to change things in what ways she can. Here, Bick and Leslie signify the two forms of paternalism: exploitive and benevolent.[34] While Bick assumes the role of Great White Father to accrue more wealth and political power at the expense of Tejanos, Leslie's activism also strips away Tejano agency for her own elevation. Thus, the novel's diner scene functions as a thematic climax wherein the chickens of racial injustice have come home to roost for the Benedict family. Not only has the exploitive paternalism of racial hierarchy affected the Benedict family, but Leslie discovers the limits of her own benevolence.

In the novel, Leslie embodies the troubling nature of white saviorism in two ways. First, her interventions on behalf of the Mexican American community are dependent on her race and class privilege. Second, in fashioning Leslie as a protagonist working on behalf of the oppressed, Ferber erased much of the historically significant Mexican American civil rights activism at the time.[35] For instance, when the body of Angel Obregon, a Mexican, returns from World War II and the undertaker refuses burial within the town of Benedict, Leslie intervenes by contacting the U.S. president and having Angel buried in Arlington National Cemetery. While this moment illustrates Leslie's wielding of power on behalf of Mexican Americans, this telling erases the more complex historical event to which it alludes. In 1949 Felix Longoria's body was recovered from the Philippines and refused service by the only funeral home in his hometown because he was Mexican. The American GI Forum, founded by Dr. Hector P. García, took up the cause of Longoria's burial and, with the help of Lyndon Johnson, was successful in having Longoria buried with full honors at Arlington. Significantly, this is the same Dr. García who helped Ferber gain access to the Mexican American community in Texas and became the basis for the character Dr. Guerra.[36] The novel, however, suppresses such Mexican American agency to underscore Leslie's benevolence. In another instance of Leslie's activism on behalf of Mexican Americans, Juana tells Leslie that "the school for Latin American children is a disgrace."[37] Leslie responds, "I know, Juana darling. We must keep on working."[38] This exchange again highlights Leslie's saviorism toward Mexican Americans. While this hints at Juana's involvement, she is subordinated to Leslie. However, during the time of the novel, Mexican American political activism had already emerged in the form of the League of United Latin American Citizens (LULAC), the aforementioned American GI Forum, and efforts to end the segregated practices of Mexican schools in the Southwest.[39] Indeed, despite the novel's progressive critique of racism, *Giant* pinned the hopes of ending racial oppression on the actions of whites, crafting a world in which aggrieved communities fundamentally lack the agency necessary to change the conditions of their lives. Here, we see the contradictory nature of white saviorism—it gestures toward liberation as it simultaneously reinforces racial hegemony.

Despite Ferber's elision of Tejano agency, the novel does expose limits to white saviorism. Immediately after this brief exchange between Juana and Leslie, they enter the diner where Leslie discovers the limits of her own power as she is unable to protect her family. As they are refused service, Leslie faces the crisis of a new social order, or at least a social order that is new to her. Significantly, Leslie does not exclaim that one should not be refused service because of race or ethnicity. Rather, she tellingly says, "You can't be talking to me!" and "You must—be out of your mind."[40] Previously, she had wielded her race and class power to shape the lives of others. In the diner, it is not the impoverished and oppressed Mexican Americans who must be protected but the Benedicts, now racially othered. Leslie's shock is quite revealing. In the past, her race and class power had insulated her from immediate experiencing of racial injustice as it simultaneously enabled her to work on behalf of others.[41] Without that position of power, her benevolence is nothing. In a potentially significant act, Leslie halts Luz from invoking the Benedict family name at the diner. Here, one must ask, was this an effort to stop the name from being sullied? Or did Leslie recognize the limits of wielding economic, cultural, and social capital codified in the name Benedict to resolve the immediate situation but not the larger system of racial injustice? To these questions, the novel is ambivalent. Leslie clearly does not want news of the diner incident to spread prior to Jett Rink's party. However, she also recognizes that this experience is no different from what has "always happened to other people."[42]

The novel's diner scene effectively challenges Leslie's saviorism by troubling the whiteness upon which it rests. While Leslie had previously used her race and class power, in the diner she refuses to invoke the Benedict name, and the owner reads her body as racially nonwhite. Not only Juana and Jordy but also the dark-haired, sallow, and thus Mexican-looking Leslie are refused service for being Mexican. After the Benedicts leave the diner, the woman working behind the lunch counter says to the proprietor that "only the kid and his ma was cholos, not the others."[43] Defending his decision to throw out Leslie, the owner says, "Aw, the old one was, black hair and sallow, you can't fool me."[44] This exchange troubles the naturalized position of whiteness as a racial category. As scholars such as Ian Haney López have noted, whiteness is a flexible social category that has accrued meanings over time. Even as white as a racial category has been expanded, this scene illustrates the tenuous na-ture of whiteness. Lacking or not demonstrating the appropriate forms of capital, Leslie loses her claims to whiteness and the power that comes with it. Moreover, Ferber's troubling of whiteness forms a complement to the racial categorization of Mexican Americans, specifically during the 1950s. While phenotypically diverse, Mexican Americans were and are legally classified as white. As Ignacio García, Laura Gómez, and oth-ers have noted, this white racial standing was contingent upon the social context.[45] Even as Mexican Americans were classified white by law, they were considered socially unequal. Ultimately, this scene undermines the category of whiteness by demonstrating its socially constructed nature. While Mexican Americans may be classified as white yet unequal, this moment illustrates how whites may indeed lose their whiteness, albeit momentarily, simultaneously challenging the power and saviorism that Leslie's race privilege wields.

The novel's diner scene functions as the thematic convergence of the narrative, wherein white saviorism, power, and the very category of whiteness are left troubled. Even as Ferber relied upon this cultural trope to fashion Leslie as a heroine, this scene undercuts white saviorism as a reliable strategy for social change. With the exposure of anti–Mexican American racism and the absence of a celebratory resolution, it is lit-tle wonder that many white Texas readers were disenchanted with the novel. Jane Hendler has argued that the non-Texas readership responded so favorably because *Giant* allowed for the celebration of U.S. wealth and power while relegating excesses and prejudices to the general backwardness of Texas.[46] Hendler's analysis speaks to the intersection of U.S. nationalism and whiteness, particularly at the start of the racial break. For a non-Texas readership, Leslie could epitomize the democratic ideals of the United States, which had just waged war against fascism, as well as the normative goodness of whiteness against the aberrant (i.e., bad and explicitly racist) whiteness she finds in Texas.[47] For white Texans, however, such disassociation was impossible and the novel cut to the bone. Thus, unsurprisingly the intervening years between the novel and the film were marked by anxiety in Texas as to how the film would depict the Lone Star State—would the novel's eviscerating critique reach a broader audience? In a much quoted comment, one Texan suggested, "If you make and show that damn picture, we'll shoot the screen full of holes."[48] Unsurprisingly, to fashion a more palatable experience for its white audience, the film not only sheds much of Ferber's racial and gender critiques, but also culminates in the redemption of Bick Benedict through a full-scale, uncritical embrace of white saviorism and the power systems that maintain it.

Take 2: Stevens's Giant, the Film

In the film's diner scene, Bick, Leslie, Juana, Jordy, and Luz stop at Sarge's Place on their way home from Jett Rink's celebration and the confrontations of the night before. As they enter, Sarge gazes at Juana and the blonde waitress hesitates to serve the Benedicts. When Bick orders ice cream for Jordy, Sarge says that he thought the child would have wanted a tamale and tells the waitress to give them what they want. The slight, however, does not go unnoticed. Leslie and Juana are visibly upset by the comment, and Bick shifts his posture slightly away from the table, his eyes tracing the movements of Sarge. Other than the palpable tension, there is no immediate conflict in serving the white Bick, Leslie, and Luz or the phenotypically othered Juana and Jordy. This tension erupts into conflict with the entrance of a working-class Mexican American family, a foil to the Benedicts. The massive Sarge tells the unnamed Tejano man to "vamooos" and that his "money is no good here." When Bick crosses the diner to intervene, Sarge grips the Tejano man by the arm like a rag doll. Hoping to use his name as a form of capital on behalf of the

Figure 3.2. Bick Benedict (Rock Hudson) prepares to intervene as Sarge (Mickey Simpson) grabs an elderly Mexican man to expel him from the diner in *Giant*. *Giant*, Warner Brothers Studios.

Tejano family, Bick tells Sarge, "The name Benedict has meant something to people around here for a considerable time." Sarge responds by asking, in reference to Jordy, if "that there papoose down there, his name Benedict too?"[49] Bick replies, "Yeah, come to think of it, it is," acknowledging the mestizo heritage of his grandson and deploying the capital of the name Benedict to provide Jordy some benefits of whiteness, at least temporarily. While Sarge remains willing to serve the Benedicts, he tells Bick, "This bunch here needs to go," still holding the man like a prop. At this point, Bick shoves Sarge and the fight begins. "The Yellow Rose of Texas" plays on the diner jukebox as Sarge repeatedly pummels Bick across the diner. While Bick does land the occasional punch, he ultimately ends up on the floor, defeated, covered in salad plates. To drive his point home, Sarge takes the sign that reads "We reserve the right to refuse service to anyone" from the wall and tosses it onto the defeated Bick.

Positioning the diner scene at the chronological end of the film fundamentally alters the way this exchange functions within the narrative. Rather than a thematic climax that opens questions about the consequences of racial injustice and chronologically foreshadows the alterca-

Figure 3.3. Bick and Sarge fight over which form of white masculinity will prevail in the United States. *Giant*, Warner Brothers Studios.

Figure 3.4. Leslie Benedict (Elizabeth Taylor) embraces the fallen Bick. While he loses the struggle, his fight wins her respect and often that of the audience. *Giant*, Warner Brothers Studios.

tion at Jett Rink's party in the beginning of the novel, the filmic iteration works as a resolution for many of the film's issues. As Hendler has noted, Bick refused to punch Jett Rink in the conflict the night before.[50] He has apparently learned when to use force, and the diner scene provides the audience with a larger-than-life fight that a stumbling drunk and substantially smaller Jett Rink could not. Moreover, the fight with Sarge comes after not only the confrontation with Jett, but also a scene where Jordan faces his father, accusing him of fighting Jett not because of the injustice to Juana but due to the insult to the Benedict name when Jett beat up Jordan in front of everyone. Thus, the diner fight provides a final opportunity for Bick to stand up for Mexican Americans and justice, not just simply his family name, fostering a resolution to the film's muted theme of racial injustice. But perhaps most important for the Hollywood narrative arc, this diner scene provides the potential for resolution in the romantic story line. When they return from the diner, Leslie and Bick sit on the couch in their Reata home. Consoling her bruised husband, Leslie tells him that he is her hero and that he was never "quite as big a man to me as you were on the floor of Sarge's hamburger joint. . . . Before we went into that place, . . . I was thinking to myself, well, Jordan and I and all the others behind us have been failures. And then it happened. You wound up on the floor, on your back, in the middle of the salad. And I said to myself, well, after a hundred years, the Benedict family is a real big success." In marked contrast to the novel, where she looked solely to the children as the potential for success in the Benedict family line, Leslie locates triumph for justice in her and Bick's generation. Such a move seemingly resolves the film's romantic and racial conflicts, ultimately foreclosing the questions of white saviorism and power raised at the end of the novel.

The introduction of Bick and the unnamed Mexican American family to this diner scene forges the film's full, uncritical embrace of white saviorism, making Bick not just Leslie's hero but likely the audience's as well. While seemingly a simple heroic act, this iteration of the diner scene reinforces the social order even as it makes the gesture against racial injustice. Unlike in the novel, Sarge allows the Benedicts to be served despite the phenotypic markedness of Juana and Jordy. Here, one must ask why they are served but not the Mexican American family. Do Juana and Jordy benefit from their proximity to whiteness vis-à-vis

Bick, Leslie, and Luz? Is it because Bick orders on his grandson's behalf? While there may be palpable tension, Bick's own family is not refused service. Bick readily deploys the Benedict name to claim authority when confronting Sarge. He does not recognize that the capital signified by the name Benedict was accumulated through the very racial hierarchy he is now protesting. Indeed, a legacy of racial injustice has positioned him for this very moment. Moreover, as the novel exposed the limits of Leslie and Luz's whiteness to benefit others, there is no question that Bick, the film's embodiment of white masculinity, can protect his own family. Notably, the gendered shift in the embodiment of white saviorism from Leslie to Bick must be recognized. While Ferber certainly centralized the role of women in her critique of the racial order, the novel also called into question the effectiveness of such efforts. In contrast, Bick's white saviorism in the film is deployed without critique. This dynamic finds common ground in Richard Dyer's examination of gender, whiteness, and empire in film. For Dyer, white women take the lead in narratives that call into question the machinations of empire—that is, "the white male spirit achieves and maintains empire; the white female soul is associated with its demise."[51] Read in this way, Bick's actions and his embodiment of white masculinity allow the film not to critique empire and its racial logics, but to continue them through another name, saviorism.

Significantly, the inclusion of the unnamed Tejano family allows Bick to embody white saviorism without facing the immediate threat to his family. Just as *Giant* has been credited with exposing anti–Mexican American prejudice and including speaking Mexican American characters, this scene has been lauded as the transformation of Bick Benedict's racial consciousness.[52] However, contrary to expectations, these agendas may actually work against each other, for Bick's transformation of racial consciousness subordinates the agency of the aggrieved community. When Bick stands up on behalf of the unnamed Tejano family, the struggle against racial injustice becomes solely the territory of whites. The mestizo bodies on the screen do not contest the situation. They merely look on in fright or are shaken and shoved as props to illustrate the race power of two herculean white men. Arguably, this scene has been confounding for many critics because of a desire to see Bick transformed from explicit racist to fighter for racial and social justice. This scene, however, more accurately exposes another shift in Bick, from exploitive paternalism to white saviorism. Here one must recognize the continuity along with the change. Bick's paternalism allowed him to see himself as aiding Mexicans while he financially and politically profited off of their exploitation. In this scene Bick's reward is more symbolic and affective—his heroism is forged at the expense of the Mexican family. Bick's transformation allows him to occupy the position of Great White Father, ultimately subordinating the struggle of Mexican Americans to the reconciliation of Bick and Leslie's relationship.[53] As Jesús Salvador Treviño has contended, "While it may be argued that showing an Anglo helping out a Mexican couple in trouble is positive, it may also have underscored the opinion that Mexicans are inherently servile, humble, ignorant and powerless. Despite countless historical incidences in which Texas Mexicans have stood up for their rights, in GIANT they must once again await help from well-intentioned saviors of the dominant society."[54] This is to critique not the effort of whites fighting for social justice, but rather their relationship to the aggrieved community. Depicting the Tejano family as passive props, this scene reinforces the century-old image of Mexican Americans as "indolent" and in need of paternalistic protection.[55] The Mexican American man in the diner is close to Bick's age but certainly not his stature. His lack of language and agency makes him merely a prop to highlight Bick's white saviorism. While this un-named man does not actively challenge white saviorism, he certainly exposes why it is so troubling.

In contrast to Ferber's novel, the film reinforces whiteness as a naturalized racial category. In this iteration, there is no racial confusion—whites are white and mestizos are undeniably Other. This change is significant in at least two ways. First, Bick does not risk losing his racial positioning and its attendant privileges as Leslie did in the novel. He stands up for the unnamed Tejano family, but he does so from the position of unquestioned whiteness. While Ferber exposed the socially constructed and tenuous nature of race, this *Giant* relies upon and reinforces Bick's whiteness in this scene, for it along with his masculinity and class standing become the source of his power. Bick's whiteness, and arguably that of Leslie and Luz, allows Juana and Jordy to be served. Bick's whiteness and the accrued capital of the Benedict name allow him to stand up to Sarge on behalf of the other family. Ultimately, without interrogating the societal making of whiteness, this scene gestures to the general unfairness of racial injustice without exposing its roots in the social and legal fictions of race. Thus, for the characters and viewers, racial discrimination may be frowned upon but the system of racial logic that undergirds it remains unquestioned.

In an equally troubling aspect, the diner scene exposes how white saviorism is enacted without threatening institutional racism. Like Leslie, film viewers are able to watch in horrified amazement as Bick is beaten repeatedly around the diner. When he finally collapses and the sign is tossed upon him, he is elevated in Leslie's eyes, and likely those of the viewers as well. However, nothing is won. The next day Sarge's Place and thousands of other private and public establishments will remain segregated. Had Bick won, nothing would have changed. But the film does not offer social change—it offers racial fantasy. As Hendler has noted, Bick's beating may be seen as punishment for his previous racial sins.[56] In the end, it is Bick, the defeated and transformed hero, who has stood up for people who cannot defend for themselves. Thus, not only does the film elide the agency of Mexican Americans, it also appropriates their unjust treatment to elevate Bick. Ultimately, while Bick's benevolent actions may provide a temporary reprieve, they do nothing to dismantle the structures of oppression.[57] Indeed, in the following and final scene, little has even changed within Bick. When Leslie tells Bick that Reata is her home and that she belongs there, he says, "You really want to know what's gotten my goat. My own grandson don't even look like one of us, honey . . . he looks like a little wetback." In response, Jordy shakes the walls of his playpen, and Bick says, "Little muchacho fires up, don't he?" This is supposed to be humorous. But like the diner scene before, this moment reveals the seductive, insidious nature of white saviorism. It asks viewers to laugh or cheer when the racial hierarchy is being reinforced—it offers comfort in the guise of change.

Finally, the white saviorism forged in the film's diner scene exposes an absence of risk to the social order outside the film. The muted racial critique and the revised diner scene illustrate significant reasons for why the film was received so well in Texas after the novel stirred so much controversy. However, we must remember the inherent contradiction of cheering on Bick Benedict, the film's Great White Hope, from the comfort of a segregated movie theater. Read in this way, the film may very well have received such popular praise because it critiqued only explicit forms of racism without addressing white supremacy's structural nature, made the concerns of aggrieved communities solely the territory of whites, and replaced an exploitive paternalism with white saviorism. But it is important to remember that not all film viewers in Texas were white. Though the refusal of service shocks Leslie in the novel and challenges Bick in the film, racial segregation was a part of daily life for Mexican Americans in the Southwest. Even as some Mexican Americans celebrated *Giant*'s public exposure of Juan Crow, others struggled to make meaning of its racial politics.[58]

Take 3: The Case of Macario García

While the imaginative realm of film deploys the diner scene to illustrate a change in Bick's character, it must be recognized that in the lived experience of southwestern Mexican Americans such refusals of service were common occurrences that were deployed not for dramatic purposes but to preserve the color line. As numerous scholars have documented, parts of the Southwest were marked by a Juan Crow system that mirrored the formal and informal strategies of oppression and sociopolitical marginalization in the U.S. South. Mexican Americans attended segregated schools, faced a racialized wage scale, were excluded from primary voting, and were denied jury service in addition to confronting segregation in places of business. Notably, Wanda García, the Italian wife of the Dr. Hector García who had hosted Edna Ferber on her visit to Texas, was refused service when she and some Mexican American friends tried to eat at a Texas café. Could Mrs. García's experience be the originating impulse behind Ferber's scene?[59] Again, however, this was hardly an isolated incident. During the 1940s, because of Mexican American activism and concern about the U.S. image abroad as the government sought alliances in the fight against fascism and then communism, President Truman established the President's Committee on Fair Employment Practices to hold hearings and investigate the prevalence of anti-Mexican discrimination. In his 1948 *Are We Good Neighbors?*, diplomat and lawyer Alonso S. Perales documented numerous refusals of service for Mexican Americans in Texas. In this light, Ferber's diner scene and its filmic revision emerged not from the ether but from the already growing consciousness of anti-Mexican white supremacy. Indeed, it is likely that the inspiration for the iconic scene came from Ferber's visit to Texas and her time spent with Dr. García or from another case that made national news, one which exposes how the dynamics of white goodness and white saviorism are interconnected with imaginings of American ideals of fairness and justice.

Michael Olivas has called the case of Staff Sergeant Macario García "'the trial of the century' that never was" because of the way it rose to national attention and receded from public memory.[60] In 1945, García returned from World War II after sustaining injuries in Normandy in June 1944 and in Germany that November. Upon his return, President Truman awarded García the Congressional Medal of Honor. When he returned to Texas, García received a citation from Robert E. Smith, chairman of the Good Neighbor Commission, and the *Houston Post* heralded the hometown hero with the story "Sugar Land War Hero." On September 9, 1945, local officials with LULAC organized a celebration in García's honor at the Richmond City Hall. The following evening, García was refused service at the Oasis Café in Richmond, Texas. The exact details of the incident in the café are unclear. While there was certainly a physical altercation, García's affidavit differs significantly from the press coverage and police charges.[61] That being said, beyond the simple refusal of service, the facts of the story are less significant to this study than the competing narratives that emerged. After the incident, García hired Houston-based Mexican American attorney Johnny Herrera. According to Olivas, even though no charges had been filed against García, there was no guarantee that charges would not be forthcoming. Herrera contacted newspaper and radio reporter Walter Winchell, and Winchell publicized the incident through his Sunday broadcast, stating that García was refused service and beaten with a baseball bat and needed medical attention.[62] Moreover, Winchell asserted that two sailors were also assaulted when they tried to help García, who was in uniform at the time.[63] However, the local paper offered an opposing account of events. According to the *Texas Coaster*, it was not until after Winchell's "erroneous" report that charges were filed:

> Winchell's misstatements regarding the incident prompted the airing of the affair locally. The Coaster had the story of the incident the day after it happened, but "killed" it in a charitable attitude toward the soldier,

who had just come back to his home town after gaining fame on European battlefields. For his action in Europe he was presented the Medal of Honor by President Truman.

Likewise, local officers did not attempt to prosecute the man until nationwide attention was drawn to the incident, and Fort Bend county began to be criticized through newspaper editorials in various parts of the nation.[64]

The *Texas Coaster*'s version of the incident differs greatly from Winchell's. Drawing upon affidavits from the café owners, the paper asserted that García was refused service "because he had been drinking."[65] The *Texas Coaster* reported that García broke several dishes and windows and struck café owner Mrs. Andrews in the mouth. Andrews's brother and business partner Pete Lower and her son Louie Payton then struggled with García, ultimately "quieting" him with a baseball bat to his back.[66] Winchell's media spotlight and the formal introduction of criminal charges transformed a sadly routine occurrence into a potential trial of the century. Herrera was joined by Phillip Montalbo as part of a politically well-connected and media savvy defense team. After former Texas attorney general and former governor James V. Allred joined the case, the trial was postponed, charges were eventually dropped, and the potential trial of the century never occurred.[67]

While the Macario García case may have been the basis for *Giant*'s diner scene, particularly the film's violent, plate-smashing conflict, the operation of white saviorism may not be readily apparent. Importantly, however, the case illustrates how the discourses and ideology white goodness need not be embodied in a Great White Hope like that of Bick Benedict. Consider the curious pattern of events and the *Texas Coaster*'s account. Charges were not immediately filed after the incident. Only after Winchell brought the weight of national attention did Fort Bend County officials bring charges against García. The lateness of this decision suggests that officials were motivated more by protecting the reputation of Fort Bend County from claims of racial intolerance. Whereas Winchell's story was one where a Mexican American war hero was refused service because of his ethnoracial background, the charges and the narrative advanced by the *Texas Coaster* seek to transform the narrative from one of white supremacy to one of a belligerent and drunken

Mexican attacking a white female who refused to serve someone in such a condition. The beating, in this narrative, reinforces white goodness as Pete Lower and Louie Payton sought to protect law and order and Mrs. Anderson's white womanhood as they "quieted" García with a baseball bat. Unlike in the film, the force of law itself was marshaled to protect the town and the practices of Juan Crow under the guise of white goodness. That is, charges were "charitably" withheld until the white supremacist practices of Fort Bend County were under national media scrutiny, at which time the charges repositioned Staff Sergeant García from a victim of racial injustice to a drunken rabble-rouser and the people of Fort Bend County from practitioners of anti-Mexican discrimination to upstanding, good, and benevolently white citizens.

The *Texas Coaster* also draws upon this discursive strategy as it seeks to counter García's and Winchell's account. In an attempt to explain why the newspaper did not report the story immediately after it occurred, and perhaps to articulate how a national voice told the story first, the *Texas Coaster* claimed to have heard about the incident but "'killed' it in a charitable attitude toward the soldier."[68] Here, the *Texas Coaster* makes legible the discursive logic of the charges, for the newspaper casts García as both a drunk and a war hero and positions the *Texas Coaster* as the paternalistic and benevolent protector of his reputation. This is an enlightening move because it demonstrates that the Mexican Other need not be a hapless victim of white supremacy, as depicted in the film, in order for whiteness to save the day. Rather as an echo of older manifestations of white goodness, whiteness may be forged through claiming to save Mexican Others from themselves—in this logic, even Mexican war heroes need saving from their lawless impulses by the organs of a white power structure. For white supremacy, the newspaper's rhetorical move is double-edged: it simultaneously recirculates the trope of the drunken, lawless Mexican and reinforces an investment in white goodness.

The Macario García incident also reveals an intersection of whiteness and U.S. nationalism. During the early to mid-twentieth century, Mexican American public intellectuals laid claim to Americanness and ideals of democracy, fairness, and equality in order to fight white supremacy. This discursive maneuver was particularly potent when framed against the global threats of fascism and communism. Indeed, Perales's *Are We Good Neighbors?* includes numerous speeches, essays, and records of testimony by Mexican Americans and Anglo-American allies that position the United States as a beacon of fairness and equality and argue that racism, particularly directed at servicemen, has no place in a democracy. Moreover, Olivas contends that Winchell's defense of García was likely motivated by the Staff Sergeant's position as a decorated serviceman and not simply because he was Mexican American.[69] Acknowledging this discursive context opens the debate surrounding Macario García's case. Arguably Winchell, local officials, and the *Texas Coaster* were engaged not in a debate simply over racial justice but in a discursive battle over race, nation, and the righteousness of America. For Winchell, it may have been unthinkable to treat a serviceman in such a way, a refusal of service that violated central tenets of respect and abstract embraces of equality. Likewise local officials and the *Texas Coaster* did not want to be viewed as having mistreated a Mexican serviceman. Although such mistreatment was likely evident to all involved, they cast their actions as protective and benevolent. While Winchell, Fort Bend County officials, the *Texas Coaster*, the café owners, and García and his defense team clearly saw the incident differently, they all seem to have agreed on one thing: all sides were invested in the belief that racial injustice is antithetical to Americanness, or more accurately the *perception* of racial injustice was antithetical to Americanness.[70] Whereas this is the organizing logic of Winchell's critique, this narrative also allows Fort Bend County officials and the *Texas Coaster* to deny the mistreatment of García and take umbrage at the accusation. Indeed, this pervasive and pernicious myth of America as a land of racial justice has long allowed whites to unwitness the racial violence of the world they inhabit and deny the persistence of inequality.

Recognizing the dynamic of white saviorism in the Macario García incident returns us to the interrogation of *Giant* with a critical question: how does one read the diner scene from *Giant* against this case, particularly if the incident in the Oasis Café was the originating impulse for the movie's penultimate scene? Here, I should note that Macario García's refusal of service resonates more clearly with the film's iteration of the diner scene. As explained earlier, the novel does include a refusal of service, but no violent conflict ensues. Reading the case of Macario García against the film, however, exposes how white saviorism can be marshaled to obscure the experiences and active struggle of people of color. For example, in the film it is Bick who intervenes on the Mexican American family's behalf as Sarge jostles the Mexican man like a puppet. *Giant* does not render the imaginative possibility of the unnamed Mexicano demanding to know on what grounds his family is being denied service, yet that is what Macario García did. As police arrived to the Oasis Café, García asserted his right to know why his rights were being withheld.[71] Importantly, however, the film's scene is not about the unnamed Tejano family or really about racial injustice. It is about the racial transformation of Bick Benedict. As Bick is washed of his racial sins and elevated in the eyes of Leslie and the viewers, the possibility of Mexican American–led activism epitomized by historical figures like Johnny Herrera, Alonso Perales, Dr. Hector García, and numerous others is unimagined and unimaginable on the screen. Tragically, when viewers initially praised—and critics continue to laud—*Giant* for exposing audiences to anti-Mexican racism, they fell for a racial sleight of hand. In truth, anti-Mexican discrimination had been gaining gradual attention for years. Including it in the heroic story line of a Hollywood blockbuster came with the cost of erasing Mexican American agency and activism.

Moreover, by staging the conflict between Bick and Sarge, the punches thrown and plates smashed become a battle over the appropriate form of whiteness and the righteousness of whiteness. Rendering the refusal of service in this way not only displays white-on-white violence but also hides white-on-brown violence. Sure the possibility is alluded to though the puppetization of the Mexican man, but Bick steps in to bear the brute force of white supremacy in the form of Sarge's fists. The film leaves unexplored the way whites could brutalize those who questioned Juan Crow. According to Winchell, García was beaten to the point he needed medical attention. The *Texas Coaster* suggested that the decorated war hero was merely "quieted" with a baseball bat. For his part, García denied that the bat ever made contact with him.[72] But white-on-brown violence can take many forms: the psychological blow of the refusal of service, the manhandling and public humiliation, the financial strain of fighting trumped-up charges, the time of life lost with a potential jail sentence. When critics laud *Giant* for showing Mexican American discrimination to a broader audience, one must ask how the audience would have responded to seeing a man brutalized with a baseball bat or being unjustly imprisoned. But that wouldn't be Bick's story; that wouldn't be a story of saviorism.

Of course, depictions of Mexican American agency and explicit race violence are unimaginable in *Giant*. Arguably that is why something so "revolutionary" could also be so popularly accepted. The film acquiesces to the logics of supremacy in another critical way, illustrating yet another entanglement of whiteness and U.S. nationalism. In *Giant*, Bick and Sarge are the embodiments of the nation fighting over its racial future for their own interests. The unnamed Mexican American man does not embody the nation. Depending on the outcome of the fight, he and his family may be able to sit at the American table. The case of Macario García offers something more complex: a decorated war hero of Mexican descent, an image LULACers thought ushered in a new era in Mexican American belonging within the United States, an image Walter Winchell could support. Yet in *Giant* the figure of Staff Sergeant Macario García is nowhere to be seen. The only sergeant is Sarge, one of the two titanic white men crashing about Sarge's Diner. By diminishing García and others who were refused service, *Giant* imagines and depicts white saviorism as an American force against discrimination. White saviorism and its national form of American exceptionalism are forces for good, fighting against discrimination and oppression, foreign and domestic. Or so the audience is asked to believe. Yet this is but one scene and one case among many. The logic of white saviorism and its intersection with and expression of American exceptionalism can be found in numerous discursive locations, particularly in the fantasies of international invasion.

White Benevolence and American Messianism in *The Magnificent Seven*

Even as the white saviorism of *Giant* and the Macario García case was inflected with nationalist impulses in the militaristic framing of the diner scene and the debate surrounding anti-Mexican discrimination and American ideals, white saviorism takes other nationalist forms as well. Consider the long-standing cinematic and political trope of (white) Americans intervening on behalf of oppressed communities abroad. For example, Clint Eastwood's unnamed stranger in *A Fistful of Dollars*

WITH FRIENDS LIKE THESE | 133

(1964) single-handedly liberates a Mexican town from rival gangs: one consisting of Mexicans and one of white Americans. Such a narrative takes the white saviorism epitomized in *Giant* and turns it outward, beyond the U.S. borders, and transforms it into a global posture. It is through such a maneuver that white saviorism intersects with and reinforces the impulses of U.S. interventionism. One of the most famous incarnations of this trope is John Sturges's 1960 *The Magnificent Seven.*

Set in 1880s Mexico, *The Magnificent Seven* is a story of a Mexican farming village that lives under the threat of a bandit named Calvera and his forty men. As the film opens, the bandits rob the town, and the villagers of Ixcatlan debate what they should do. The village elder tells them to fight, go to the border where guns are "plentiful," and purchase the weapons needed to drive off Calvera and his men. When three villagers travel across the border to the United States, they meet Chris (Yul Brynner), who convinces them it would be cheaper and smarter to hire gunmen. As they agree, Chris assembles a premier team of gunslingers to rid the town of the lawless bandits. The heroes travel to Mexico, arm and train the townsfolk, fight Calvera and his men, are betrayed by the villager Zotero, defeat the bandits, and importantly transform the village by giving the farmers the courage to fight for themselves.

This iconic Western is a revision of Akira Kurosawa's 1954 *Seven Samurai. The Magnificent Seven* shares many elements of Kurosawa's original where a village of Japanese farmers face starvation at the hands of a band of forty marauding bandits. The villagers' only recourse is to hire a group of samurai to defend them. *The Magnificent Seven*'s shift from samurai to predominantly white U.S. gunfighters does more than transform a film about medieval Japan into a popular Western. This maneuver fundamentally alters the tale by overlaying a national-racial system of meaning onto a story that originally interrogated social caste. That is, the Western repositions the narrative in a different discursive context wherein a tale of courage and honor accrues racialized and nationalist dimensions as the mostly white embodiments of U.S. masculinity intervene abroad to allegedly ensure safety and spread freedom.

Here the dynamics of whiteness and U.S. nationalism converge again. As Steve Martinot has argued, white supremacy and American exceptionalism share a common cultural structure—both are charged with virtue and impunity. Together these attributes form the basis for the messianism that underwrites discriminatory treatment at home and imperialist actions abroad.[73] According to Martinot, this "messianism," or what I have been describing as "saviorism," is a constitutive element of U.S. political culture and is evidenced in the discourse of spreading democracy in Afghanistan, Iraq, and other countries. Moreover, the practice of U.S. messianism is hardly limited to the past thirty years. U.S. messianism and its racial-nationalist logics can be found in the Mexican-American War, Manifest Destiny, the Spanish-American War, as well as twentieth-century conflicts that emerged as proxy battles with the Soviet Union like the Korean War and Vietnam War.[74]

Through *The Magnificent Seven*, this cultural structure of U.S. white saviorism finds expression in film. In his analysis of Cold War–era U.S. cinema, Stanley Corkin has argued that *The Magnificent Seven* and other Westerns evidence the political thought and discourse of the time. For Corkin, John Wayne's 1960 *The Alamo* and John Sturges's *The Magnificent Seven* "offer powerful emotional pleas for the extension of U.S. power to bring about social conditions throughout the world that will replicate those that exist in an idealized vision of the United States."[75] While Corkin's historical contextualization of *The Magnificent Seven* within the debate surrounding the U.S. role in the fight against the communism in the third world is well reasoned and incisive, Martinot's theorization of U.S. white messianism pries open analysis of the film and its political ideologies in two critical ways. First, U.S. imperialist interventions have a history that extends well before and long after the mid-twentieth century. Thus, although the film may be read strictly within the moment, it may also be read tropologically in a long signifying chain, the longue durée of U.S. imperialism and white supremacy. Second, Martinot's model exposes how the nationalist logics Corkin examines are also racially organized. In other words, *The Magnificent Seven* is a filmic expression of not simply the benevolent powers of Americanness in the world, but also the powers of whiteness in the nonwhite third world, a move that fashions whiteness against Mexico and Mexicans.

The Magnificent Seven renders U.S. saviorism beside and against the equally well-established trope of the Infernal Paradise where Mexico is cast as seductively beautiful and dangerously corrupt. Importantly, the Mexican government was aware of and concerned about the potential nationalist and racial meanings permeating the film. While the film was

shot in Mexico, the government censor Jorge Ferretis demanded changes
to the script because he felt it showed his country in a negative light. For
example, he required that the villagers initially go to the border to buy
guns and not simply hire U.S. gunmen. Moreover, he objected to a line
that suggested Mexicans were too poor to hire American gunmen.[76] The
censor's critiques illustrate a concern about representing Mexico and
Mexicans as poor and vulnerable. The change to having the villagers
seek weapons for *self*-defense does afford them more agency than in Kurosawa's original and certainly more agency than the unnamed Tejano in
Giant. However, the efforts of the censor and the Mexican agency were
quickly short-circuited in the revised script.[77] To maintain the narrative
structure, Chris informs the villagers that they would be better off hiring
gunmen. Moreover, in a move that reinforces the national-racial logics,
Chris first suggests that they reach out to the *rurales*, Mexico's mounted
police force that patrolled rural areas of the nation from the 1860s to the
1910s. The villagers respond that they have twice gone to the rurales, but
after the rurales left the village, Calvera returned to pillage again. This
moment establishes both that the Mexican government cannot protect
its citizenry and that U.S. gunmen are needed to bring about peace and
order. Even though the censor got his wish that the villagers not immediately request the help of U.S. gunmen, the film ultimately reinforces
the Infernal Paradise trope in suggesting that Mexico is a place of instability that the government cannot control. Moreover, whether or not the
villagers initially sought men or guns, they quickly acquiesce to the need
for seven saviors.

While the film clearly constructs a U.S. saviorism against Mexico as
an Infernal Paradise, the racial implications of these gun-slinging saviors may be less apparent. Although the characters of Chris, Vin (Steve
McQueen), and most of the gunmen are unquestionably white Americans, Bernardo O'Reilly is of mixed Mexican and Irish ancestry, and the
youthful Chico is Mexican. At first glance, the inclusion of Bernardo
and Chico seems to disrupt the Great White Savior motif, for these two
Mexican-descent gunfighters also contribute to the rescue of Ixcatlan.
However, these characters epitomize the logics of whiteness and U.S.
nationalism during and after the racial break. Even as Bernardo and
Chico are used to deploy Mexicanness, they are portrayed by the white
actors Charles Bronson and Horst Buchholz, respectively. Indeed, in

keeping with the times, all of the film's lead roles were played by white actors.[78] Furthermore, Eli Wallach thrilled reviewers with his portrayal of the villainous Calvera. Evidencing the ability of Wallach to inhabit racial scripts, reviewers described him as an "illegal hombre" with "shifty, roguish eyes," a "dark, dirty, stubbed face," "a figure of towering rascality, ruthlessness and cunning as the scourge of Ixcatlan."[79] This ethnoracial discrepancy between the characters and the casting works on two levels. In the realm of narrative, the multicultural but predominantly white United States stands for goodness against a monocultural, corrupt other. Here, echoing *Giant*, the United States incorporates people of color in order to further its underlying logics of white goodness and American exceptionalism. With a critical eye, the film does not expose the U.S. embrace of multicultural cohesion but rather enacts a contest between white men, even those playing brown men—a contest to serve the needs of white nationalist fantasies.

Importantly, the white goodness that undergirds the film's messianic impulses is not simply fashioned in juxtaposition to Calvera's embodiment of the corrupt Mexican Other. Rather, the film first establishes white goodness as Chris and Vin confront and defeat an instance of racial injustice in the United States. Early on in the film, when three Mexican villagers travel to the United States, the audience is introduced to a local conflict. The local undertaker tells a Yankee salesman that he cannot perform a burial. When the salesman interjects that he didn't know the man who died, he just saw him fall down dead, the undertaker explains that Old Sam was an Indian and "there's an element in town that objects" to him being buried in Boot Hill alongside whites. It is at this moment that Chris steps forward to drive the hearse, Vin offers to ride shotgun, and the eventual leaders of the seven become partners. Through their bravery, sense of righteousness, and gun-fighting prowess, Old Sam receives a burial. Reminiscent of *Giant* or the commission hearings discussed earlier, this scene positions racial intolerance as something that has no place in the United States. The film's protagonists defeat bigotry with bravery and guns to assert a proper Americanness and whiteness. Importantly, as this scene establishes Chris's and Vin's whitely heroic bona fides, it also perpetuates the pernicious belief that racism solely takes the form of overt bigotry. Thus, this moment establishes white saviorism through the simultaneous elision of other forms of racial domination. Moreover, one would be remiss not to note that Old Sam allows for the rearticulation of two anti-Indigenous tropes— the vanishing Indian and the drunken Indian. That is, Old Sam has disappeared prior to the scene, present only through the coffin and the words of white men. Also, as the Yankee salesman says "I'm walking down the street, and a man drops dead in front of me. For two hours people kept stepping over and around him without lifting a finger," viewers may fairly place Old Sam in a long chain of signification of drunken Indians in the white American imagination. Thus, through recognizing how Old Sam fits into the discursive tradition of white supremacy, this scene exposes how even the film's formative action of white goodness is based on the recirculation of supremacist imaginings. In this way, white saviorism is not simply a response to injustice—white saviorism is also dependent upon and rearticulates racism. Ultimately, it is the goodness of Chris and Vin established in this scene that underwrites the American messianism of their conflict with Calvera as well as their invasion and salvation of the Mexican farming village.[80]

As the seven travel to Mexico, their juxtaposition to Calvera elucidates both their human complexity and the core elements of U.S. white saviorism. It is critical to note that *The Magnificent Seven* marks a shift in genre toward the revisionist Western.[81] Rather than simplistic constructions of pure heroics versus dastardly villains epitomized by the white hat, black hat motif, this film renders more complex protagonists through the film's treatment of criminality, trauma, and greed. While the seven gunfighters are certainly heroes, they are far from saintly. As Corkin notes, "the force is quintessentially American in that it is made up of a gallery of 'types' that define the nation."[82] However, each of the seven is more than a "type." With varying degrees of development, they—unlike the villagers and Calvera—are rendered with human complexity as exposed in their initial motivations for taking the mission. For example, Harry Luck is motivated to protect the town because he believes that the villagers know of a hidden treasure, and he continually tries to elicit their secret riches. Another gunfighter, Lee, joins the seven because he is on the run from the law and needs the meager twenty dollars offered to pay off his room and board from hiding out. Even the leaders of the seven, Chris and Vin, are motivated not simply out of their sense of justice but in part out because life in the settled West offers little for them. These elements of the revisionist Western reinforce key aspects of whiteness. Through their various motivations, the seven gunmen signal how whiteness is allowed to inhabit a type of human complexity. The bandit Calvera, however, lacks the complexity of the heroes. He is motivated simply by greed and power. Thus, read against the depiction of Calvera, the seven are not simply allowed complexity but also embody white virtue. When the seven first confront the bandits, Calvera asserts that he and the Americans are "in the same business" and offers to split the spoils of the village. For Calvera, his pillaging is driven by greed and justified as the natural order of things. Later, as Calvera drives the seven out of the village, he asks Chris, "Why a man like you took the job in the first place?" While Chris responds that he had been wondering the same thing and Vin asserts that "It seemed to be a good idea at the time," Calvera's question brings to the fore that the gunmen were motivated not simply by adventure or need but ultimately by a sense of righteousness. This contrast to Calvera is augmented in the next scene when the heroes decide to pick up their guns, return to the town, and fight because of their honor and pride. These moments are significant in two interrelated ways. First, they reinforce the traditional Western theme of honor, exposing how a revisionist approach still adheres to core genre elements.[83] Second, that sense of honor and righteousness is forged in opposition to the absolute greed of Calvera.

This cultural structure of U.S. saviorism takes on greater significance toward the end of the film. In a plot twist, the seven are betrayed by the villager Zotero and Calvera takes the town and their guns, allowing the seven heroes to return to the United States with their lives. When they are given their guns back, they return to the town out of honor and pride. Echoing the discourses of Manifest Destiny and foreign wars, they must clear the town of bandits. That is, in this pivotal fight, the seven do not keep the bandits from coming in. Rather, they must drive the corrupt Mexicans out so that the good Mexicans can thrive. As such, the film concludes with an invasion where the U.S. heroes are greeted as liberators. Such a move reinforces the naturalized position of white goodness, American exceptionalism, and U.S. imperialism through a logics of saviorism. This film's conclusion enacts the nationalist fantasies of U.S. imperialism. Land is cleared. Bad guys are defeated. Democracy and civilization can now flourish. The United States can retain its status as a beacon of promise awash in a sea of corruption. Here the dynamics of white saviorism and U.S. messianism converge to map the racial-nationalist-imperialist impulses that have underwritten U.S. interventions in Vietnam, Iraq, and elsewhere.

Critically, while white saviorism and U.S. interventionism are forged against the Infernal Paradise trope, it is the protracted encounter with the villagers, Mexican Others embodied, that reveals a metamorphosis of the gunmen.[84] Indeed, as Daniel Cooper Alarcón notes, encounters with Mexico and Mexicans often perform a transformative function within the U.S. racial imagination.[85] The personal transformations are particularly noticeable in the two Mexican-descent members of the seven. While Bernardo starts off as a solitary hired gun who has fallen on hard times, he builds a relationship with the village children, acknowledges his mixed Irish and Mexican heritage, dies saving a child, and according to the village boys will be remembered as a hero for years to come. Even as the character is not fully developed, the film suggests that Bernardo had largely hidden his Mexican heritage and concludes with his embracing and being reintegrated into Mexicanness. Similarly, at the outset Chico is an impetuous and unskilled young gun who desired to team with Chris and the other established gunfighters.[86] By the end, however, he has fallen in love with a young woman from the village and chooses to stay in Mexico, returning to life as a farmer. This personal transformation also reverberates through the racial meanings at the end of the film. While the seven included two nominally Mexican characters among the predominantly white U.S. saviors, the film concludes with a clean racial division: Mexico is returned to the good Mexicans, as the one surviving Mexican member of the seven Chico remains in Ixcatlan and the white saviors return home. Such a move troubles the good intentions behind white saviorism and furthers the imagination of the United States as a racial state.

Unsurprisingly, the adventure in Mexico and the encounter with Mexicans also leave a mark on the leaders of the seven. Prior to being ridden out of town, Chris and Vin discuss their desire to settle down. Their transformation is exposed when Vin explains that on the first day in Ixcatlan he began thinking about putting down the gun-fighting life, settling down, and raising some cattle. Importantly, Vin confides this to Chris because he knows that Chris feels similarly about the village. This is a marked contrast to Chris and Vin's inability to settle down established earlier in the film. After facilitating the burial of Old Sam, Chris and Vin had questioned the viability of settling in the U.S. frontier town because the only job is bagging at a grocery store. Both were reticent to reject the ways of the wandering, hired gunman for the domesticated life. Even though the desire for adventure may have initiated their mission, Chris, Vin, and the others ultimately embrace honor as their reason to fight Calvera. At the end of the film, however, Chris and Vin have changed, at least partially. They see the possibility of settling down even as they leave town. This dynamic proves interesting for two distinct reasons. First, we again see how experiences of the Mexican Other are subordinated to the stories of white saviors. That is, in the final moments we must again recognize that the film was less about the villagers and more about the character of the men who saved them, a theme punctuated as Chris and Vin ride not west into the sunset but north for the border. Second, reading the film as an articulation and celebration of white saviorism and U.S. interventionism, Chris and Vin's inability to settle down gestures toward the future. U.S. imperialism and white saviorism await. Calvera has been vanquished. The two leaders ride into the horizon, and new days, new territories, new adventures will arise.

And new days and new interventionist adventures did arise. *The Magnificent Seven* spurred sequels and knockoffs. In *The Return of the Seven* (1966) the men of the village are captured and enslaved by a band of gunmen hired by a wealthy rancher named Lorca. Chico's wife travels north to find Chris, who reconstitutes the seven and saves the Mexican village again.[87] Here one must wonder about the effectiveness of the original seven's training of the villagers and Hollywood's attitude toward Mexicans' ability to defend themselves if the village was able to be taken yet again. Luckily the villagers are so close to the Great White Hope of the United States as they are "so far from God."[88] The same year also saw the release of *The Professionals*, which depicts a band of U.S. guns hired by a wealthy, white U.S. businessman to save his Mexican wife from the ruthless revolutionary leader Raza (Jack Palance).[89] Reminiscent of *The Magnificent Seven*'s embrace of soft multiculturalism, the heroes of *The Professionals* are nominally diverse, consisting of three white men (Burt Lancaster, Lee Marvin, and Robert Ryan) and one black man (Woody Strode) who is given few lines. They rescue the Mexican wife Maria

(Claudia Cardinale) and learn that she had not been kidnapped by Raza but had left her husband for him. After killing all of Raza's men, these heroes turn on their employer, demonstrating not just their military prowess but also their sense of righteousness.

Of course, filmic depictions of white saviorism and U.S. interventionism are not relegated to the 1960s. *The Magnificent Seven* and other filmic imaginings of cross-border white saviorism have circulated on television and other discursive locations as well. Indeed, I remember being introduced to these classics while watching television on Saturday and Sunday afternoons in the 1970s and 1980s. Growing up in Chicago's western suburbs, I learned the logics of white goodness and U.S. messianism, and they seemed natural even as I still did not understand the location of Mexico and Mexicans in my formative racial imagination. Such recirculation forms a popular education and hidden curriculum of whiteness on the border. I remember well sitting in Mr. Falk's seventh-grade social studies class when my classmates proudly asserted that the United States was the best country in the world because we had won every war. Perhaps we had all been watching the same movies, taking in the same stories, learning the same hidden curriculum. Without missing a beat, Mr. Falk merely said, "What about Korea? What about Vietnam?" Sadly the adherence to U.S. white messianism still propels the nation into conflict: in Afghanistan, in Iraq, in Syria through the war on terrorism and in Mexico and Latin America via the drug war. If we seek to end perpetual warfare, perhaps we should confront the logic that makes it not just possible but inevitable. Here it is imperative to confront the fact that the logics that underpin U.S. nationalism are intertwined with those of white supremacy. Alas, Antoine Fuqua is directing a remake of *The Magnificent Seven* scheduled for release in 2016. The remake will star Denzel Washington, Vincent D'Onofrio, and Chris Pratt. While the film is being directed by the African American Fuqua and while the characters' racial makeup differs from the original, one can expect the underlying nationalist messianic logics of the film to remain. According to the trailer, Washington and Pratt will lead a multiracial band of American gunfighters not to save a Mexican village but on a mission to liberate a U.S. town. Ultimately, this remake suggests not just Hollywood's lack of original material and original thought but also the secure marketability of old American exceptionalist narratives wrapped up in newer special effects and slightly more diverse casting. Here we are reminded that the project of imagining the United States as a racial state is not simply about phenotype. Rather, it is about the coterminous overlay of nationalism and white supremacy, in this case the discourse and ideology that structure whiteness and Americanness as virtuous and as acting with impunity.

Border Patrol Rescue Narrative and the Benevolent Nation

Although U.S. white messianism structures imperialism and interventionism, a nationalist incarnation of white saviorism is deployed not only outside the nation's borders. Rather, it also plays a crucial role in the discourse of border protectionism. Today this United States as humanitarian savior trope can easily be found in what I call the "Border Patrol rescue narrative." The U.S. Border Patrol was founded in 1924 as part of the Department of Labor and charged with halting illegal entries from Mexico and Canada. In 1933, the Border Patrol was moved into the recently consolidated Immigration and Naturalization Service (INS). After the September 11, 2001, attacks, the U.S. government reorganized many of its policing agencies. As a result, the U.S. Border Patrol was relocated into U.S. Customs and Border Protection as part of the U.S. Department of Homeland Security.

Most of the press releases from the U.S. Customs and Border Protection (CBP) and the media coverage of the Border Patrol focus on apprehension of undocumented immigrants and seizures of illegal drugs. Together, these stories emphasize the role of the Border Patrol in protecting the U.S. borders and the U.S. citizenry. Indeed, the citizens are cast as protected from drugs and sex offenders. For example, an April 3, 2015, press release tells of Border Patrol "agents seizing more than $3.5 million worth of marijuana" and "arresting two convicted sex offenders."[90] Another release describes the seizure of more marijuana and the apprehension in separate incidents of four men, all of whom were undocumented and "had previous criminal convictions of sexual crimes to include sexual assault of a child."[91] The stories presented in these press releases are far from unique. Rather, they work as two distinct points on an ongoing narrative chain about the U.S.-Mexico border and the role played by the Border Patrol. As such these stories render the border a site of vulnerability and protection against external threats. However, a significant number of press releases and news articles focus on incidents where the Border Patrol renders aid or otherwise "rescues" people. Importantly, the border protection and rescue narratives do not simply emerge from active journalism alone. The CBP media relations team writes and disseminates numerous press releases each year, ultimately shaping and driving these narratives.[92] These press releases along with other sites of CBP discourse form an official narrative of transnational migration, the structure of which we have seen before: there are heroic good guys, lawless and greedy villains, and innocent Mexicans (as well as other Others) in need of protection.

Reading a wide selection of Border Patrol press releases and media coverage, elements of the genre readily take shape. Here I am less interested in individual instances, and more interested in how the formulaic nature of official press releases reveal the narrative of Border Patrol heroism. Arguably, it is the rescue narrative's formulaic nature that gives it power, for it is a structure that both allows for endless repetition and causes it to align with broader racial and nationalist narratives.[93] Iterations of the Border Patrol rescue narrative typically have four components: a declaration that the Border Patrol rescued an individual or a group, a description of the circumstances that necessitated the rescue, a statement of how the Border Patrol was alerted, and an articulation of the means of rendering aid. Importantly, not all of the rescues are of immigrants. Many reports detail how the Border Patrol locates and renders aid to lost or injured hikers as well as assists other government agencies in emergency response situations.[94] The cases involving undocumented immigrants, however, have an additional element. At the end of the rescue the immigrant is turned over for processing, that is, readied for detention and deportation.

Revealing the overdetermined desire to cast the Border Patrol as heroic saviors, the official press releases are quite flexible with their use of the term "rescue" when immigrants are involved. Most commonly, stories detail unquestionable rescues performed by the Border Patrol. Often alerted by lost or injured immigrants calling 911 or other immigrants who have found help, the Border Patrol searches out and renders aid to those who need it. For example, on September 22, 2014, after an undocumented immigrant called 911, the Border Patrol's Search,

Trauma, and Rescue (BORSTAR) unit located and transported him to a hospital.[95] In June 2013, CBP reported that the Tucson sector of the Border Patrol had "rescued 177 people who were unable to continue due to heat related illnesses."[96] These examples illustrate that one should not discount the dangers of crossing. However, the discourse of rescue is applied to other situations as well.

In many press releases, the Border Patrol is described as rescuing immigrants caught at border checkpoints as they are hiding in trunks, hidden compartments, or freight vehicles. For example, a May 29, 2015, press release reports that "U.S. Border Patrol agents from the Rio Grande Valley Sector rescued two undocumented immigrants from inside the trunk of a car."[97] In these cases the need for rescue is less definite. To be sure, being transported in such a way is dangerous and can be deadly.[98] Similar degrees of danger, however, can be found in most undocumented crossings of the U.S.-Mexico border, for the Rio Grande, the Sonoran Desert, and other unfamiliar terrain can all be deadly. Moreover, casting these checkpoint apprehensions as rescues is undermined when the migrants repeatedly turn down the offer of medical attention.[99] Being locked in a car trunk, hidden compartment, or truck with no means of escape is certainly dangerous. However, these incidents at checkpoints could be better described as apprehensions, for the Border Patrol is arresting migrants who are not in distress. These press releases reimagine apprehensions and border policing as humanitarian and life-saving missions. Depicting these checkpoint apprehensions as rescues has less to do with the immediate danger posed and more to do with the construction of Border Patrol agents as humanitarian heroes in a broader narrative of transnational migration, good and evil. Here one may legitimately ask if such a rhetorical strategy may work beyond border checkpoints: can apprehensions in the Sonoran Desert be emplotted into a rescue narrative?

Read against the grain, other iterations of the Border Patrol rendering aid trouble the too easy narrative of Border Patrol as saviors. For example, a May 4, 2015, press release describes an incident wherein Border Patrol agents received a 911 call "from a group of distressed immigrants." However, when agents "located and rescued two subjects . . . two other subjects fled the area."[100] The press release is unclear as to whether the same immigrants who called 911 were the ones who were "rescued." Either way, by fleeing the Border Patrol, two of the migrants gesture toward the possibility of another story. Perhaps this was more arrest than rescue. The fact that two of the migrants fled their "rescue" also forces a critical question: how does one account for the involuntary nature of some Border Patrol rescues? Here another example is useful. An August 28, 2013, press release reports an incident when Border Patrol agents came across four men trying to cross the Rio Grande into the United States: "When agents made contact . . . , two of the four men absconded to Mexico. A third subject attempted to abscond to Mexico but was swept away by the fast moving current. Border Patrol agents quickly rescued the distressed man."[101] While there should be no doubt that the man needed aid, this press release, because it is framed within the broader rescue narrative, does not account for the fact that the immigrant was initially seeking not rescue but escape from the Border Patrol. Moreover, the policing efforts to apprehend him are what necessitated a rescue in the first place.

Here a note of clarification is required. I am not dismissing that there is danger in undocumented migration, nor am I suggesting that agents should not render aid. Rather, by reading these rescue narratives against the grain, I expose how they are not merely documents of reportage. These narratives are charged with ideological power; they shape, open, and foreclose ways of understanding the world. While the Border Patrol may be rendering aid to those in need, emplotting these as rescues winnows down a complex reality into a simplified tale of heroism. Moreover, such stories of humanitarian saviors perform valuable cultural work for the nation.

The nationalist function of the rescue narrative is both epitomized and further troubled in what was likely meant to be a feel good, humanitarian story. According to a February 23, 2015, release, CBP officers at Houston Intercontinental Airport rescued a stowaway squirrel on a flight from Costa Rica. An officer and agricultural specialist "caged the squirrel without incident," provided it with food and water, and turned the animal over to the U.S. Fish and Wildlife.[102] While it may be tempting to draw an analogy between the rescue of the squirrel from the dangers he faced and his quarantine and the treatment of human migrants, what is most revealing about this story is not the saved squirrel. Rather, this story exposes the way the Border Patrol rescue narrative humanizes agents of the state. Border Patrol agents, like the CBP officers, are not simply beat cops charged with policing the nation's borders—they are imagined to be humanitarians who will help even a poor, innocent squirrel.

To better comprehend how the Border Patrol rescue narrative renders agents as benevolent humanitarians of the state, one must place these stories in the broader narrative of transnational migration that U.S. CBP tells. Echoing back to the chapter's earlier interrogation of white saviorism, CBP casts the Border Patrol's rescuing mission against the heartless villains in the story: the coyotes and human smuggling networks. According to the CBP website, the CBP is responsible for stopping not only terrorists and drug traffickers, but also human traffickers. The CBP states that one of its missions is to fight human trafficking, which is not the same as but is often linked to human smuggling. According to the CBP, human trafficking is not relegated to the sex trade but may also include migrant agricultural work, sweatshop factory labor, and domestic servitude. Like the dangers of undocumented migration, human trafficking is very real. Human trafficking is characterized by the use of "force, fraud, and coercion" to propel migrants into a life of servitude.[103] However, CBP uses the linkage and conflation of trafficking and smuggling to craft its broader narrative of transnational migration. In this maneuver, the CBP argues that Border Patrol agents are heroes protecting victims lacking agency. This discursive strategy is extended in the rescue narratives. When describing the extraction of migrants from the Rio Grande, the Texas brush land, or the Sonoran Desert, it is not uncommon for the narratives to declare that "human smugglers are ruthless criminals who view the immigrant not as a human being, but as cargo."[104] Likewise, as migrants are "rescued" at border checkpoints, the press releases make statements like "rescues such as this highlight the risks ruthless criminal organizations take with immigrants' lives for monetary gain. All of the subjects were offered medical attention but declined."[105] Even as the CBP website acknowledges the distinctions between human trafficking and human smuggling, these press releases repeatedly demonstrate the agency's linkage and conflation of the two. While there is an undeniable truth in the dangers of much transborder migration, these rhetorical deployments are purposeful in propagating and recirculating a long-enduring nationalist and racialized story. The specter of human trafficking (i.e., modern-day slavery) is deployed to strike against coyotes and human smugglers as well as to render the Border Patrol agents as those fighting on behalf of migrants and embodying a national humanitarian mission.

The Border Patrol rescue narrative is essential to forming the discourse of border protection. The Border Patrol spends most of its material resources and rhetorical energies limiting undocumented immigration and protecting against threats described as external to the United States: terrorists, drugs, and criminal entrants. This discourse is evidenced in abundance on the CBP website, media releases, and other official statements that position Border Patrol officers as agents of the state holding the line against potential chaos. Such rhetorical positioning along with the increased militarization of the border exposes elements of the United States as a police state, inhumane and inhospitable. The Border Patrol rescue narrative, however, complicates matters, reimagining the agents of border protection not simply as a militarized police force but as a humanitarian one. These rescue narratives find common ground and seek to perform similar work to international exercises of soft power when the U.S. military delivers aid in disaster stricken countries.[106] While U.S. military humanitarianism purportedly seeks to win the hearts and minds of people in other countries, the Border Patrol rescue narrative is pitched largely for U.S. audiences, to convince them of the humanitarian saviorism of the nation-state.[107] April Shemak makes a parallel argument in her incisive analysis of Coast Guard photographs from the 1990s and their visual rhetoric.[108] According to Shemak, the U.S. Coast Guard has actively deployed a discourse of hospitality while interdicting Haitian refugees in international waters. Coast Guard photos and captions tell of Haitian migrants "relaxing" and servicemen providing hygienic products and "rescuing" migrants from their vessels. In contrast, Shemak dutifully illustrates how such a narrative masks the fact that migrants are often unwillingly detained in their rescues and that the Coast Guard narrative recirculates white supremacist tropes about Haitians.[109] Likewise, the Border Patrol rescue narrative overwrites that their rescues are also apprehensions. Indeed, given the flexible use of "rescue" described earlier and given that Border Patrol rescues of undocumented immigrants end with their apprehension, detention, and deportation, might we ask whether all apprehensions might be recast as rescues. Ultimately, the Border Patrol rescue narrative produces and reinforces the exceptionalist image of the United States as innocent and kind. The Border Patrol seeks to halt undocumented migration and protect the United States from external threats all the while lending a humanitarian hand—it is militarization with a smile. Here one may note a striking yet uncomfortable commonality with the nativism discussed in the previous chapter. Just as nativist fears and hate are dependent upon a discourse of white victimhood, so too does a continual militarization of the United States require a guise of humanitarian benevolence.

The Border Patrol rescue narrative also performs valuable cultural work through what it elides, beyond militarization. The push-pull factors that create and structure immigration as well as factors that increase the need for rescues are absent from press releases and often mentioned only in passing in news coverage concerning rescued immigrants. It is unsurprising that the CBP does not address politically volatile issues such as NAFTA, Mexico's political instability caused by the war on drugs, the U.S. political gridlock on immigration reform, and Operation Gatekeeper. However, it is fundamental to recognize that the immigrant rescues and Border Patrol heroism are largely dependent on these factors. Without acknowledging the push-pull dynamics, the Border Patrol rescue narrative casts migrants as emerging ex nihilo at the border, facing danger and in need of U.S. humanitarianism. This is a neoliberal sleight of hand where economic and structural forces are elided, and individualism is augmented through the "choices" of migrants and coyotes. This elision positions the U.S. agents as saviors without acknowledging governmental and corporate complicity in the conditions that foster migration. For instance, the omission of Operation Gatekeeper is particularly crucial to the functioning of the Border Patrol rescue narrative. Operation Gatekeeper was launched by the Clinton administration in 1994. Through increased border fencing, personnel, and other resources, the Border Patrol sought to dramatically reduce undocumented border crossings near San Diego and other populated areas of Southern California. Ultimately, the efforts funneled migrants east, away from heavily policed areas and into the deadly Sonoran Desert. Unsurprisingly, in the late 1990s, the Border Patrol and the U.S. government saw the number of migrant deaths skyrocket, creating a humanitarian disaster and a potential public relations nightmare. In response, in 1998 the Border

Patrol created a special emergency tactical unit known as BORSTAR to facilitate emergency rescues. In other words, the unit most responsible for Border Patrol rescues and their resulting narrative emerged from the crisis spurred by Operation Gatekeeper. By emphasizing the rendering of aid without acknowledging how border policing exacerbates the dangers migrants face, the Border Patrol rescue narrative asserts humanitarian bona fides for the United States as it simultaneously eschews responsibility.

In contrast to official CBP discourse, Luis Alberto Urrea's *The Devil's Highway* (2004) troubles, and at times plays into, the Border Patrol rescue narrative. Urrea's book blends history, journalism, cultural criticism, and techniques of fiction to tell the story of the Yuma 14/Wellton 26. In the summer of 2001, a group of immigrants became lost in the desert that connects Sonora, Mexico, and Arizona. Fourteen of the immigrants died, and the Border Patrol located and rendered aid to the remaining twelve. Notably the twelve survivors were not deported because they made a deal with prosecutors to testify against the guide who abandoned them in the desert. Urrea's narrative renders a more complex understanding of transnational migration than the standard rescue story. Although *The Devil's Highway* recognizes that those atop smuggling networks make their money off of the desperation and suffering of others, they are not Urrea's only villains. Unlike the Border Patrol rescue narrative, *The Devil's Highway* spends significant time exposing how economic forces, U.S. border policies, and geographic elements like the desert create the need for smuggling networks and together work as an often unseen coalition of villains to both foster migration and place immigrants in danger.[110]

The Devil's Highway also seeks to humanize both migrants and Border Patrol agents, two groups that are routinely stereotyped in popular political discourse. Urrea explores the immigrants' motivations for crossing and their suffering in the desert, and he acknowledges that the Border Patrol is often isolated from U.S. communities.[111] Moreover, Urrea examines the psychological taxation that comes from agents' dual responsibility to both hunt and save immigrants. As Urrea states, "If it was the Border Patrol's job to apprehend lawbreakers, it was equally their duty to save the lost and the dying."[112] Interestingly, here Urrea draws upon an element also found in many iterations of the Border Patrol rescue narrative. Several press releases note that agents must "shift" from a mode of tracking and apprehension (i.e., hunting) to one of rescue.[113] In reality, however, hunting and rescuing are not so easily disaggregated. As Urrea recognizes elsewhere, the militarization of the border and agents' hunting mission have led migrants and their coyotes to pursue more dangerous routes.[114] In other words, the hunting causes the rescue. Furthermore, the same techniques—clearing the land and scouting for tracks of crossing—as well as the same resources—radio, GPS, land and air vehicles—are deployed for the rescue. While Border Patrol agents may rightly need to compartmentalize human hunting apart from rescue, and while press releases and media coverage may largely frame them as distinct, hunting and rescue are imbricated, intertwined, part of a much more complex narrative of transnational migration. Recognizing such calls into question the moral coding of the United States in pervasive nationalist narratives of exceptionalism and saviorism.

Ultimately, the Border Patrol rescue narrative illustrates the intersection of whiteness and Americanness through their common internal logics. Again, this coterminous relationship is not relegated to phenotype. There are many nonwhite and Latino Border Patrol agents, and I avoid the essentialist trap of suggesting that they are motivated by "a kind of rabid self-hatred."[115] Nor do I simply link this embodiment of Americanness and whiteness to the history of immigration law and policing that has made the United States a white-majority nation. Rather, I am interested in the discursive and ideological commonalities between American exceptionalist humanitarianism found in the Border Patrol rescue narrative and supremacist dynamics of white saviorism. As evidenced in official CBP discourse, the agents are positioned as embodiments of the U.S. fight against heartless coyotes and drug smugglers. The Border Patrol regularly rescues the victims of human smuggling. In this narrative, the agency of immigrants is erased as they become "victims" and their apprehension and eventual deportation are at least partially occluded. Here, we see a common structure to that explored in *Giant* and *The Magnificent Seven*. The United States and whiteness—figured as the Border Patrol, Bick Benedict, and the seven gunfighters—rescue the helpless Mexicans from human smugglers, bigoted whites, and Mexican bandidos. In the end whiteness and Americanness, and often whiteness as Americanness, save the day, and the underlying logic of U.S. white saviorism is secured and recirculated. Of course, beyond its erasure of complexity, a problem with the logic of saviorism is that it elicits and requires gratitude from the aggrieved communities. Those who fight for their rights and their survival are reimagined as simply victims who must be grateful as their agency is erased. This narrative propels gratitude toward agents of a government who have contributed to the danger migrants face in the first place. Here, there is only one appropriate answer: as *Latino Rebels* responded to Bill Maher's racist saviorism that opened this chapter, "No mames!"

The Trouble with White Benevolence

At first glance, some may be struck by the disparate nature of the cases examined in this chapter: a political comedy skit, an epic drama exploring the changing social order in Texas, the refusal of service to a Medal of Honor recipient, a classic shoot-'em-up Western, the stories of Border Patrol heroism. These moments stretch across genre, place, and time. Can they really be laid side by side? Placing these historical and discursive moments in conversation reveals a common underlying structure. White American righteousness and humanitarianism is imagined against Mexicans in need, in need of protection from anti-immigration activists, bigoted proprietors, Mexican bandidos, and ruthless human smugglers. Ultimately, this common structure organizes the continuity of history and the long endurance of white supremacy discussed earlier.

What makes these moments, and white saviorism generally, so troubling is their seductive nature. They may be lauded as revolutionary or at least positive. However, these seemingly enlightened works actively perpetuate racial hierarchies, relying upon, recirculating, and occluding critical aspects of racial inequality. They reinstantiate notions of white American goodness not always against the image of threatening Mexicans that propels nativism but through the imagining of Mexicans in need of benevolent protection. Indeed, after the racial break when nativists like those discussed earlier or those targeted by Maher may be seen as déclassé, whiteness is able to endure, cast itself in a better light, and reimagine itself into the future. Paula Ionide has argued that white racial fantasies provide affective rewards. For Ionide, whiteness relies upon historical amnesia to forge what James Baldwin has called a "willed innocence."[116] Whites may fantasize about meritocracy and a color-blind, Melting Pot nation of immigrants, but those narratives elide systemic inequality. Together these form the "psychological, economic, civil, social, and cultural wages of whiteness."[117] Just as nativist fantasies of an Aztlán-reconquista rely upon an investment in a white victimhood and forge besieged solidarity, narratives of white American saviorism reinforce and extend the affective investment in goodness. Through this logic, white goodness is not simply innate and within but can be expressed outwardly for the benefit of Others. In actuality, however, white saviorism is about benefiting whiteness. Narratives of white American saviorism may provide an affective reward and script fights for racial justice and humanitarianism, but such narratives both obscure the broader system of inequality and require its maintenance into the future. Bick's heroic triumph asks viewers to forget that Mexicans will still be barred from Sarge's and many other establishments the day after the fight. The Border Patrol rescue narrative erases the economic policies and militarization of the border that have placed migrant lives in danger. Moreover, white saviorism does not simply rely upon oppression in the present but requires it in the future. The examples discussed in this chapter all evidence moments of political, racial reconciliation, but the logic of saviorism requires aggrieved communities to return to subordinated statuses and be placed in perpetual danger so that they can be saved yet again. Thus, Bick may be the hero as Mexicans are continuously excluded, the Magnificent Seven may ride again as another Mexican villain captures the town, and the Border Patrol will continue to rescue migrants as long as economic and immigration policies place them in danger.

In recent years, many scholars and activists have explored how white folks may participate in the struggle for racial justice. The discourse of allyship has become prevalent on college campuses and social justice circles. Here, racial-justice-oriented whites may become allies of people of color, working for the betterment of others and an end to inequality. Mia McKenzie and others have critiqued the position of ally when it lacks an interrogation of what whites have to gain or lose from the struggle, treating them instead as neutral observers who may simply opt in to activism.[118] While not rejecting allyship entirely, David Shih has reframed allyship beyond an effort to help people of color. Writing about white allies' relationship to Asian Americans in particular but with a message for all whites who hope to ally themselves with aggrieved communities of color, Shih contended, "You shouldn't aspire to be allies on behalf of Asian Americans. . . . You should be allies in the fight against white supremacy."[119] What strikes me as dangerous about "ally" is the way it can be marshaled as a totalizing identity, bracketing whites off from systemic inequality. "Ally" may seduce whites with the affective reward of thinking they are "the good ones," ironically investing them in a central tenet of white supremacy: goodness, a goodness that easily slides toward saviorism. This does not mean that antiracist whites should not ally themselves with others for racial liberation. Rather, we must be vigilant against the many wages whiteness offers.

White participation in multiracial organizing cannot succeed if whites demand to be saviors. Solidarity work is not sexy; it requires participants to do jobs not for affective, symbolic, or economic rewards but because those jobs advance the collective struggle together. Placed within this context, the benevolent white saviors are by no means allies, although they may posture themselves as such. The narrative of white saviorism requires a continual degradation of aggrieved peoples, the erasure of structural oppression, and the revivification of a core element of white supremacy: white goodness. Whether one frames the struggle as an allyship for the liberation of all or a fight for whites and people of color to dismantle white supremacy, one thing is certain: the struggle does not need friends, stories, and saviors like these.

4

Deep in the Heart of Whiteness

White Desire and the Political Potential of Love

Nothing to show but this brand new tattoo.
But it's a real beauty,
A Mexican cutie,
How it got here I haven't a clue.
—Jimmy Buffett, "Margaritaville"

One of the most popular and enduring songs of the late twentieth century, Jimmy Buffett's 1977 "Margaritaville" is seemingly ubiquitous. It is probably fair to suggest that most white people in the United States over the age of thirty know the tune if not the words. This line where the singer describes his new tattoo as "a real beauty, / A Mexican cutie" encapsulates a key dynamic in the foundation of whiteness on the border: the romanticization of things Mexican and often Mexicanas.[1] Of course, Buffett is neither new nor unique. This musical moment is but one point in a broad, ever-sprawling discursive constellation, and this line is more than evidence of a singer spending a night "drunk in Mexico."[2]

Notably, the image does not require description beyond a "Mexican cutie." The audience can fill the gaps, for the line draws upon and contributes to a long chain of visual, literary, and musical signification: the Erotic, Exotic Mexicana. Consider the image of the demure and potentially sultry Mexicana from cinematic history. The images from *Duel in the Sun* (1946) and *The Wild Bunch* (1969) typify this trope.[3] The look, those eyes, speak of unspoken desire and desirability. Whether describing the "Mexican cutie" from "Margaritaville" or the Mexicana from *The Wild Bunch*, one must recognize that this image is *not* a woman; this image is *not* a Mexicana. Drawing upon Gerald Vizenor's *Manifest Manners*, this is a type, a trope, a discursive maneuver deployed to invoke and reinforce social scripts.[4] Importantly, as the image from *Duel in the Sun* illustrates, the bodies need not be actual mestizas or Mexicanas, for this Mexicana Pearl Chavez was played by the white Jennifer Jones. Deployments of white women in Mexican roles continue to fulfill the racial script, demonstrating how the Erotic, Exotic Mexicana is a discursive formation overlaid and inscribed upon material bodies.[5] Moreover, as this chapter explores, these tropic embodiments are not simply objects of desire but critical fulcrums in the construction and imagination of white masculinity.

Importantly, however, the "Mexican cutie" is not the only way the dynamics of whiteness emerge in "Margaritaville," for the song deploys broader romantic impulses as well. After listening to the song, no one will doubt that Buffett loves Mexico and Mexicans, or at least his ideas of them—synecdoches for margaritas and good times. Indeed, one may well consider "Margaritaville" a love song, and that declaration of love functions as an occlusive force, foreclosing the legibility of racial hegemony. Here, another example may be useful. A few years ago, I sat across the table from Gwen. I had just explained my discomfort with a mutual acquaintance. Let's call him Jeff.[6] His comments, made in earnest and in jest, about ethnic Mexicans and other people of color weighed heavily upon me, and I was hoping for an ally and understanding. Gwen, however, saw things differently: "Jeff can't be racist. I know him; he's a good person. He *loves* Mexicans and Mexican culture; his first wife was Mexican. Did you know that?"[7]

Gwen's deployment of love and goodness provides a rich point of departure, for it illustrates key aspects of racial hegemony in the contemporary United States. First, Gwen understands racism to be a malfunction in the proverbial content of one's character. In contrast, most scholars and activists concerned with racial justice recognize that white supremacy emerges from and is characterized through social structures, actions, and language. Second, because racism is often popularly characterized as explicit bigotry and hatred, assertions of goodness contradict and obscure the possibility of white supremacy. Gwen was present when Jeff made the pertinent comments. Does her perception of goodness and love of all things Mexican cause her to "unwitness" these words?[8] Confronted with claims of love and goodness, how does one respond?

Figure 4.1. Pearl Chavez (Jennifer Jones) gazes offscreen at Lewt McCanles in *Duel in the Sun*. *Duel in the Sun*, MGM.

Figure 4.2. Unnamed Mexicana tosses her hair and gazes upon the white American protagonists of *The Wild Bunch*. *The Wild Bunch*, Warner Brothers Studios.

To be clear, I do not want to suggest that Buffett harbors explicitly racist or nativist sentiments.[9] Rather, I find common ground between Buffett's love song and Gwen's assertion that Jeff cannot be racist. In both, claims of love potentially foreclose interrogation of troubling racial dynamics because love and white supremacy are framed as mutually exclusive, but as Frank Chin and Jeffery Paul Chan argued years ago, "There is racist hate and racist love."[10] While racist hate may be readily apparent, racist love performs crucial work for white supremacy as it binds oppression to seemingly positive representations. Working at the intersection of love and white supremacy, this chapter dives deep into the heart of whiteness. Like "Margaritaville," this chapter draws together these two romantic impulses, declarations of love to Mexico and Mexicanas. As will be explored throughout, both are linked through a common logic: Mexico and its inhabitants function as an Other, unmoored from modernity and charged with erotic power. Ultimately, these romantic impulses more than limit the representational possibilities of Mexico and Mexicanas. White desire both organizes and obscures white supremacist and heteropatriarchal power relations. Mexicanas are often charged as premodern, prefeminist, and thus idealized objects of desire. They become the eroticized Infernal Paradise incarnate. Such depictions may be used to foster a mythos of white male desirability and superiority. These imagined unions of white men and Mexican women also serve to displace and police Mexican men and white women. Through examining how representations of Mexicanas are deployed in Texas country music and the work of well-known transnational matchmaker Ivan Thompson, this chapter exposes the deep-seated sexual racism central to the U.S. national-racial project.

White Desire; or, The Romantic Impulses of Colonialism and Racism

White supremacy has never been able to sustain itself on fear and hatred alone. Articulations of white goodness and heroism have structured and reinforced claims of innocence and victimhood. This has been the case since the creation of racial difference as a system of meaning, and it is even more critical within the post-break era when white supremacy has worked hard to smooth its rough edges of explicit domination and degradation, making these "positive" aspects of whiteness more crucial for racial hegemony. As George Lipsitz has contended, combating white supremacy is rendered much more difficult when confronting the discourses of white desire and romanticization.[11] Thus, making legible the troubling nature of white desire and its romantic impulses is an essential step for scholars and activists. Through an examination of white fascination with the blues musician Robert Johnson and the story of him selling his soul to the devil at the crossroads, Lipsitz exposes white desire as a means of asserting authenticity through a connection to a racial Other and romanticizing individuality.[12] As a precept of this book, however, disparately racialized communities do not necessarily experience white supremacy in the same ways. Therefore, white desire and romance take different shapes and forge distinct aspects of whiteness against the Mexican Other. Through whiteness on the border, Mexico is cast as a timeless, potentially chaotic Infernal Paradise and Mexicanas are gendered and sexualized embodiments of this national-racial trope.

Of course, such romantic impulses of domination are not unique to U.S. racial hegemony. Indeed, in his foundational examination of the way discourse organizes imperial endeavors, Edward Said noted that national (and racial) relations were framed through gender paradigms.[13] As such, European nations were imagined as penetrating the feminized Others, potentially protecting and civilizing them as a form of benevolence. This gender and sexual frame was more than metaphor. Sex was a critical component of European imperial projects.[14] Anne McClintock has incisively moved Said's observation beyond seeing gender and sexuality as a discursive frame for colonial relations.[15] Rather McClintock demonstrates how eroticization and fetishizations of the Other were central to the organizing logics of commodity racism and nineteenth-century imperialism. Indeed, she exposes how in both colonial and anticolonial projects women and land were cast as anachronistic and ahistorical against men as agents of history, a move in line with U.S. depictions of Mexico and Mexicanas.[16]

Examining contemporary U.S. culture, bell hooks has theorized how the impulses of colonial transracial desire function. For hooks, through the eroticization of women of color, mass culture reenacts "the imperialist, colonizing journey as narrative fantasy of power and desire, of seduction by the Other."[17] Like with colonial postures of benevolence discussed earlier, transracial desire may well be used to maintain the racial order as it does not require whites to step out of or challenge positions of power. According to hooks, "To make one's self vulnerable to the seduction of difference, to seek an encounter with the Other, does not require that one relinquish forever one's mainstream positionality. When race and ethnicity become commodified as resources for pleasure, the culture of specific groups, as well as the bodies of individuals, can be seen as constituting an alternative playground where members of dominating races, genders, sexual practices affirm their power-over in intimate relations with the Other."[18] Here, hooks's description of the "alternative playground" is particularly telling. A playground invokes pleasure solely for the agents of play. In other words, the bodies of women of color are rendered merely for the pleasure, adventure, and play of whiteness. Moreover, through play*ground*, hooks underscores the relationship between women's bodies and land as colonizable territories. This is particularly resonant for how both Mexico and Mexicanas are cast as sites of white masculine desire and escape.

Through Said, McClintock, and hooks, we see that white desire's targeting of Mexicanness does not emerge ex nihilo nor materialize solely from U.S.-Mexican history. Rather, this romantic form of supremacy is a discursive and ideological tool that may be used to structure and legitimate racial-national power relations across time and space. Indeed, perhaps it should be unsurprising that Daniel Cooper Alarcón drew upon Said's model of an Orientalized Other to describe and theorize Mexico's place in the U.S. imagination as an Infernal Paradise.[19] Said, however, was concerned not solely with Orientalism, but also with opening the possibility for a critical Occidentalism.[20] Shifting the axis from East/West to South/North provides a similar intervention, looking to how deployments of romanticized Mexico and Mexicanas organize the logics of U.S. white supremacy.

Here an important question must be addressed: in what ways do romantic impulses shape and constrain the representations of Mexico and Mexicanas? While Mexico is often rendered as timeless, traditional, and lawless, Mexicanas are characterized as carriers of "traditional" gender norms, vulnerable to a corrupt and modernizing world around them, and in need of protection by white men. Mexicanas are imagined as both desirable and desiring, and when they make that fateful connection with the subject of white desire, the attachment is deeper than language. While the implications of these dynamics will be elucidated shortly, two observations should be noted. Just as la Mexicana's eroticization is bound to representations of Mexico, so too does white desire evidence the logics of U.S. nationalism via American exceptionalism. Moreover, despite its soft façade, white desire and its romance are linked to and form the other side of the Latino Threat narrative.

Texas Country Music Deep in the Heart of Whiteness

Today, romantic depictions of Mexico and Mexicanas are perhaps most prevalent in the discursive location of country music, forming a dominant and reoccurring thread in the subgenres of outlaw and Texas country music. From the 1960s to the early 1980s outlaw country was popularized by musicians such as Merle Haggard, Waylon Jennings, Willie Nelson, and Hank Williams Jr. who rejected the Nashville scene and reveled in rebellious and often antiauthoritarian behavior. This musical tradition has had a substantial influence on more recent musicians like Robert Earl Keen, Ryan Bingham, Pat Green, Jack Ingram, and others who have popularized Texas country music.[21] Numerous songs from these musical traditions invoke Mexico as a foundational Other to the United States. In "Sonora's Death Row," "Mariano," and "Seven Spanish Angels," Mexico figures as a site of potential lawlessness and violence. In "Drunk in Mexico," "What Happens in Mexico," and others, Mexico is an escape from the pressures of modern work and life in the United States. And, of course, the Erotic, Exotic Mexicana figures most prominently within this musical tradition.

Here, a note on genre is required. Within country music, there is a perceptual divide between mainstream artists who record in and are signed to Nashville labels and those who come from, record in, and are signed to smaller labels in Texas and elsewhere. Arguably, the prevalence of the Mexican Other in Texas country music emerges in part from geographic proximity as well as the racial-national discursive traditions upon which this music draws. However, while romanticization of Mexico and Mexicanas is more prevalent outside the more "popular country" of Nashville, this discursive practice is far from the fringe. Historically there has been a strong, devoted following for outlaw and Texas country in the Southwest and throughout the United States. Indeed, in recent years, the rise of satellite radio and Internet venues like Pandora and Spotify have allowed this music to reach audiences more regularly and in a larger scale, forging an imagined community of listeners.[22] Moreover, the romanticization of Mexico and Mexicanas has emerged in the music of more popular country artists. Consider the reference to a "bartender . . . from the islands . . . [with a] body . . . [that has] been kissed by the sun" in "Toes" by the Zac Brown Band from Georgia. Of course Brown also croons, "all the muchachas they call me big poppa / When I throw pesos their way."[23] Rather than dividing these musical subgenres, it is more apt to recognize that widely popular musicians with Texas or outlaw roots carry on this tradition to the mainstream. In this way, what could be a localized trope takes on a national scale of the U.S. racial imagination. Moreover, whether within or outside of the mainstream, romantic invocations of Mexico and Mexicanas are bound to performances of white cowboy masculinity and neoconservative nostalgia.

This examination of Mexican representations in country music is not the first foray for the field of Chicana/o studies. Here, it may be wise to acknowledge and place this analysis in critical conversation with the work of José Limón. In his *American Encounters*, Limón examines cultural texts such as the films *Giant* and *High Noon* and Marty Robbins's popular country song "El Paso" to contend that the 1950s marked a turning point in Texas Anglo-Mexican relations. For Limón, prior to the 1950s, Mexican Americans experienced explicit forms of racial domination, whereas the mid-twentieth century was characterized by ambivalence.[24] While this can be seen in the shift from explicit material forms of race violence such as lynching and voter suppression of the late nineteenth and early twentieth centuries, Limón identifies a representational shift in cultural texts as well. He demonstrates that numerous earlier songs eroticized Mexicanas, yet the white cowboy protagonists failed to "cross the line," choosing instead to remain with white women over the "sexy Latina."[25] Here, this turn of phrase is quite evocative as one must inquire if the cowboy is crossing a racial border or moral line. Nevertheless, Limón contends that "El Paso" and other 1950s texts mark a shift, where white cowboys did "cross the line" and the "wicked" Felina is transformed into a caring woman as she embraces the dying cowboy at the end of the song.[26]

Limón's analysis is a critical point of departure for exploring manifestations of anti-Mexican racialization in contemporary country music. First, the shift from dominance to ambivalence central to his analysis could be more usefully characterized as Winant's racial break discussed earlier. Such a move reframes Limón's insight. Rather than understanding the 1950s as a shift in localized Anglo-Mexican relations, Texas in the 1950s reflects a broader global realignment of white supremacy. That is, instead of finding ambivalence as Limón asserts, the racial break exposes how many of the material and symbolic forms of domination continued as they were encoded in seemingly more positive aspects of whiteness. Thus, troping upon Limón's description of Mexicans' experience of immigration to the United States as a move from "worse to bad," I would hesitate in treating history as a progress narrative. Importantly, Limón recounts the pride and joy which he and his teenage friends found in "El Paso."[27] Drawing upon Raymond Williams, Limón contends that these cultural texts marked a shift in the "structure of feeling" for Mexican Americans, a structure of feeling that enabled empowerment.[28] Perhaps he is correct; "El Paso" did openly incorporate influence of Mexican music, and these 1950s texts did provide seemingly more positive Mexican figures with whom Mexican Americans might identify. However, as I demonstrated about *Giant* previously I would contend about "El Paso" now—these texts do not simply contest white supremacy as much as they mark shifts within, reinforce, and maintain the U.S. racial status quo, propelling it into the future. Like Limón, I read Anglo-Mexican social dynamics through Gramsci's models of "war of position" and "war of maneuver."[29] Gramsci's "war of maneuver" describes the use of force, whereas the "war of position" is the slow effort to control influence and achieve hegemony. While a youthful Limón was listening to and perhaps seduced by "El Paso," one should recognize that there were and are other racialized listeners as well. Perhaps the war of position has merely changed its tune as racial hegemony is propelled forward with and through romantic impulses. That is, as Lipsitz, Chin, and hooks have examined how white desire and racist love may structure white supremacy, romantic images of the Mexican Other may also be understood as a crucial component in a racialized war of position.

The post-break dynamics of white desire are readily illustrated in the song "The Seashores of Old Mexico." Originally written by Merle Haggard, "Seashores" was recorded by Hank Snow and Freddy Weller in the early 1970s.[30] Haggard later recorded the song in 1974 and again in 1987 as a duet with Willie Nelson on their second joint album: *The Seashores of Old Mexico*.[31] However, this song should not be seen as a remnant of an older tradition. In 2005 the song was reborn when the more Nashville mainstream musician, with Texas roots, George Strait recorded it for his *Somewhere Down in Texas* album.[32] In some ways, "Seashores" is both old and new, traveling from classic outlaw country roots to Nashville stardom.

"The Seashores of Old Mexico" tells the story of a young man who runs from the law in Tucson, Arizona, and heads to the border.[33] Once in Juarez, he loses his money to "one bad señorita" and continues south to Manzanillo, Colima, Mexico.[34] There, one night he meets a "newfound companion, one young señorita" with whom he will "start [his] life over on the seashores of old Mexico." The story is not unique. We have heard it all before, however often only as discrete elements. Consider the wealth of tropes "Seashores" draws together into one narrative arc. Our white American hero, probably the cowboy type, is on the run from the law. The United States is positioned as a space of modernity, governance, and restriction. The young hero must escape across the border to find "freedom, a new life, romance." Mexico, as Infernal Paradise, is timeless freedom ripe for the taking, a chance at rebirth. Alas, do not forget the "one bad senorita made use of one innocent lad." We have seen this trope as well, no? The wicked Mexicana is but one iteration of the erotic, exotic, a gendered embodiment of the Infernal Paradise. Perhaps Robbins's "wicked" Mexican girl Felina has stepped out of his song and into "Seashores" to rob our whitely innocent country singer hero. Importantly, the theft reinscribes the hero's innocence, and we can no longer ask why he was running from the law in the first place. After he travels farther into Mexico, the singer finds himself sleeping "on the seashores of old Mexico." There he is awoken by the young Mexicana "who offered a broken hello." As Alarcón has noted, this trope of Mexicans speaking with broken English is an old one that reinforces a linguistic/racial hierarchy wherein Mexicans are positioned—often in Mexico—as less articulate and intelligent.[35] Finally, the cowboy merges the young Mexicana, her love, and her body with the Mexican land as he "found what [he] needed on the seashores of old Mexico." This discursive maneuver reinforces the linkage between the Infernal Paradise and Mexicanas discussed earlier. Just as the "one bad señorita" was an infernal experience for the singer, so now this young Mexicana is the paradise he finds.

However, one trope remains unexamined in the song, a discursive turn foundational to white desire. We cannot ignore that it is the young señorita who desires our lawbreaking yet innocent cowboy hero. Remember that it is she who shyly, coyly, alluringly approaches him:

> After one long siesta, I came wide awake in the night.
> I was startled by someone who shadowed the pale moonlight.
> My new-found companion, one young senorita,
> Who offered a broken hello,
> To the gringo she found on the seashores of old Mexico.[36]

This narrative moment cannot be overlooked, for it speaks back to a long tradition not simply of eroticizing Mexicana bodies but of casting those bodies as desiring of white masculinity. As de León has argued, such discursive maneuvers served to legitimate the U.S. conquest of the Southwest.[37]

In this moment, "Seashores" echoes and prefigures other iterations of Mexicana desire for whites. Recall the images from Hollywood cinema discussed earlier. Now consider the images above from the George Strait video for the song. The unnamed señorita casts her gaze down at the video's lead actor, her eyes turn away from the sea to look at George Strait at the video's close. These looks are but points in a long chain of signification. Obviously, the gaze does not end with these women and their acts of looking. As Laura Mulvey so critically argued, the camera functions as the male gaze, locking visual objects into frame to feed the desire of dominance.[38] The gaze, however, like all tools of power, is not solely gendered. In his analysis of how racial codes are inscribed upon black bodies in the contemporary United States, George Yancy speaks back to a long black intellectual tradition to elucidate the power of the white gaze.[39] Placing Mulvey and Yancy into conversation, one may easily suggest that in these images, the gaze is white and male and located within the United States. Recognizing the role of the gaze, we are left with multidimensional, triangulated looking. The camera, a prosthesis

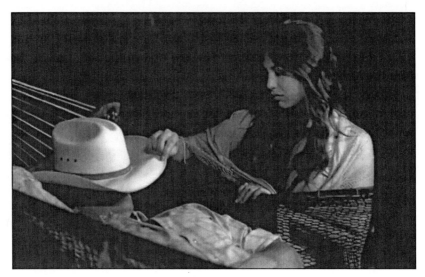

Figure 4.3. A Mexicana discovers her gringo object of desire sleeping on the beach in George Strait's video for "The Seashores of Old Mexico."

Figure 4.4. Years later, the Mexicana looks lovingly offscreen at the gringo protagonist (George Strait) as he croons of their first chance encounter. From George Strait's video for "The Seashores of Old Mexico."

for U.S. white male desire, looks onto the Mexicana, who in turn looks to white masculinity as an object of desire. In this triangulation, whiteness does not simply or solely desire the Mexican Other. Rather, here la Mexicana is a prevalent yet impermanent discursive figment of the white imagination. As the Mexicana is looking back at whiteness, we see the ultimate object of white desire. That is, whiteness desires itself, and of equal significance whiteness desires itself desirable. In this vein, the eroticization of Mexicanas is never simply about constraining the Other, but also about forging whiteness. However, since whiteness is an ideology and set of discursive and social practices, one must recognize that while the gaze serves U.S. white masculinity, white men are not the only viewers of this image or this trope across cinematic history. As I have argued elsewhere, such viewings seek to interpellate the audience to think whitely, seducing them into the naturalness of the racial-national project.[40]

This reading of white desire and desirability is shorn up when one considers the verses following the señorita's introduction:

> She spoke of Sonora and swore that she'd never return,
> For her Mexican husband, she really had no great concern.
> 'Cause she loved the gringo, my red hair and lingo:
> That's all I needed to know.[41]

Here the singer is juxtaposed to the woman's husband. Mexican masculinity is the counterpoint to the hero-cowboy's white masculinity. She refuses her Mexican husband and chooses the gringo and his language that she apparently does not speak. Beyond fashioning white desirability, this moment also reinforces a racial-sexual hierarchy in a manner common in U.S. cultural production. Nick Browne has explored how Hollywood films fail to depict healthy consensual relationships between men of color and white women. According to Browne, this "ideology of sexual relations" imagines and sanctions white men as having unrestricted access and freedom of choice within heterosexual unions as it simultaneously constrains the choices and healthy sexual partnerships of women and people of color.[42] Like with Hollywood romance, "Seashores" renders la Mexicana's rejection of her Mexican husband for whom "she has no great concern" as an expression of sexual choice.

Here, the sexual racism of the U.S. national-racial project is naturalized through consent and desire. While "Seashores" explicitly places white masculinity in opposition to Mexican masculinity, this dynamic is always at play even when Mexican men do not enter the narrative of white desire. As Adrienne Rich has argued, the logics of compulsory heterosexuality contend that men have the right of unfettered access to women's bodies and sexuality.[43] By desiring white masculinity, la Mexicana is figured as implicitly rejecting the possibility of romance with Mexican men in what becomes an unstated contest between racialized masculinities.[44]

One should also note how the initial encounter in the George Strait video simultaneously invokes and displaces Mexican men in another way. As our white cowboy hero sleeps on the seashore, he is discovered by the young señorita. As a hat is covering his face, she does not know what she will find, yet she lifts it, gazes down, and smiles with allure. Prior to her discovery, however, his sleeping pose signifies upon the iconic trope of the sleeping Mexican discussed earlier. In the iconography of the video the Mexican man is simultaneously present and absent, as the echoes of this supremacist trope reverberate across time.[45] Of course, the young señorita lifts the hat not to find a Mexicano but to discover the object of (white) desire, the cowboy-singer-hero. What did she expect to find on the seashore? A Mexican man? Perhaps a light-skinned Mexicano considering that the actor's arms are exposed? Or was there an overdetermined suspicion that a gringo lay below the hat? Either way, this depiction of white cowboy masculinity invokes and displaces the Mexicano in another way. Recall that the original cowboys were the Mexican vaqueros. However, the celebration and romance of white cowboy culture relies on the elision of its Mexican roots. Thus, while it is clear that white desire targets Mexico and Mexicanas for eroticization and romanticization, one cannot ignore that Mexican men are part of this racialized equation. Through depicting Mexicanas as desiring whiteness, these discursive maneuvers cast Mexican men as unworthy of desire and unequal to bearers of U.S. white masculinity.

This juxtaposition of racialized masculinities is not relegated to the realm of cultural production. In *Love and Empire*, Felicity Amaya Schaeffer notes that in actual transnational marriages, Latin American women do often choose between a violent patriarchy in their home countries and benevolent patriarchy in the United States.[46] While this may be the way Latin American women frame their life choices, the juxtaposition of white and Mexican masculinities in U.S. cultural production forges and naturalizes a racial hierarchy where it is nearly unimaginable that Mexican women would see anyone, any *body* other than U.S. white men, as the ideal object of their desire. But recall that *these* Mexicanas are but figments of the U.S. racial imagination. Thus, a critical question must be asked: what needs are secured by rendering whiteness desirable?

More than simply asserting racial hierarchies through gender relations and cross-border romance, "Seashores" exposes another wage of whiteness. W. E. B. Du Bois and David Roediger have demonstrated that whites receive psychological wages for group loyalty and participation in a system of white supremacy.[47] Likewise drawing upon Lipsitz, I have noted that the recreational fear and hate of nativism fosters a psychological wage of belonging. Moving beyond this song and its narrative, one may make a similar move. This long tradition of casting whites as desirable through looks and longings of Mexicanas and against Mexican men points to an ugly wage indeed. White singers and listeners are able to see themselves as desirable and superior to Mexican men. Such a reading troubles Limón's ambivalence, for beyond a representation that is both good and bad, "Seashores" and its discursive tradition illustrate how the seemingly good can be marshaled to secure domination by other means.

Deploying the Erotic, Exotic Mexicana as an object of and tool for white desire is hardly limited to "Margaritaville" and "The Seashores of Old Mexico." For those familiar with Texas country music, it is a common, dominant thread that courses below the critical radar. The examples abound. However, not all of the songs in the tradition engage the trope in the same way. Consider Tommy Alverson's "Una Más Cerveza" and Kevin Fowler's "Señorita Más Fina." Alverson sings of escaping his hectic life in the United States through a Mexican vacation. Like the singer of "Seashores," he meets "up with a girl down there but she did not speak the English."[48] Alverson quickly asserts that he "probably coulda had her too, but all I knew how to say was / Una más cerveza por favor señorita."[49] This seems to signal a significant departure from Haggard and Strait, for in Alverson's song language is a barrier to a thoughtful cross-border romance. However, Alverson then continues to sing of how he woke up the next morning naked and "lying face down in the sand."[50] Perhaps language was not such an obstacle after all. Did he meet a "bad señorita" as we've seen in "Seashores"? A young and innocent señorita, perhaps? Or did he simply spend the night "drunk in Mexico"?[51] Alas we will never know for the lesson of the song is that the only words needed to enjoy Mexico are "una más cerveza por favor señorita." In Fowler's "Señorita Más Fina" the singer recalls his efforts to woo a young woman by the name of Rita Flores:

> She was hotter than the Mexican sun
> She's one sweet chiquita
> My latino lolita
> I knew right then she had to be the one[52]

Fowler declares to her that he will "be your little gringo / Marry you and take you away." The language barrier emerges for Fowler as well:

> Yeah she never caught my lingo
> Because I was a gringo
> She didn't understand a word I'd say
> She say "mi no comprende"
> But that smile on her face
> Told me I should try it anyway[53]

Here Fowler's reference to the language barrier and its potential transcendence proves meaningful. La Mexicana smiles at the singer; beyond language she induces him to "try it anyway." She may not know him but she can desire him, for what could be more natural?

To be sure, Alverson's and Fowler's songs mark a departure from "The Seashores of Old Mexico." More akin to "Margaritaville," they invoke humor and revelry. Simply put, they are party songs that draw upon hackneyed clichés of la Mexicana. These songs, however, should not be read simply as parodies. Rather, despite and through their absurdity, these songs draw upon, reinforce, and disseminate the logics of whiteness on the border. First, they both depict the way in which Mexico and Mexicana bodies become sites of excess, revelry, and erotics. Second, these songs replicate the tropes of the erotic Mexicana and white desire. Both singers yearn not just for a Mexicana, but for the Mexicana to desire them. The language barrier does not matter for this is love at first sight. In a mix of honesty and humor, these songs declare a logic of "please love me; I'm white." Remember Fowler's desire to be "your little gringo / Marry you and take you away." He will benevolently rescue her from this Infernal Paradise and take her to the superior United States that so many white heroes seek to escape. Taken in isolation these songs or this line might easily be read as a smug, repugnant articulation of white supremacy. Such a narrow reading, however, is a mistake. Recognizing whiteness on the border as a discursive constellation suggests that these border texts emerge not simply from songwriters but from an ideology and broad system of language that circulates it. Indeed, the songs discussed so far are but a few well-known or explicit examples of a long musical tradition. Songwriters and performers like all people are interpellated subjects, swimming in a sea of discourse. Buffett, Haggard, Strait, Alverson, Fowler, and the countless others do not forge these ideas ex nihilo—they have drawn on a long, enduring set of ideas, images, and stories about Mexico and people of Mexican descent.

Critically, however, the dynamics of white desire that underwrite songs like "The Seashores of Old Mexico," "Una Más Cerveza," and "Señorita Más Fina" need not be so explicit. They may well exist just below the surface, an unseen and surging ideological current as in the case of Robert Earl Keen's "Maria." For the uninitiated, Keen is one of the most well-regarded and prolific songwriter-musicians in Texas music over the last four decades. Since 1984, he has recorded eighteen albums and his songs have been performed by numerous popular and little-known musicians. Indeed, written by Keen and recorded for his 1989 *West Textures* album, "Maria" has also been recorded by the more popularly recognized George Strait on his 1998 *One Step at a Time* album.[54] In "Maria" the singer depicts a night of romance and declares his love for the eponymous Mexicana, for whom he "never meant to fall."[55]

Keen's "Maria" diverges from the previous examples in that it does not explicitly suggest how whiteness desires its own desirability. However, "Maria" exposes how women's bodies are encoded with racial-national meanings. Moreover, unlike the songs discussed earlier, there is no explicit declaration of Maria's Mexicanidad. She could be Mexican, Mexican American, Latina, or, in a generous reading, of another ethnic background. That being said, the discursive tradition of Mexicanness

upon which whiteness on the border relies structures her characteriza-
tion and the relationship within the song. Ostensibly, Maria is part of a
textual landscape so embedded with racial and national tropes that it is
unnecessary to identify her as Mexican within the song. Rather, through
invocations of the symbolically charged "cross of gold" and other elements, Maria is positioned as the Mexican Other.

The song draws upon the Mexican Other through both Maria's allure
and her unstated geographic location. The singer declares,

> I never meant to stay an hour
> I thought that I was passin' through
> Another town along the highway
> I never meant to fall for you
>
> Well, I can't speak for you, Maria
> I only know the way I feel
> When I sleep with you, Maria
> There's nothin' left for dreams to steal[56]

Clearly, Maria evokes seductive potential as the singer has fallen for her.
Not only does he desire her, but she has captivated his romantic impulses
when he meant to just pass through. The location of her in "another
town along the highway" does not strictly place her in Mexico. However,
it shares much with the tradition of an Orientalized Mexico. Like many
depictions of Mexico, Maria's location is unmoored from time—it exists
outside of the modernity of the singer's life. As in "Seashores" and "Una
Más Cerveza," Maria and her location become an escape for the singer.
Moreover, Maria fulfills his needs. He is able to open up with her and
share secrets. This move signifies upon a long tradition. As Alarcón
contends, the deployment of Mexico as an Infernal Paradise is often
characterized by the figuring as Mexico as a meeting place between Old
and New Worlds, a place of timelessness, where exotic people and landscape form the "symbolic backdrop against which a spiritual quest is
played out."[57] In this way, "Maria" is not about the eponymous Maria but
about the white cowboy hero singer.

This song concludes with a significant conflict. The night ends, "the
sunlight brings the morning," and the singer must make a choice:

When the sunlight brings the morning
I cannot tell you what I'll do
But I've a mind to take you with me
And I've a heart to stay with you[58]

Note the juxtaposition between "heart" and "mind." The singer invokes the mind and its signification of rationality with taking her with him to an implicitly racialized white U.S. space. In contrast, his heart, signifying emotion and potentially irrationality, would keep him in this Mexican Other space. Here, the song draws upon one of the core elements in juxtaposing the United States to Mexico, and whiteness to brownness. Like Said's model of Orientalism as well as Mills's critique of the Racial Contract embedded in Enlightenment thought, the Other space is rendered as outside history, eroticized, and irrational in order to construct a subjectivity—the Occident, European man, or, in this case, U.S. whiteness—that is encoded as rational, self-governing, and a force of history.[59] Through Maria, the singer may access an Other space, and Maria may well desire that they stay together. Of course, Keen's song does not explicitly articulate a racial-national dichotomy. Rather, these logics course through unstated and without need of utterance largely because this is an old, entrenched, and continuing discursive tradition.

Finally, one should also note that Maria does not seem to have much choice here, even if the singer recognizes that he "cannot speak for you, Maria." Will he stay? Will he go? The song does not provide an answer. However, reading "Maria" within the Infernal Paradise tradition, it is unlikely that he *can* stay. Unless the U.S. white man is running from the law as in "Seashores," this discursive tradition suggests that Mexico ultimately becomes inhospitable. While the singer yearns for Maria, it is unlikely that he will be able to stay with her. In fact, one need only listen to the following two tracks on Keen's *West Textures*. Both "Sonora's Death Row" and "Mariano" invoke the Infernal Paradise trope and render Mexico as a place of potential violence and chaos for both Mexicans and Anglos alike.[60]

In contrast to Limón's declaration of ambivalence, this strand of country music draws upon an old colonial and racial discursive tradition in the post-break era. This is demonstrated in both songs in which the Erotic, Exotic Mexicana figures significantly as well as those that fashion Mexico as an Infernal Paradise. Critically, Mexico and Mexican women do not simply occupy this role in country music. James Taylor's "Mexico," the Grateful Dead's "Mexicali Blues," Sublime's "Caress Me Down," Dirty Heads's "Lay Me Down," and unfortunately many other songs suggest the pervasive presence of white desire of Mexico and Mexicanas across a spectrum of U.S. cultural production. Whether in music, film, or other cultural forms, white desire is never simply about erotics or love. Rather these deployments pay symbolic and psychological wages. As these songs have shown, the United States is constructed as modern and rational against the timeless frontierscape of Mexico. Even as the protagonists seek to escape U.S. modernity, two observations stand out. First, such an escape is often temporary, is forced, or leads to their downfall. Second, regardless of outcome, the United States embodies attributes of modernity against Mexico's supposed Otherness.

One of the most significant benefits that this tradition offers to whiteness is repeated depictions of whites as desirable and the reinforcing of a racial "ideology of sexual relations," a trope repeated across genre and time so much that the desire for whiteness or U.S. white masculinity appears natural. Writing about contemporary racism more broadly, Eduardo Bonilla-Silva contends that characterizing racism and racial stratification as natural is central to maintaining the status quo.[61] Thus, one should recognize that the repetition of these tropes across time forges a central aspect of the U.S. racial project. Whiteness looks in the mirror, hears its own song echo back across time, seeing and hearing what it most longs for, its own naturalized, superior desirability. Importantly, this is such a rich discursive tradition that the racial codes need not be made explicit. As shown in Keen's "Maria," white desire and the eroticized Mexican Other form a structure for the story, charging it with meaning that can slip under the critical radar if one does not listen closely.

This discursive and ideological tradition does not simply provide an intellectual map of anti-Mexican racialization. These discourses structure and shape behavior. Moreover, such tropic deployments are not relegated to country music. For example, writing not about Mexicanas but Puertoriqueñas and Latinas more broadly, Judith Ortíz Cofer recalls a moment when a man "serenaded" her with "Maria" from *West Side Story*. Another time Cofer and a companion were aurally assaulted by a drunken man in front of his daughter. After a mixture of singing and bellowing "Don't Cry for Me, Argentina," "He began to shout-sing a ditty to the tune of 'La Bamba'—except the lyrics were about a girl named María whose exploits all rhymed with her name and gonorrhea."[62] The eroticization of Mexicanas and Latinas in the U.S. white imagination forges an ideological justification for such behaviors. The myth of the Latin woman, to borrow Cofer's phrase, compounds compulsory heterosexuality: men have unfettered access to women's bodies, and Mexican women are always already accessible to and desiring of U.S. white masculinity. That is, in the white racial imagination, because la Mexicana is figured as always potentially desiring white men, asserting one's right to access and tasteless wooing, requests for beer, and songs about sexually transmitted diseases are not recognizable as expressions of sexual racism. These practices are cast as revelry, fun, humor, excess, and love. Indeed, white desire may simultaneously reproduce and obscure a racial-sexual hierarchy. Not only does this discursive tradition elevate white men against Mexican men through the objectification of Mexicanas, but white desire for Mexican women also becomes an outlet and narrative frame for revanchist claims against feminism. As will be explored shortly, such a logic underwrites many white men who seek Mexican wives.

Cowboy Cupid and Cross-Border Romance

As can be seen, the romantic impulses of white supremacy abound in the fictional experiences of literature, film, and music. Critically, however, whiteness on the border and its declarations of love for a Mexican Other are not relegated to these discursive locations. They are also written onto and frame lived experience. Recall that Arnoldo de León and Jason Ruiz examined the trope of the Erotic, Exotic Mexicana in the travel writings during the nineteenth-century conquest of Texas and U.S. traveler accounts of Mexico under the Porfiriato, respectively.[63] Of course, as Cofer's experiences illustrate, whiteness on the border is not simply tethered to a remote past. Moreover, these romantic impulses have also taken shape in the business of cross-border matchmaking. Internet agencies like AmoLatino.com and Rosebrides.com specialize in matching U.S. men with women from Mexico and other countries.[64]

Epitomizing the logics of white desire, latinwomansite.com advertises their services with the slogan that among the wide selection of Latinas, customers should "Choose yours!" and SexyLatinWoman.com asserts "Get Up Close with 1000s of Hot Latin Girls and Fulfill Your. . . ." InternationalLoveScout.com generously explicates the diversity among Mexicans for its largely U.S. audience:

> Mexican dating can cover the gamut. You can meet sophisticated, intelligent, and accomplished women in Mexico City, often referred to as "Chilangas." . . .
> On the other hand, you can find Mexican mail order brides from Oaxaca with strong indigenous roots. These *hot Mexican women* may not exhibit the urbanity and sophistication of their Chilanga sisters, but they bring *strong family* and *moral values*, not to mention a *great beauty*, often derived from their Mayan and Incan ancestors.[65]

Here, one must acknowledge the way InternationalLoveScout.com tropes upon the Erotic, Exotic Mexicana through invocations of hotness, family, and Indigenous beauty. Importantly, however, such services are not entirely new. Throughout the twentieth century, mail-order agencies provided photos, personal information, and addresses to U.S. men who paid for their quest for a bride from abroad. In contrast to these earlier mail-order programs, contemporary matchmaking websites and agencies offer a host of services—from facilitated gatherings and translation services to support groups—that assist romance and partner compatibility. One of the pioneers of modern cross-border matchmaking, Ivan Thompson established a business of matching U.S. men and Mexican women prior to the Internet era, styling himself as the "Cowboy Cupid."

Prior to his career as Cowboy Cupid, Thompson spent much of his life in the horse business as a breeder. In 1989, he found himself divorced, lonely, and living in Anthony, New Mexico. He decided then to look south for a wife, putting an advertisement in the Juárez, Mexico, newspaper "about a gringo looking for a Mexican wife."[66] While an acquaintance would eventually introduce Thompson to Chayo, the Mexican wife he would marry and divorce twice, Thompson began actively arranging marriages between U.S. men and Mexican women, marketing himself as the Cowboy Cupid. As Thompson described the career shift, "You know I was a cowboy for a while and finally switched over, just stumbled into . . . the woman business."[67] In the pre-Internet era, Thompson advertised in "weekly car publications" and other venues.[68] By the mid-1990s, his business and marketable personality garnered him modest national attention as stories about Thompson appeared in the *Enquirer*, numerous newspapers, and television shows like the celebrity and entertainment program *Extra* and the Spanish-language talk show *Christina*. In 1999 Thompson self-published *Cowboy Cupid*—a mix of memoir, "how-to guide" for finding Mexican brides, and political musings. In 2005 Thompson and his business became the subject of Michèle Ohayon's documentary *Cowboy del Amor*. Thompson still maintains his website cowboycupid.biz, where he boasts that he is "the *tried in fire* matchmaker you can trust to honestly and tirelessly work with you to successfully meet and marry a Mexican woman." Today Thompson's services are far from unique. With the proliferation of online transnational dating and marriage services, he is joined by the aforementioned amolatino.com, rosebrides.com, and numerous others. Like Thompson, these services rely and capitalize upon the gendered racial script of Mexicanas as traditional, family-oriented, and exotic.[69] Thompson's *Cowboy Cupid* and *Cowboy del Amor*, however, expose not simply how Mexicanas are eroticized or how white desire is manifested. Rather, the words and work of Thompson illustrate crucial dynamics of racist love, namely how romance may be used to both articulate an antifeminist politics as well as reinforce racialized-gendered hierarchies.

Here, a note of focus and clarification is necessary. In recent years, ethnographers like Howard Campbell and Felicity Amaya Schaeffer have explored the rich complexity of international romance and marriage. Privileging the words of local participants in his research, Campbell has cautioned scholars against imposing moral judgments on those who engage in cross-border relationships.[70] Campbell and Schaeffer effectively demonstrate how Latin American women are not reducible to hapless victims, but rather are agents who navigate a complex set of economic, national, racial, gender, and sexual relations.[71] In this way, the work of Campbell, Schaeffer, and others is critical in uncovering the messiness of everyday life. In contrast, I am not concerned with actual relationships per se. Rather, I interrogate the discourses and ideologies that shape and constrain these relationships. Even as Campbell and Schaeffer expose the complexity of these relationships, these relationships are still embedded within the discourses and ideology of white desire.[72] Indeed, hinting at the impact of the logics of white supremacy in Mexico, one of Campbell's Mexicana research participants asserts the naturalness of looking to Anglo men as ideals of love and beauty: "after all, who isn't a sucker for light skin and blue eyes?"[73] Ultimately, pairing cross-border matchmaking with the earlier examination of music makes two observations readily apparent. First, the romantic impulses of whiteness do not end with passive listening. Second, this discursive tradition shapes attitudes and orders social relationships.

Prior to examining how cross-border romances may be deployed to instantiate an antifeminist politics, conceal racial hierarchies, or foster white goodness and belonging, one should recognize the process by which Thompson facilitates transborder marriages. In his *Cowboy Cupid*, Thompson offers a "how-to guide" for establishing cross-border romances. Ever the benevolent cupid, Thompson states that "there's no reason for any man who reads this, to be lonely or be without a wife, if he has a little money and the huevos to do something about it."[74] Note how Thompson deploys hegemonic masculinity—one must have the *huevos* (balls)—as a prerequisite for finding a wife in Mexico. Then, Thompson advises that U.S. men go beyond border towns and travel via bus into Mexico's interior. Once they arrive and locate a midrange hotel near the center of town, the men should put an advertisement in the local newspaper and on radio; for example, "A 57-year-old American from Texas looking for a wife 23 to 40 years old, slender, a non-smoker and with no more than 2 children."[75] Men can advertise for translators the same way. According to Thompson, "your phone will be ringing by the time you get" back to the hotel.[76] From there, Thompson suggests scheduling fifteen-minute interviews: "I tell the men not to narrow their selection down to one, because things happen. If there are two or three you like and something happens to one, you haven't wasted your time and money."[77] After the men have interviewed and selected their Mexican wives, Thompson offers insight into the process for tourist and fiancée visas. Based on Thompson's guide, the process seems simple, and importantly, his description invokes marriage as a marketplace. Indeed, his logic finds common ground with the latinwomansite.com declaration that customers should "Choose yours!" In this logic, Mexican women are cast as interchangeable products in the marriage market.[78] In actuality, these women do have agency, although it is asymmetrical and circumscribed, and Thompson alludes to the potential for Mexicanas to make choices: if "something happens to one." Critically, Thompson does not frame this "something" happening as a Mexican woman making a choice. Reminiscent of Browne's "ideology of sexual relations," only white men are imagined to have unrestricted access (i.e., choice) when it comes to racialized and sexualized partners. Ultimately, Thompson's description overrides the challenges to U.S. men that Mexicana agency might offer by assuring reader-clients that their time and money will not be wasted if they have a backup choice for these otherwise exchangeable Mexicanas. With such a business-like accounting of the process, one may ask, where is the romance?

The business-like accounting of the process covers up the ongoing racialized impulses in the ongoing U.S. romance with Mexico and Mexicanas. In the book and documentary, Thompson does not explicitly eroticize Mexicanas as "sexy señoritas" as is so abundant in the music discussed earlier. While Campbell notes that "American men looking for Juárez women . . . construct an image of dark, sultry, attractive *mexicanas* who are both sexually hot and available, yet devoted to family and eventually to the 'right' future husband," Thompson does not actively invoke the sexualized Mexicana in *Cowboy Cupid* or *Cowboy del Amor*, emphasizing instead the trope of Mexicanas as family-oriented ideal mothers.[79] Of course, the trope of Mexicanas as mothers and caretakers of white men is not far from depicting them as desiring and desirable—in both cases a racialized femininity is deployed to serve and center white masculinity. However, part of the power of this sexualized racial trope is that it doesn't need to be articulated. Recall Jimmy Buffett's nondescript "Mexican cutie" and how it draws upon a long chain of signification. Like Buffett and others, Thompson does not need to specifically depict eroticized Mexicana bodies if they are already present in the U.S. racial imagination. Moreover, one should note that such bodies are vividly displayed on his website.

For the most part though, Thompson's romanticization relies on much more than unquestionably sexualized Mexicanas. Rather, his romanticization also emerges as he juxtaposes Mexicanas to U.S. women who are imagined as selfish, career-oriented feminists. Consider that

Figure 4.5. An image from Ivan Thompson's website where he advertises his match-making services and deploys the image of the "sexy señorita." www.cowboycupid.biz.

Thompson initially sought a Mexican wife when he found himself "lonely and burned out on American women."[80] This juxtaposition is made more explicit in Thompson's dedication of *Cowboy Cupid*, "to Rush Limbaugh's Femi-Nazis and the other women's libbers who make a book like this possible." Here, Thompson does not explicitly deploy the image of the "sexy señorita," but he does deploy Mexico and Mexicanas in particular as the ahistorical, traditional Other to U.S. modernity. La Mexicana becomes an implicit anchor in a binary relationship to U.S. women. As U.S. women are characterized as asexual "Femi-Nazis," Mexicanas become the sexualized alternative. Reminiscent of the triangulation explored earlier in the case of "The Seashores of Old Mexico" where white desire links white masculinity and la Mexicana through a rejection of Mexican masculinity, Thompson's rhetoric brings together white masculinity and la Mexicana to reject the politics of U.S. feminism. Importantly, this is not unique to Thompson. Schaeffer also uncovers how such a discourse frames U.S. men's expectations of Mexican and other Latin American women.[81] In this juxtaposition, Mexican women are rendered traditional, family-oriented, and submissive against the specter of a caricaturized U.S. feminism.

The juxtaposing of U.S. (white) feminists to la Mexicana is a critical component of Thompson's discursive repertoire for both responding to critics and consolidating a "besieged solidarity" among the men that make up his clientele.[82] Perhaps unsurprisingly, not all who hear of Thompson's exploits are seduced by his humor and business of cross-border matchmaking. Those who have written him letters complain of Thompson's fees, the morality of his business, and the way such a business fosters Mexican immigration. Significantly, however, Thompson re-deploys these otherwise critical letters for his own rhetorical purposes. In both *Cowboy Cupid* and *Cowboy del Amor*, Thompson includes a let-ter from Mary, who argues that Mexicans immigrate but do not wish to assimilate, instead demanding special treatment and rights. Responding to Thompson's assertion of "Mexican women being very traditional," Mary states,

> This is surely because they don't have the brains to do anything else but be wives and baby-making machines.
>
> Believe me, I am well aware of how Mexican women are. I have a Mexican sister-in-law who married my brother-in-law strictly to gain citizenship, and is now in the process of getting a divorce, right after her husband completed building a new home for her.
>
> Wake up and smell the roses, Mr. Thompson. There are a lot of American women right here who are lonely, also. We don't need any more illegal aliens crossing our borders to take away from citizens of our country.[83]

Mary's letter runs the gamut of anti-Mexican nativism, from anchor babies and low intelligence to refusal to assimilate, and instead of "they're taking our jobs," she asserts that *they're taking our men*.

Because Mary is a woman and frames much of her nativism through gendered concerns, Thompson's response is both markedly antinativist and antifeminist. While he does contend that Mexicans have historical precedence in the U.S. Southwest long before U.S. whites, much of his response focuses on what he sees as wrong with U.S. women: "If you don't want to stay home, take care of kids and be a housewife, why should it piss you off for someone else to want to do this. Do not be mad at me for filling the void that you and women like you created. . . . And if there are a lot of lonely American women, they can get off their fat rears and do something about it."[84] This response bears significance in a few ways. First, writing against U.S. feminism, Thompson juxtaposes U.S. feminist modernity to the image of the traditional, subservient Mexicana. Here, it is critical to note that both the nativist Mary and the antinativist Thomp-son share vast ideological ground. Both Mary and Thompson agree that Mexican brides fill the void left by or are in conflict with U.S. feminism.

At the center of this exchange between Thompson and Mary is the concept of what Amy Kaplan has termed "manifest domesticity."[85] Kaplan and others have examined how domestic politics of the home are linked to domestic politics of the nation. In her investigation of nineteenth-century women's writing, Kaplan exposes how women did not occupy separate spheres but were crucial to various domesticating projects of the home, nation, and empire. Mary's letter makes claim on that space, asserting whiteness through her desire for unions between (white) American men and (white) American women. Mary's argument about the home is simultaneously a vision for the nation. As Kaplan's work suggests, home and nation are inextricably linked. In this regard, Mary's letter reveals that men are not alone in the wielding of sexual racism. Through the logics of nativism, to police entry into the politics of the home is to police entry into the politics of the nation and vice versa. Moreover, her letter demonstrates how white women may not ally themselves with men and women of color against heteropatriarchal white supremacy. Like Mary, they may accept the false notion that people of color are their domestic competition.

Thompson, in contrast, offers a partial inversion of the manifest domesticity Kaplan located in the nineteenth century. Because he sees white women as abandoning their roles in the home, he and other men must look outside the nation to recruit new, Mexican women to take their places. While both Thompson and Mary tacitly agree that family and nation are interconnected, Mary sees this move as a betrayal of a racial-sexual-national compact. Thompson considers his efforts to bring Mexican women and their supposedly prefeminist ideal femininity as a means for revitalizing the nation. One may recognize this strategy as one of replenished patriarchy, where la Mexicana is drawn upon to displace U.S. feminist women and Mexicana feminism is unimaginable. As such, Thompson's neoconservative nostalgia for traditional gender roles requires the guise of racial liberalism. Thompson's vision rests on the embrace and maintenance of a racial-sexual hierarchy. Echoing the logic found in "The Seashore of Old Mexico," white American men are positioned at the top and Mexican men are relegated to an unimaginable choice. In this case, however, brown and white women are set in locked competition for white masculinity.

Clearly Thompson scripts U.S. white feminists as the root cause behind the need to look south of the border for romance. However, this rhetorical maneuver does not function solely as a pithy response to female critics. Because this narrative is deployed in the dedication and is echoed by Schaeffer's informants, one should recognize how this triangulation of U.S. feminism, la Mexicana with her ascribed traditionalism, and U.S. masculinity forges a sense of besieged solidarity among white men. That is, by including his response to Mary, Thompson imagines community with his male readership, viewers, and potential clients. This solidarity is built upon the notion that U.S. white masculinity is under siege. Just as songs like Creager's "Long Way to Mexico" and Zac Brown Band's "Toes" suggest Mexico as a potential escape from the forces of U.S. modernity, so too does Thompson charge la Mexicana as a means for escaping the modernizing impacts of U.S. feminism.[86] Both moves, of course, erase the possibility of Mexico's modernity and Mexicana feminism. However, there is a long history of feminisms in Latin America, feminisms that often go unrecognized as such in the United States. Indeed, Schaeffer demonstrates that women who engage in these matchmaking services are exerting feminist agency and sensibility.[87] Ultimately, reading la Mexicana as a premodern antithesis to U.S. feminism illustrates how gender and the crisis of patriarchy are sutured onto a racial and national binary.

Beyond framing la Mexicana as a foil to the specter of U.S. feminism, Thompson's responses to nativists also elucidate the dynamic complexity of whiteness, for he positions himself and his male clients as potential model citizens in the multicultural world. For example, one letter to Thompson states, "Tell your Mexican women to stay in Mexico, because we are tired of supporting illegal immigrants. Let them marry their own kind in Mexico."[88] Notably, the nativist writer was male, and Thompson did not respond with an attack on feminism. Rather, Thompson responds by asserting that unless the writer is a "full-blooded Indian," he and his ancestors "came from somewhere else."[89] This rhetorical maneuver is telling in at least two ways. Notably, Thompson invokes the "nation of immigrants" trope in asserting that only Indigenous people have unquestionable claim to U.S. lands. While this has been a popular proimmigrant strategy over the past few decades, one must note that it also erases the complexity of U.S. immigration history and uneven power dynamics. As Ian Haney López has demonstrated, the U.S. population has historically been majority white and is often imagined to be so not by happenstance, but because of years of racially restrictive and constitutive immigration laws.[90] The "nation of immigrants" trope elides that some who came to the United States came as slaves, others came free with the ability to naturalize, some arrived without even being allowed to become citizens, and still others were restricted from coming to the United States. Deploying this trope serves to both contest nativist exclusion and reinforce a historically empty, feel-good liberalism that casts the United States as a model of inclusion, eliding the historical realities that prove otherwise.

Beyond the response itself, the rhetoric of including the letter and response suggests how Thompson wishes to distance himself from nativists. He presents himself as outwitting the letter writer, and his response positions himself as not nativist and thus an upholder of the multicultural U.S. vision. However, a rejection of nativism should not be confused with a refutation of whiteness. Reminiscent of the white benevolence described previously, Thompson invokes a whitely goodness against the rhetoric of anti-immigrant nativism. This move is significant for the post-break era in which the United States is imagined to be a multicultural nation and a beacon for others.[91] Joe Feagin, Richard Dyer, and numerous others have demonstrated that whiteness has long been charged with the connotations of goodness and innocence.[92] Prior to the racial break, white goodness was forged against savage and nefarious others in disparate ways. Consider the cultural work performed by the "sexually aggressive black man" or the "corrupt and thieving Mexican." While these racist tropes continue today, after the racial break whiteness also maintains its assertion of goodness by incorporating and co-opting some aspects of multiculturalism. As Jodi Melamed argues in *Represent and Destroy*, today the racial capitalism of white supremacy relies on positioning the multicultural United States, which remains invested in the logics of whiteness, against monocultural Others.[93] Indeed, through the rejection of racial nativism and through the rhetoric of cross-border romance, Thompson reveals another aspect of white desire: whiteness desires not merely to be itself enticing, as explored earlier—whiteness desires to be and imagines itself as the embodiment of goodness.

The linkage between white desire and cross-border romance does not simply end with the appearance of white goodness. Rather, white desire and its resulting illusions of goodness work to mask white supremacy in action. For example, in *Cowboy Cupid* Thompson uses his affections to explain away seemingly distasteful actions and ideas. Signifying upon an old I'm-not-a-racist-because trope, Thompson presents a story from his past to assert his wife's Mexicanness as a frame and inoculation against claims of racism. In the chapter titled "Possible Kin Folks," Thompson recalls an incident in 1959 when he was eighteen years old, working on a ranch, and living with a white friend named Pat and five Mexicans in a workers' house.[94] The story revolves around the cooking responsibilities at the house and, of course, race. According to Thompson, "Now me, Pat and the five Mexicans were all living in the same house. This led to problems because they were right messy and I kept a pretty neat house. Besides that, I cooked for me and Pat and if we filled our plates once or went to the restroom, those other guys would have all our food ate up. This was very irritating to me and later on led to my downfall."[95] Before detailing his retaliation against his Mexican housemates and the fallout, Thompson pauses his narrative to assert his love for Mexicans and deploy "strategic color blindness": "And I'm wondering if I'm over here to look after cattle or be a cook for a bunch of Mexicans. Now, I sure don't want anybody to get their hackles up, because I love Mexicans—my wife and children are Mexicans and I really wouldn't have cared if they had been Chinese, I would have taken the same action."[96] In retaliation, Thompson cooks beans together with dog food and leaves it out for his Mexican housemates. According to Thompson, the Mexicans ate second and third helpings and did not get sick until he showed them the can of dog food, which started a "Junior Alamo."[97]

Before one explores Thompson's rhetorical maneuvering and the dynamics of whiteness in this incident, it is imperative to ask the question: what exactly was it that bothered Thompson so much to warrant retaliation against his housemates? The potential answers are plentiful. Perhaps he was irritated because he didn't think they were contributing equally.[98] Certainly he considered the food to be for both him and Pat and not the Mexicans. But why? Thompson's narrative does not go into great detail as to how such living arrangements should have worked. The Mexican housemates may well have understood the food to be communal. Despite these possible reasons for grievance and miscommunication, Thompson points to another reason when he states that he wondered if he was "over here to look after cattle or be *a cook for a bunch of Mexicans.*"⁹⁹ Thompson's strategic color blindness is fascinating, for while he declares that he wouldn't have cared if his housemates were Chinese, one must wonder if he would have cared if they were white. Would he have gotten his "hackles up" if he was not serving racialized others? This moment suggests that Thompson's grievance was not simply about sharing food but about a violation of racial privilege and hierarchy. Was the offense not the distribution of food but that *he,* a white man, was doing labor *"for a bunch of Mexicans"*? Here one must recognize how the gendering of labor plays into the dog food incident. There are no women at the ranch who perform "women's work." Rather, there is a white man irritated that he has been doing "women's work" for Mexican men. One clearly cannot look into Thompson's mind from over sixty years' distance. However, Thompson's telling suggests that he bristled at the loss of social standing, the loss of his wages of whiteness and patriarchy. Such a reading is augmented when one considers that at the time of this incident, 1959, Mexicans still faced legally enforced segregation in many parts of the Southwest.

Beyond the incident itself, Thompson's I'm-not-a-racist aside proves enlightening in the way his claim of love seeks to obscure, yet relies upon, anti-Mexican racialization. Thompson states "I love Mexicans—my wife and children are Mexicans." This moment is useful in exploring how his wife's Mexicanness frames the recollection. Importantly, the dog food incident happened nearly thirty prior years to Thompson meeting and marrying Chayo. In truth, his relationship to his Mexican family has nothing to do with an incident that took place long ago. Rather, by rhetorically drawing upon his Mexican family, Thompson seeks to hide from readers the possibility that his actions were in any way malicious or racially motivated. Ultimately, through the framing of the incident with his wife's Mexicanness and his love for her, readers are both supposed to accept the affection at face value and apply Thompson's contemporary seeming goodness and whitely innocence onto another time in his life.

Interestingly, Thompson does not simply invoke his Mexican family and romantic impulses as a prefatory interjection to the dog food anecdote. Rather, he draws upon them again in the final lines of the chapter.

After coming to the conclusion that his trick successfully taught a lesson to "that particular group of Mexicans," Thompson returns to his family and the present: "Now that I have a Mexican family, makes me wonder if any of those fellers might be kin. I may ask someday, if there's anyone in the family that is bad to chase cars."[100] This rhetorical move again seeks to inoculate Thompson from claims of racism. After all, it was all in fun and for the purpose of a joke. Importantly, this invocation of family and romance moves in the other temporal direction from his earlier effort to frame the story. There, Thompson used the current moment to alleviate the potential reading of racism in an incident from the past. Here, Thompson pulls the five Mexicans forward in time. Such a move is important. While the first mention of his family asserted his postracial and good white bona fides onto the past, this move fosters the ability to read Thompson against the grain. That is, what exactly does Thompson think of his "Mexican family"? One should consider the rhetorical situation of the moment. Thompson notes that he "may ask someday" about relatives chasing cars. Perhaps Thompson knows that such a query and its racial logics will not go over well; otherwise he would have already asked. However, in this moment, his Mexican family is not the audience of his humorous anecdote—the assumedly white reader whom Thompson has given a how-to guide to finding a Mexican wife is his audience. That racialized reader is the recipient of the joke.

While the dog food anecdote may be merely read as evidence of Thompson's homespun humor, such a reading forestalls key insights. As with the construction of the Erotic, Exotic Mexicana discussed earlier, Thompson's anecdote obscures and reinforces racial hegemony in key ways. Perhaps most notably, Thompson's act of feeding dog food to his housemates and the punch line about chasing cars position Mexicans (kinfolk or not) as less than or not quite human. Read beyond the limiting frame of intent, these actions find common ground in the long history of white supremacy, from Enlightenment philosophers constructing a savage and uncivilized Other against the model of universal (read: European and white) man to the use of nature and animalistic metaphor to describe Mexican immigrants in the United States.[101] These moves suggest a racial hierarchy repackaged as humor and romance. Moreover, while the anecdote is surely told for the purposes of humor, one cannot ignore that the Mexican housemates and Mexican family are not laughing. They are the butt of the joke. Such a realization is critical for interrogating the racial logics beyond the incident and its purported humor.

The dog food incident and its telling elucidate another key aspect of whiteness: belonging. After two of the Mexican housemates went to the hospital, Thompson was taken to the sheriff's office, where he met with the sheriff and representatives of the association that oversaw the Mexican worker program: "When I walked in, the sheriff said, 'Ivan these men told us you told them they were dogs, so they should eat like dogs.' I said, 'J.B. that ain't right, but now that you mentioned it, it is a good idea.' Then J.B. told me to tell my side of it. I told about half of it before I broke down and laughed. Looked like 'Sing Along with Mitch' 'cause everybody in there laughed right along with me. Anyway, they told me not to leave town or they would send the U.S. Marshal after me."[102] This moment illustrates what Joe Feagin has described as the frontstage/backstage dynamics of racial discourse in the contemporary era. According to Feagin, the frontstage characterizes how whites talk about race in the company of people from other ethnoracial backgrounds. In contrast, the backstage consists of how whites perform race talk in front of other whites.[103] As Kenneth Ladenburg has demonstrated, Feagin's frontstage/backstage model forms a critical fulcrum for exposing the dynamics of racial humor and making vulnerabilities of white supremacy legible.[104] In this moment, the frontstage is gestured to through the potential seriousness of police action should Thompson decide to leave town. The laughter in the sheriff's office, however, demonstrates the social function of the backstage, a place characterized by a type of racial and ideological belonging where ideas and acts considered troubling in mixed company can be uttered freely, without fear of being labeled racist or retrograde. Indeed, this is evidenced again a few days later when another (white) man who "worked Mexicans" asks Thompson about the incident, only to declare that it "was the funniest thing he ever heard."[105]

Importantly, as the incident is retold in *Cowboy Cupid*, Thompson forges another backstage collectivity or racial belonging with his readers, real and imagined. That is, those same readers who receive a "how-to guide" on finding a Mexican bride are also imagined to find the humor in feeding dog food to Mexicans and wondering if one's own Mexican kinfolk might be given to chase cars. Here one finds strange and significant common ground between Thompson's critique of U.S. feminists and his dog food anecdote. In both situations, Thompson seeks to build solidarity among those who see themselves as under threat of a loss of racial and gender power, whether that be from women in the workplace or Mexicans who may see a white man as someone who could cook for *them*. One may ask how white desire plays into these instances to imagine a U.S. white male community. The trope of la Mexicana is not as central in these moments as it is in the country music discussed earlier. La Mexicana, however, plays a critical role in Thompson's discursive repertoire as well. Recall that she is a figment of the U.S. racial imagination, a tool for securing power. Through Thompson, la Mexicana, while less an object of desire, functions as the antithesis of U.S. feminism and also as an emblem of white multicultural goodness. In both cases, she is essential to imagining and consolidating whiteness. Whereas in country music la Mexicana has been deployed to render whiteness desirable, here this trope fosters both white goodness and solidarity.

As noted earlier, white supremacy does not survive and thrive by hatred and fear alone. Rather, white desire and racist love are key to the maintenance of white supremacy, carrying it into the future. Not only do these romantic impulses make it difficult to fight continual systems of material and symbolic inequality, but they also render troubling racial logics invisible to the uncritical eye. Recall the popularity and commonplace nature of the songs discussed earlier, or contemplate how some journalists have responded to Thompson's use of romance and humor. In particular, in reviews of *Cowboy del Amor*, film critics have called attention to Thompson's problematic logic and his ability to escape critique. For example, writing for the *Dallas Observer* Melissa Levine concludes that the filmmaker "gives Thompson so much rope to hang himself with that he tends to slip through some pretty large loopholes. And no matter how charming his cowboy colloquialisms and brazen self-promotion, he's still a raging sexist whose business exploits disadvantaged women. Watching *Cowboy del Amor* is like sitting in a room with someone who's making funny racist cracks; you can't help but laugh, but you feel sullied by the implicit collusion."[106] Levine's analysis here is insightful, for she readily notes not just Thompson's sexism but also how his homespun humor may deflect charges of sexism. Moreover, Levine's review is significant in what it fails to name. While she compares watching the film to listening to racist jokes—here one should recall Feagin's backstage—and while she asserts the "disadvantaged" position of these potential brides, her review casts Thompson solely as sexist and breaks down when it comes to naming the racial logics behind Thompson's matrimonial-entrepreneurial endeavor. Perhaps more telling of the occlusive power of romance, Pat O'Brien from the *Press-Enterprise* of Riverside, California, exemplifies the way romance renders illegible the force of white supremacy. O'Brien begins the review by acknowledging that "it would be easy to dismiss Ivan as bigoted and misogynistic. After all, he thinks Mexican women are more compliant than American women."[107] However, the next sentence erases the possibility of racism: "But part of Ivan is well-meaning, compassionate and hopelessly romantic."[108] This reviewer's emphasis on romantic intent inoculates Thompson against charges of bigotry. Embracing a model of intent forecloses the possibility of holding Thompson accountable for troubling words and deeds. Reminiscent of my conversation with Gwen that opened this chapter, claims of romance and desire provide a discursive and ideological escape route wherein perceived goodness is incompatible with and mutually exclusive from white supremacy. Here we must recognize that white supremacy does not lie simply, deeply within the human heart. It courses through stories, music, images, and other discursive forms as it organizes the racial imagination and social structures in the United States and globally.

White Desire and the Prosthetic Imaginary

As stated from the outset, the Mexican Other performs crucial work in the construction of whiteness as Americanness, allowing whiteness and American exceptionalism to be ideologically coterminous. Heretofore, I have focused on white desire and articulations of white cowboy masculinity. For some, the linkage between whiteness and Americanness—the imagining of the nation-state as a racial state—may not be clear. Of course, as this chapter has explored white U.S. masculinity and the eroticization of Mexico and Mexicanas, the racial binary maps across the national border. Moreover, one could simply and easily argue that white cowboy masculinity functions as a synecdoche for an imagined America. Certainly, other scholars have noted how national meanings have been ascribed to this trope throughout its history. Whether in the early antecedent of the frontiersman like Daniel Boone, the iconic John Wayne and Clint Eastwood of Hollywood Westerns, or the twenty-first-century image of George W. Bush clearing brush on his Texas ranch, riding horses with the president of Mexico, or asserting a "Cowboy Diplomacy," this image of western, rugged individualism looms large in the imagining of America.[109] However, cowboy masculinity as national and racial icon is hardly the only element that links the romantic impulses of whiteness to American nationalism.

There is a long history of Other spaces in the formation of the U.S. national-racial imagination. Perhaps the most useful analog and antecedent can be found in the cultural work on the U.S. frontier as described by Frederick Jackson Turner, often referred to as his "frontier thesis." Turner contended that the expanding frontier was essential to American exceptionalism.[110] For Turner, the frontier was more than simply a means for tracing the development of U.S. history. Rather Turner contended that the frontier, as the line between "savagery" and "civilization," was essential to forging the national character of individualism.[111] Turner also recognized the formative power of the frontier beyond personal attributes: "the frontier promoted the formation of a composite nationality for the American people," for "in the crucible of the frontier the immigrants were Americanized, liberated, and fused into a mixed race, English in neither nationality nor characteristics."[112] Without stating it directly, Turner described the frontier as essential to throwing off Old World identities and becoming American *and* white, or perhaps becoming American *by becoming* white.[113] While contemporary historians may challenge the broad strokes and elisions of Turner's historical method, few would contest that his description of the significance of the frontier captures a key dynamic of the white U.S. racial-national imagination.[114]

As Turner wrote his famous frontier thesis, the western frontier as a distinct line of expansion and settlement was closing.[115] Reading Mexico and Mexicans against this frontier tradition suggests that Mexico may well function as a prosthetic imaginary at the death of the West. Echoing the role of the frontier, U.S. white men escape civilization and modernity by traveling south to Mexico, a timeless Other space with the potential for rebirth. In "The Seashores of Old Mexico," it is both the land (i.e., seashores) and the Mexicana body (i.e., the arms of the young señorita) for which the white cowboy hero escapes U.S. law and forges a new life. Ivan Thompson and other men who seek Mexican brides "cross the line" in order to, among other reasons, reject the gains of contemporary U.S. feminism. By securing Mexican brides, they potentially replenish patriarchy in the name of tradition and reproduce the nation.[116] Through claiming to love Mexico and Mexicans, they can tell off-color jokes and engage in white racial communion.

This romanticization of and desire for Mexico and Mexicanas— charged as premodern and prefeminist—is a projection of the U.S. racial imagination, and these dynamics are not exclusive to renderings of the Mexican Other. Nathan Irvin Huggins, Fredric Jameson, and others have examined how utopian or idealized renderings of an Other both mark and mask an ideological and identitarian crisis. Huggins argued that staging an infantilized black faith in *The Green Pastures* temporarily ameliorated the crisis of faith in white audiences.[117] Similarly, Jameson contended that white ethnics have been used to represent that utopian time when organic human connection was possible.[118] As expressions of a prosthetic imaginary, representations of Mexico, Mexicans, and Mexican Americans fulfill the fantastic needs of whiteness on the border. Mexico is the timeless Other space where white Americans can escape the alienation of their workplaces, homes, and contemporary society. Mexicanas are rendered with a museum-like femininity—shorn from history and modernity—so that white men can hark back to an imagined past without ever inhabiting masculine gender roles that they no longer find desirable.

However, returning to the discussion of "whiteness on the border" in the introduction, "border" does not solely refer to the geopolitical line dividing the United States from Mexico, nor does it simply signal the perceptual divide between brown and white. The border also marks the limiting edge where whiteness is both fortified and fragile. Here we must remember that Mexico is not the frontier. Thompson, his readers, and his clients may want traditional wives, but he cannot go back in time. Mexican women will bring their own feminism with them. Tommy Alverson may want to escape his workaday life in "Una Más Cerveza," but at some point he will have to put down the beer and return to work. Perhaps only the cowboy hero of "The Seashores of Old Mexico" can stay across the border, but this is hardly his choice. As a wanted man, he can never return. Ultimately, the Infernal Paradise tradition works against notions of widespread settlement. Recall the way in which *All the Pretty Horses'* John Grady Cole leaves Texas as his grandfather's ranch will be sold. In Mexico he falls in love with Alejandra, only to wind up in a Mexican prison and eventually to be cast out of what he imagined to be a potential new home.[119]

Mexico as prosthetic imaginary marks a site of dynamic tension between fear and loving, anxiety and romance. In this way, white desire is the complementary opposite of the Latino Threat. While the Latino Threat narrative articulates anxieties about how immigration and a perceived refusal to assimilate will change the ethnoracial and political makeup of the United States, white desire imagines in Mexico and la Mexicana the potential for escaping modernity and replenishing U.S. white patriarchy. White desire and the Latino Threat, however, should not seen as mutually exclusive. As complementary opposites, white desire and the Latino Threat are mutually interdependent because as one expands the border and the nation, the other fortifies and polices them. While this may seem contradictory, this is exactly the dynamic of nation and empire; the nation must be protected even as it desires and intervenes in others to expand its reach of empire. While white desire expands the nation, the Latino Threat polices the nation-state as a racial state. Indeed, when the U.S. Senate debated renewal of the Violence Against Women Act (VAWA), Senator Chuck Grassley worried that new protections for immigrant women against domestic violence would create potential ways for immigrant women to game the system.[120] Grassley's concerns targeted undocumented women and immigrant women who were engaged to U.S. men and were on fiancée visas. In grouping them together, Grassley located all immigrant women as a locus of the Latino Threat, a move that undergirded his opposition to the revised VAWA.[121]

Toward a Politics of Cross-Border Love

For some the problematic nature of racial and gendered tropes in country music and cross-border matchmaking may seem self-evident, and thus there is no need for critical examination. As one friend put it, "regressive colonialist politics in country music, who would have guessed?" This quick response, however, is not sufficient. Antiracist scholars and activists need to interrogate everyday and surprising manifestations of white supremacy. Critically, the discourse of white desire is both: it is the status quo racial logics that course through these romantic stories of Mexico and Mexicanas, and it is surprising for some participants because articulations of love and romance are framed as antithetical to white supremacy in the popular imagination. Thus, making the interrelationship of romance and racial domination legible is critical not simply for examinations of the past, but also for justice struggles of the present. Importantly, writing off regressive politics of cross-border romance in country music may have another consequence as well. That is, while there is a long tradition of desire and exotification in whiteness on the border, not all depictions of Mexico and Mexicanas fall into this romantic paradigm. Some cultural expressions seek not to satisfy white desire but to foster a form of cross-border understanding. The danger in this assertion is to fall into the ideological trap of white goodness, to say these cultural texts and their producers are model whites. Such is not my desire. Rather than simply exemplifying a "good" white, this other tradition within Texas country music makes visible systems of power and other possibilities for cross-border relationships. Indeed, drawing upon the work of María Lugones, I argue that songs like Jack Ingram's "Inna from Mexico" and the Dixie Chicks' "Long Time Gone" gesture toward the possibilities of "world" traveling and cross-border love.

In her *Pilgrimages/Peregrinajes*, Lugones works through the obstacles that hinder coalitions between women of color and white women as well as among women of color.[122] Lugones contends that women of color travel to and inhabit white worlds often and involuntarily.[123] For Lugones, world traveling is foundational for identifying with and building loving relationships with others. She argues that "this travelling across 'worlds' [is] partly constitutive of cross-cultural and crossracial loving."[124] Ultimately, Lugones's model of world traveling allows travelers to recognize elements of the self in others, identify across and through differences, and form loving relationships. While Lugones particularly frames world traveling as a necessity for women of color, her model exposes the possibility of cross-border love and its transformative potential for whites as well. To be clear, Lugones articulates that world traveling should not be confused with middle-class leisure and colo-nialist travels. Thus, she imagines a form of cross-cultural engagement that goes beyond those depicted in "Margaritaville," "The Seashores of Old Mexico," and "Señorita Más Fina." In leisure and colonialist travels, whites are more likely to encounter figments of the U.S. racial imagina-tion, tropic projections of the Mexican Other ascribed to flesh and blood bodies. Although Lugones suggests that playfulness is a requirement for world traveling, she is not invoking playfulness as drunken revelry or sexual conquest. Rather, she sees the required playfulness as the "open-ness to being a fool . . . not worrying about competence, not being self-important."[125] Such playfulness is foundational to breaking down rigid borders between self and other so that "we can understand *what it is to be them and what it is to be ourselves in their eyes.*"[126] It is through this seeing the self in and through the other that Lugones's world traveling and cross-cultural love find imperfect articulations in Ingram's "Inna from Mexico" and the Dixie Chicks' "Long Time Gone."

At first glance, Ingram's "Inna from Mexico" may appear yet another country song about a white man and a Mexican woman. Written by Bruce Robinson and Jack Ingram and recorded on Ingram's *Hey You* (1999) album, "Inna from Mexico" describes the life situation of a Mexi-cana immigrant from the eyes and words of a U.S. white male. Inna came from Mexico to find a job in the United States, perhaps working "on rich girls' nails."[127] Her migration to and labor in the United States is motivated by economic duress and her need to provide for her twelve-year-old daughter she left behind. Inna holds to the dream that life will get easier and one day her daughter will be able to join her, "But just like every other dream so far / She knows that one probably won't come true."[128] According to the song, the hardships Inna faces in the United States are unrecognized by her friends in Mexico, who "think she's got it made."[129] After establishing Inna and the economic conditions that have shaped her cross-border existence, the song turns its narrative focus to an exchange between the singer and Inna:

> I met Inna at a grocery store
> We were waiting in line
> I asked her who the Barbie doll was for
> You'd thought that I had asked her who died

So I started to apologize
Man, I was just trying to kill some time
But I still cant get Inna from my mind
But I will never look behind
Cause I can see it in her smile looking at her eyes
Yeah, that's right, she keeps her smile when she's about to cry[130]

From this moment, the song shifts back to the chorus that reasserts Inna's perseverance and the lack of understanding from those in Mexico who think that her life in the United States is easy.

To be sure, "Inna from Mexico" is no "Seashores of Old Mexico." This song speaks back to, builds upon, and challenges the trope of the Erotic, Exotic Mexicana. Rather than a feminized escape from modernity, Inna signals and makes legible the economic forces that propel migration and structure survival and suffering. While Schaeffer notes that many U.S. men seek brides from south of the border because of the impact of neoliberalism, "Inna" exposes the impact of those same neoliberal policies.[131] She does not immigrate to achieve a sanitized American Dream. She is not the romantic salve to the perceived wounds of U.S. white masculinity. Inna migrates out of necessity for the economic survival of her family. Of course, the song is not simply about Inna, for she also impacts the singer. Could this move be seen as an eroticization of vulnerability where Inna satisfies the needs of white goodness? Perhaps. But it is important to note that the singer does not save Inna. He cannot. No Great White Hope can wave away the power of neoliberal capitalism. The interaction between Inna and the singer echoes the trope of the Mexicana found in film, music, and other sites of the U.S. imagination. He looks at her. She looks at him. He focuses his gaze on her eyes. But she does not desire him. In her, he finds not his own naturalized superiority. Rather, he finds suffering, a suffering that does not simply reinforce the easy stories we tell about the world, but a suffering that could potentially challenge the singer's understanding of the world and self. Returning to Lugones, the singer's encounter evidences a form of world traveling, seeing himself and the world through Inna's eyes for a brief moment that impacts him across time.

If "Inna from Mexico" invokes and troubles the trope of the Erotic, Exotic Mexicana, the Dixie Chicks' "Long Time Gone," written by Darrell Scott for his album *Real Time*, provides a divergent example of how the political imagination need not capitulate to the logics of white desire and romance. The Dixie Chicks covered Scott's "Long Time Gone" for their *Home* (2002) album and charged it with new meaning in their video for the song. The song focuses on the United States, depicting and lamenting the loss of agricultural livelihood—"Looking out on a vacant field. Used to be filled with burley t'bacca"—rural to urban migration signaled through a move to Nashville and "Living from a tip jar, / Sleeping in my car," and the mainstreaming of country music away from traditional and outlaw roots epitomized by Merle Haggard, Johnny Cash, and Hank Williams Sr.[132] In keeping with a prominent thread in country music, the song articulates a clear nostalgia for a time, place, and way of life "long time gone." As Genaro Padilla has demonstrated, nostalgia often voices an implicit critique of the present, and this is certainly the case for this song.[133] The natural question arises, however: what does "Long Time Gone" have to do with Mexicanness and the U.S. racial imagination? The answer is found in the video.

The Dixie Chicks' video for "Long Time Gone" maps the experiences of Mexican immigrants onto those of U.S. southern whites. The video takes place in Reynosa, Mexico, with the Dixie Chicks singing on the streets, in markets, and in a pool hall. The video intersplices these scenes with others depicting three men as they walk north and cross the symbolically charged river. The video closes with the men entering the United States, and as such the narrative offered by the lyrics is fundamentally reframed. By placing the experiences of rural southerners in the same imaginative space of Mexican immigrants, the video seeks to foster a cross-border empathy. The video takes that familiar narrative of white rural nostalgia and "travels" the story and viewing audience to the "world" of Mexican immigrants and the communities they leave behind. The viewers are asked to see themselves in others, identify, and love.[134] No longer are Mexico and people of Mexican descent simply and completely an Other through which to establish whiteness or whiteness as Americanness. "Long Time Gone" establishes economic struggle and experiences of loss as the grounds for a cross-border empathic understanding. This is a particularly interesting move when one considers that whiteness as a political, ideological, and social manifestation was created out of the exigency to split working-class whites from people of color who shared the same economic interests.[135]

I do not wish to suggest that Ingram's "Inna from Mexico" and the Dixie Chicks' "Long Time Gone" are beyond critique, pure and innocent in intent and practice. One may question the centrality of white humanity and the use of the white gaze in "Inna from Mexico." For "Long Time Gone," one may challenge the role of the white gaze as the Dixie Chicks take in the exotic Other in their "tour" of Mexico.[136] While Lugones maps the dynamics of cross-cultural love necessary for coalitionist struggle, these songs are but imperfect gestures as to how this politics of love and world traveling may find its way into cultural production. "Inna from Mexico" and "Long Time Gone" are significant because they demonstrate ways of thinking beyond the romantic impulses of white desire. How can we describe these discursive and political moves? What are they to be called? Influenced by Lugones, I posit that these cultural texts exhibit the grounds of empathy and potential for cross-border love. To be clear, I do not mean romantic love. This is not a racist love of a fetishized Other. This politics of love illustrates the ability and need to see oneself in others and others in oneself. This love is not color-blind, but love as a force that recognizes ethnoracial and social differences and propels one to work through them. Gesturing toward a cross-border love, these songs offer something different, a critical way of entering, challenging, and reconfiguring the brown-white binary in the U.S. racial imagination.

Conclusion

Imagining and Working toward Gringostroika

A Pilgrimage to Pedro

It is late February 2015, and I am headed to the Disneyland of anti-Mexican racialization. South of the Border is a Mexican-themed tourist trap located in Dillon, South Carolina, that lures travelers on their way to Myrtle Beach or otherwise traveling the New York City–Florida corridor. I had heard about South of the Border from Louis Mendoza, who had visited there as part of his 2007 trip across the United States.[1] When the opportunity came about to speak at UNC, Chapel Hill about whiteness on the border, I knew that a trip south would be necessary: part research excursion, part pilgrimage to a dystopian fantasyland of Mexicans within the U.S. white imagination. Before my trip, I was assured by Ariana Vigil that many Latinas/os in North Carolina have stories about their encounters with South of the Border. Friends from the area shared their recollections—mixtures of horror and humor—and made sure I would travel the main route via I-95 so as not to miss the racially encoded billboards. On each the image of South of the Border's mascot Pedro beckoned. For the uninitiated, Pedro is South of the Border's cartoon Mexican, draped in a serape and donning a sombrero, sometimes standing, but often lounging on a cactus for rest. The signs did not disappoint: "Pedro's Weather Report: Chili Today–Hot Tamale!," "You're always a wiener at Pedro's," and "Don't be a lost injun, make a reservation!"

Today, South of the Border is a large complex of attractions deployed to lure in families and separate them from their money. This tourist destination offers a hotel, seven souvenir stores, six restaurants (one shaped like a sombrero), an arcade, amusement rides, a reptile exhibit, and other attractions on several acres. This local tourist empire, however, grew out of a small grocery store. In 1949 Alan Schafer partnered with his father as they took over his grandfather's store. Because North Carolina had limited how much beer businesses could store at a time, Schafer relocated the family business south of the North Carolina-South Carolina border and emphasized beer sales, under the name South of the Border Beer Depot. Schafer began selling tourist souvenirs only after a road-weary salesman sold him some stuffed souvenirs for cash to get home. Over the years, Schafer became a local political player. He ran behind-the-scenes political campaigns, lobbied for gambling, and spent a year in federal prison for voter fraud. South of the Border diversified and grew over the years as well, playing upon the location south of the North Carolina border to allude to and signify upon *the* border of the U.S. racial imagination. Pedro became an icon for advertising, but even though he signals the Mexican Other, his naming bears the traces of other forms of racialization. South of the Border had hired several Lumbee Indians to work at the hotel. When an early guest began referring to these Indigenous workers as Pedro—or Pedros—Schafer found the name for his iconic Mexican.[2]

When I arrive, I am surprised by the size of the destination, the vastness magnified by the emptiness and quiet as it is just opening for the day. One white former Carolinian told me that the place had lost some of its luster over the years. However, I am visiting in the middle of winter, at the start of the day: what must this place look like during peak season? I travel the grounds, see the attractions that are open. Sadly, the tower and sombrero-shaped observation deck are closed, due to high winds, the employee tells me. The gift shops are all open though and increase in activity as lunch hour draws near. Perhaps unsurprisingly, the vast majority of souvenirs are cheap, Mexican-themed, and made in China: T-shirts, ponchos, back scratchers, snow globes, and much, much more—most adorned with sleeping Mexican Pedros. But not all is Mexican. Capitalism, nostalgia, and white supremacy are rarely so discrete. Small sections of gift shops are dedicated to items invoking Pacific Island exoticism and Native American spirituality for sale. Reminding visitors that there is more than one type of border state in U.S. history, Union and Confederacy souvenirs are readily available as well. At South of the Border, you can one-stop-shop for a Civil War–era hat, a Pedro doll, and a dream catcher. What more could your racial imagination need?

Figure C.1. Among the range of kitschy souvenirs at South of the Border, one can find shelves of sleeping Mexicanos. Photo by author.

Beyond its oddity as a site and expression of the U.S. racial imagination, South of the Border exposes significant aspects of whiteness on the border. Perhaps most notably, the park is located far from the U.S. Southwest. Even as it began as a reference to the North Carolina–South Carolina border, the name accrued and signified upon the more iconic border and its racial logics. This illustrates how whiteness forged out of anti-Mexican representations is not a regional phenomenon. Rather, it is a national project with a regional style, and considering the global reach of the U.S. culture industry, it may well be described as a national project with international implications. Furthermore, South of the Border does not couch its anti-Mexican discourses in terms of hatred or outright inferiority. Embodying the logic and rhetorical positioning of the post-break era, the tourist trap deploys Mexicanness through attempts at humor and affection. Indeed, along with its troubling renderings of all things Mexican, South of the Border's website also boasts of the destination's southern hospitality: "South of the Border is proud to be a part of the rich history of hospitality that's made the South famous, and keeps visitors coming back each year."[3] Of course the myth of southern hospitality is old, and it has never excluded active white supremacy. If anything, southern hospitality and other regional postures of niceness conceal social inequalities.[4] Finally, South of the Border suggests the linkages between disparate racializing projects, illustrating how the images and scripts applied to one community may be applied with little modification to others. The park is located within the U.S. South—so far from Mexico and haunted by the legacy of antiblack racism—and one must wonder if the smiling Pedros are but ghosts of other Others. The United States has had a long history of antiblack characterizations, from minstrels and Sambos to lawn jockeys and golliwogs. Might it be that the countless Pedros of this dystopian racial fantasyland perform similar cultural work at a time and in a place when explicit antiblack renderings would be déclassé? Moreover, consider the way local Lumbee Indians were key to the naming of Schafer's Mexican icon. Here, South of the Border exposes how the brown-white binary may rely upon, evoke, play upon, and reinforce other racializing projects.

The Pedros, of course, are not just small figurines and dolls. They do not merely adorn coffee mugs and T-shirts. Outside, as I walk the grounds, I come across many a Pedro, five, ten, twenty, ninety-seven feet high. Pedros standing by the road. Pedros among donkeys and dinosaurs wearing sombreros. Pedros, eyes gleaming. Pedros smiling. Pedros open-mouthed and silent. I stand below a giant Pedro and wonder what the visitors who come throughout the year see. A brown reflection of Sambo? A humorous, kitsch-filled wonderland? I wonder what Pedro sees. What is behind his eyes? His smile? His mask? But Pedro sees nothing, you see. As William Nericcio may suggest, Pedro is but a Mexican mannequin. We must turn our gaze from Pedro to his Geppetto, the hands and minds that made him what he is. For Pedro, you see, is but a reflection of white fantasies.

The Sensibility of White Supremacy

Whiteness on the border is a discursive and ideological network wherein representations of Mexico, Mexicans, and Mexican Americans are used to forge both whiteness and Americanness, or more accurately whiteness as Americanness. Whiteness on the border and its Mexican Other

Figure C.2. A giant Pedro statue greets visitors to South of the Border in Dillon, South Carolina. Photo by author.

are manifested in seemingly disparate locations: in political rhetoric and fiction, in film and news coverage, in music, in memoir, on online dating sites, in myriad other spaces left unexamined. In all of these discursive sites, a brown-white binary emerges as whiteness and Americanness are interchangeable and coterminous against the Mexican Other. As such, the nation-state is imagined as and becomes a racial state.

But what to make of this discursive constellation stretching across such a wide field of activity? The Mexican image in the white mind exists across and performs ideological work in visual, textual, aural, erotic, and political fields. Taken in isolation, one iteration may have limited power and seem an oddity. However, through reading tropologically, scholars, activists, and artists must recognize how these depictions of the Mexican Other weigh upon, speak back to, and connect with each other. Such a sprawling discursive system not only shapes the imagination in numerous spheres but also causes the Mexican Other to become over-determined in both its production and reception over time. This vast symbolic reservoir does not simply exist in an ether of representation. Rather, whiteness on the border interpellates its subjects so that these renderings of Mexico, Mexicans, and Mexican Americans are as nearly unremarkable as they are foundational to whiteness as Americanness.

Here a brief meditation on Jacques Rancière's distribution of the sensible may be in order. In his rejection of a hierarchal model of discourse and an attempt to explain seemingly spontaneous political uprisings, Rancière theorized the distribution of the sensible as "the system of self-evident facts of sense perception," a terrain constituted by that which is visible, audible, speakable, in other words, sensible.[5] For Rancière, this terrain marks a common imagined and perceptual ground, and the various "coordinates" within the distribution of the sensible signal political and perceptual subjectivities. Rancière's distribution of the sensible is foundational to understanding political culture, for it offers at least three critical interventions. First, Rancière names "the system of divisions and boundaries that define, among other things, what is visible and audible within a particular aesthetic-political regime."[6] Rancière also acknowledges that which falls outside the distribution of the sensible—images that cannot be seen, stories that cannot be heard within a given regime. Second, in describing a "system of self-evident facts of sense perception," Rancière signals how hegemonic consent is naturalized. In other words, that which is visible, audible, and sensible maps the terrain of what can be understood—what is sensible is self-evident; what is unsensible is also unthinkable. Together these first two interventions suggest that Rancière's model recognizes a dialectical relationship wherein one's ideological positioning shapes the perception of what is sensible, and simultaneously the sensible positions (interpellates or assigns coordinates to) one within a field of perception. Finally, Rancière's model places all forms of expression including the artistic and the political on a level discursive field. As Rancière suggests and as *Whiteness on the Border* demonstrates, there is no clear break between cultural thought and expression and political thought and expression. Music and film give expression to cultural narratives and logics in ways similar to political rhetoric. Rancière's distribution of the sensible makes legible that Pedro, South of the Border, nativist articulations of Aztlán, and country music about escape to Mexico with Mexicanas are not simply discrete, isolated examples. Rather, they are interconnected points within the terrain of the sensible. In this way, as a discursive and ideological network, the representations of Mexicanness are linked across discrete locations and weigh upon each other.

Mapping the terrain of the sensible, anti-Mexican racialization fashions whiteness as Americanness in ways beyond a simple vilification.

While claims of a reconquista and the browning of America position U.S. whites as innocent victims, other cultural expressions render white Americans as fighters for social justice, as humanitarians, as desirable and superior, as anything but racist. Although these aspects of whiteness have long been at play, they have accrued greater significance from the mid-twentieth century onward as white supremacy has reconfigured itself to endure well into the future.

In a sense, this discursive and ideological constellation that I have begun to map may be described as a national racial fantasy constituted of interlocking racial and political scripts. Drawing upon the work of Donald Pease and Natalia Molina, we may see how ideas, images, and stories shape the world in which we live. Pease illustrates how American exceptionalism operates as a state fantasy that subjects the U.S. citizenry: "American exceptionalism defined America as having already achieved the condition of the ideal nation that normally incited national desire."[7] The result is twofold: American exceptionalism makes Americans content with the nation-state they have, and because they imagine the United States as an ideal, they seek to export Americanness through imperialism. Critically, Pease's state fantasy of American exceptionalism shares much of the discursive and ideological terrain of whiteness. Whiteness is often positioned as the uninterrogated ideal against which other racialized groups must be measured. Moreover, Pease exposes how American exceptionalism requires the active and continual disavowal of the U.S. histories of imperialism and injustice.[8] This systemic un-witnessing finds a crucial analog in Charles Mills's description of white supremacy as *"an inverted epistemology, an epistemology of ignorance, a particular pattern of localized and global cognitive dysfunctions . . . , producing the ironic outcome that whites will in general be unable to understand the world they themselves have made."*[9] Both American exceptionalism and whiteness require an active disavowal to forge a dangerous inverted epistemology. In her *How Race Is Made in America*, Molina explores and theorizes the cultural work of racial scripts. For Molina, racial scripts are the stories told about and ascribed to racialized groups over time. Molina demonstrates how these scripts are not attributable to one group alone or limited to one moment in time. Rather, white supremacy draws upon these scripts as rhetorical tools, deploying them as necessary to perform critical discursive and rhetorical work across the uneven churn of history. As a set of racial scripts that accrued to Mexico and Mexican-descent people in the nineteenth century and endured with little alteration, whiteness on the border has become naturalized over time, the informal logics of racial life in the United States. The work of Pease and Molina echoes that of Rancière, exposing the political and cultural work of narrative. As a racial and national fantasy, as a discursive and ideological terrain, whiteness on the border shapes, gives order to, and obscures lived reality.

Importantly, Molina also recognizes that racial scripts do not emerge without response. Aggrieved communities have also engaged in what Molina calls "counterscripting."[10] While whiteness on the border is an enduring U.S. racial tradition, it has been mirrored by a wide array of responses by Mexican Americans. Since the inception of the brown-white binary in the United States, people of Mexican descent have actively negotiated, contested, and at times embraced whiteness. In the late nineteenth century, Mexican American author María Amparo Ruiz de Burton ended her novel The Squatter and the Don by imagining a connection between the working-class white settlers and the dispossessed Californio elite. Ruiz de Burton lamented that if legislators did not act properly, against the power of monopoly capitalism, then her cross-class, cross-ethnic group of Californian whites "must wait and pray for a Redeemer who will emancipate the white slaves of California."[11] Drawing upon colonial New Spain's and Mexico's own systems of white supremacy, Ruiz de Burton staked her claims on U.S. citizenship through racial standing. Of course, she was not alone. Many have relied upon the Spanish myth to claim the rights and privileges of whiteness, and some still continue to do so today.[12] In the mid-twentieth century, Mexican Americans adopted a more complex negotiation of whiteness. Legally classified as white and socially ascribed as nonwhite, Mexican Americans made legal and political arguments that they deserved the full rights of citizenship. While this move did not invoke the specter of racial purity to achieve belonging, this whiteness strategy did divide Mexican Americans from other peoples of color who could not lay claim to whiteness.[13] Moreover, Mexican American assertions of citizenship also sometimes coincided with a distancing and demonizing of Mexican immigrants.[14] With the rise of Chicana/o cultural consciousness in the 1960s and 1970s, another strategy emerged. Rather than embracing whiteness or Americanness, Chicana/o scholars, activists, and artists rejected calls for assimilation and recuperated long denigrated Indigenous ancestry. While not without their own limitations, Chicanismo and the rhetorical embrace of indigeneity signaled a fundamental shift in the response to whiteness. Here Mexican Americans were not seeking inclusion into whiteness, a category based on the exclusion of others. They were arguing for rights without inclusion into whiteness. These three cases—the Spanish myth, the Mexican American generation, and Chicanismo—should not be seen as historically discrete moments, completely severed from one another. Instead, they embody rhetorical and strategic responses to the brown-white binary. Just as white supremacy has built a substantial set of racial scripts and images, so too have people of color historically developed a sophisticated discursive repertoire to navigate and survive this terrain.

Importantly, however, scholars and activists must also recognize that a rigid application of the brown-white binary elides the messiness and complexity of lived experience. While whiteness may be fashioned against a Mexican Other, Mexican Americans may well participate in the system of exclusion. Mexico's history of anti-Indigenous attitudes is mirrored in Mexican American thought. Consider how the writings Ruiz de Burton and Jovita González explicitly, and the Spanish myth implicitly, denigrate Indigenous and mestizo peoples.[15] Moreover, as Josefina Saldaña-Portillo and others have noted, the Chicana/o embrace of indigeneity often figured Indigenous peoples as part of a distant past and largely failed to develop coalitionist ties with contemporary Native peoples.[16] Such a move shows the ideological ground of Mexico's white supremacy as well as that of the United States. A strict application of the brown-white binary causes other erasures as well. Not only does it erase Mexico's cultural and political modernity and cast Mexican Americans as perpetually foreign, it also elides Westernized aspects and contributions of Chicana/o culture. In her autobiography, Chicana feminist, activist, and punk musician Alice Bag describes how her affinity for glam rock and punk created a social distance between her and Chicana/o activists in her youth: "I was excited to think that I was finally old enough to be a Chicana activist and maybe even a Brown Beret, but the people I met that day snickered and whispered conspiratorially to each other as I walked toward their table. Instead of telling me about their organization, they asked me why I was wearing what I was wearing. They made me feel rejected even thought they didn't outwardly insult me; their sideways glances and smirks let me know what they thought of me."[17] The character Aurora Esperanza from Brando Skyhorse's *The Madonnas of Echo Park* offers an analogous situation and powerful analysis when she tells of her love of the English singer Morrissey: "I never understood why when a white person likes a musician who's not white, they're cool, but if a person who isn't white likes a musician who is, they're a freak or, worse, a sellout."[18] Whether deployed for the U.S. racial project or internalized within an aggrieved community as a form of sometimes strategic essentialism, the brown-white binary erases the most difficult theoretical observations: "that life is complicated" and people are complex.[19] As Mexican Americans are rendered a racial and national Other to whiteness, recognition of their contributions to U.S. culture may well be constrained. As the case of Alice Bag suggests, if punk, glam, or other social locations are scripted as white, then there is no space for a Chicana punk in the racial imagination. Here, we see that whiteness on the border is not simply a racial and national project. Rather it is a project that shapes and limits the stories that can be told, those that appear sensible, those that are not only legible but legitimated.

A rigid application of the brown-white binary holds another danger as well. As I stated at the outset, I do not wish to foreclose an understanding of the volatile, multiracial nature of the U.S. racial project. Whiteness on the border does not exist in isolation or ex nihilo, and I hope future scholars will continue to explore how it is bound to other forms of racialization. When white Americans first came into regular contact with Mexico and Mexicans, they drew upon racial scripts of African Americans and Natives. The U.S. border policies that are so attuned to targeting Mexicans and Central Americans today have their origins in anti-Chinese attitudes and policies of the past. The power of white supremacy is explosive, and its targets are in some but not all ways interchangeable. Should we need yet another reminder, we can merely consider how quickly 2016 presidential candidate Donald Trump went from decrying Mexicans as criminals and rapists to assailing Muslim refugees as terrorists who must be excluded from the nation. His rhetorical prowess at stoking the national-racial fervor of his supporters is not unusual in U.S. history. It is sadly common.

Mapping the Future Gringostroika

Whiteness on the border maps numerous stories and logics that structure white supremacy and U.S. nationalism. Critically, these cultural
narratives and the representations of Mexicanness that undergird them
should not be seen as fanciful entertainment alone, completely divorced
from lived reality. This set of cultural logics shapes human interaction,
gives order to governmental policies, and expresses a wide-ranging field
of ethnoracial beliefs. As part of the U.S. political culture, whiteness
on the border dehumanizes people: rendering Mexicans and Mexican
Americans perpetually foreign in order to naturalize the whiteness of
the United States and cast white Americans as innocent victims, figuring
Mexicans and Mexican Americans as under threat from forces of evil
in order to shore up the goodness and heroism of American whiteness,
imagining the naturalized superiority of white American masculinity
through an ideology of sexual relations that polices the romantic relationships of white women and people of color. These stories erase the
human complexity of brown and white alike, propelling a national fantasy forward into time as they curtail introspection. They limit what is
sensible, making the racial order appear natural and inevitable. In other
words, as these stories order lived experience, they function as the crucial terrain in the struggle for hegemony.

As scholars, activists, and artists seek to revisit and dismantle the
force of whiteness on the border, the work of Stuart Hall and Antonio
Gramsci may provide useful guidance. In particular, Hall's reading of
Gramsci's relevance to race and ethnicity is instructive in two ways for
contesting these manifestations of whiteness. First, via Gramsci, Hall
reminds us that classes and ethnoracial groups are neither natural nor
homogenous. Rather than speaking of an organic working class versus a
capitalist bourgeoisie, Gramsci framed the struggle as between those who
serve the interests of capital and those who fight it.[20] As such, working-
class people may well align themselves with the rich and some elites may
align themselves with the struggle against capital. This is a critical point
particularly after the racial break. Not only have some people of color
been incorporated into and aligned themselves with the interests of white
supremacy, but Hall and Gramsci provide a way of thinking through a
genuine white antiracist allyship in the struggle against white supremacy.

Second, through Gramsci, Hall reminds us that just as group unification is always in process, so to is hegemony.[21] That is, hegemony, the cultural narratives that give order to and naturalize oppression, is never complete but always in process, in contestation. As such, resistance is not merely possible, but always occurring. Moreover, just as hegemony is fostered through a wide set of social and discursive locations—schools, media, political rhetoric, and so on—so must counterhegemonic efforts engage those sites of discourse and ideological reproduction.

Ultimately, Gramsci is particularly useful for the examination and contestation of whiteness because of the way he accounts not just for the stories and logics that organize consent, but also for what remains invisible, what Rancière would describe as outside the distribution of the sensible. For Gramsci, hegemony takes its force not just because it organizes consent, but because that consent is rendered natural and freely given. As such, coercion and systems of power seek to hide below the surface of the sensible. Counterhegemonic struggles, in turn, must make the coercion and power legible in order to gain position in the struggle. That is, the struggle against and for hegemony requires broadening the terrain of the sensible. This has been a common strategy within critical whiteness studies, ethnic studies, and antiracist activism in the United States. As numerous scholars have noted, whiteness occupies the dangerous position of ideal and unstated norm, an aspect that has grown to be more of a challenge with the rise of color blindness. As such, whiteness embodies a critical linkage in the ideas of Gramsci and Rancière—whiteness achieves hegemony as it seeks to remain outside the distribution of the sensible.[22] For scholars and activists, a consistent strategy has been to make whiteness visible and strange, simultaneously denaturalizing and decentering it.[23] Matthew Jackson has used the rhetorical term "enthymeme" to describe this aspect of whiteness. Simply put, an enthymeme is an argument that is dependent upon an unstated premise, a logical structure that relies upon a hegemonic silence. Stating an enthymeme has two effects. It brings unstated assumptions to the fore and denaturalizes them, potentially disrupting the fabric that holds the discursive community together. Arguably the enthymetic aspect of whiteness is what allows it to maintain its presence—whiteness is the secret everybody knows but few can speak because it rests below the surface as an unstated assumption.

In recent years, there has seemed to be a growing cultural and political emphasis on making whiteness visible and disrupting its naturalized position. However, such a maneuver is not enough. Here an example is useful. In 2008 folk and country musician Tom Russell recorded "Who's Gonna Build Your Wall?" as a response to the growing anti-Mexican nativism. The song was also included in the 2012 *Border Songs* compilation that sought to foster awareness of immigration rights activism and raise money for No Más Muertes, a group that provides water for migrants who cross the Arizona desert. In a standout moment, the song shifts the listener's attention from Mexican immigrants to whiteness: "But as I travel around this big ol' world / There's one thing that I most fear. / It's a white man in a golf shirt / With a cell phone in his ear."[24] This move is significant in the way Russell turns attention to whiteness and economic exploitation. Russell makes legible that immigration is spurred on by the practices of a white elite. As a result, Russell's imagined white working-class and middle-class listeners may align themselves with Mexican immigrants. While providing a savvy and powerful moment, the song also reinforces limited visions of Mexicans. The song renders Mexicans through various forms of labor: cleaning staff ("Who's gonna wax your floors tonight / Down at the local mall?"), landscapers ("Who's gonna mow your lawn?"), and child care providers ("Who's gonna wash your baby's face?"). While these are common immigrant professions, Russell's song exemplified two limits of the imagination. First, immigrants are valued solely as laborers who contribute to the quality of life of U.S. citizens. They are not valued as people. Second, their labor reinforces dominant racial scripts of what *kinds* of work Mexicans "naturally" fit into. Reading the song in this way both shows how one can make whiteness visible and underscores the need for radically transforming the distribution of the sensible through counterscripting.

Critically addressing whiteness and its enthymetic nature is different from the counterscripting Molina describes. For Molina, counterscripting describes the strategic rearticulation of how people of color are racialized. Counterscripting whiteness requires first making its dynamics audible, speakable, and visible to its practitioners. While there has been a long emphasis on counterscripting people of color, scholars, activists, and artists must also focus on, engage, and disrupt the enthymetic dynamic of whiteness. In the previous chapters, I have mapped out strategies for such scholarship: the unstated aspect of Mexican invasions is white fear, Mexican vulnerability is the manifestation of white goodness, and the sexy señorita is but an expression of white masculine desire for its own desirability and is used to maintain a racialized and gendered power structure. But other enthymetic aspects of whiteness on the border exist. In this book and in U.S. political culture perhaps the most foundational anti-Mexican enthymeme is the unstated belief that American equals white. Indeed, it is the powerful and pernicious other half to rendering Mexican-descent people as perpetually foreign. Dismantling whiteness on the border will require making this false equation visible, disrupting it, and making people confront its consequences. Dismantling whiteness on the border is not enough, for cultural workers must build a new world, reconfiguring the terrain of the sensible through counterscripting and radical acts of the imagination.

Heretofore, I have focused on whiteness produced via anti-Mexican racialization during and after the racial break. Here we must remember that Winant's model is not a totalizing shift where the world starts anew. Rather, the racial break marks the global realignment of the political and cultural aspects of racial formation. Like an earthquake felt the world over, the tectonic plates of race have broken from each other, realigned, and solidified their positions again. But Omi and Winant expose more than a model for thinking of racial formation in the past and present. They also outline a cyclical trajectory of racial politics: unstable equilibrium, crisis, absorption, insulation, unstable equilibrium, and so on.[25] Here, one may recognize unstable equilibrium as an expression of hegemony and the other stages as contestation over and reestablishment of hegemony. Turning this model away from the past and toward the future, dismantling whiteness on the border requires radical acts of imagination that will not be absorbed into or insulate racial hegemony.

The struggle for hegemony and against whiteness on the border requires bringing new perspectives, concepts, images, and stories into view, and invoking the enthymeme is but one strategy. The ongoing and future project to dismantle whiteness, U.S. nationalism, and their relationship may best be conceptualized through Guillermo Gómez-Peña's term "gringostroika." The performance artist coined the term and began to map the concept during the early 1990s, to him a moment of crisis and possibility. The time was marked by the end of the Cold War, the height of the U.S. culture wars, and the advent of NAFTA. Through gringostroika Gómez-Peña imagined an alternative possibility to the rising ethnonationalism and the New World Order. The term draws upon the concept of perestroika, the "restructuring" of the Soviet society and economy under Gorbachev and corresponding thaw in the U.S.-Soviet relations. By joining perestroika to gringo, the common term for American whites, Gómez-Peña gave name to a breakdown of brown-white binary thinking.[26] Gringostroika is a critical intervention against whiteness on the border both because it names the linkages between racial and national projects and because it imagines their dissolution, gesturing toward a new future.

While Gómez-Peña conceptualized gringostroika in the 1990s, I redeploy it here as the counterpoint to whiteness on the border, describing the same political and aesthetic project but stretching it beyond its historical moment of emergence. Using the work of Gómez-Peña as a point of departure, one finds that he has modeled a variety of strategies for naming, disrupting, and transgressing these interlinked national and racial projects. For example, in his poem "Freefalling toward a Borderless Future," Gómez-Peña invokes a hemispheric humanism that rejects artificial divisions as he celebrates migrations and icons of mixedness.[27] In their well-known "The Couple in the Cage" performance, Coco Fusco and Gómez-Peña re-created and undermined the colonial gaze as they dressed as imaginary Indians from the equally imaginary island of Guatinaui. As Gómez-Peña and Fusco toured the United States, Latin America, and Europe as part of the quincentennial of the Columbian "discovery," audiences watched and engaged with the artists as they performed the expectations of the exotic, Indigenous Other. While this piece did not invoke a brown-white binary in a strict sense, it illustrates the power of troping upon and troubling dominant racial logics and redirecting the gaze at those in positions of power. In many of his performance pieces, Gómez-Peña constructs Mexican characters through assembling the seemingly disparate costume choices of lucha libre masks, charro regalia, Indigenous headdresses, and an assortment of other pieces that signify difference. Here again, Gómez-Peña performs engagements with and disruption of the U.S. racial imagination. These characters, these images stretch, tear, and reconfigure the terrain of the sensible. Although these characters certainly invoke aspects of stereotypical Mexicanness, they are so strange that they cannot be contained. In other words, Gómez-Peña's characters are no Pedro of South of the Border; they are not the Mexicans whom whiteness is looking for. Finally, in a photo of his "Warrior for Gringostroika" character, Gómez-Peña draws together multiple tactics for disrupting the U.S. white racial imagination. His character dons a leopard print lucha libre mask along with a charro jacket and pants, jacket undone and arms pulling it back to expose his bare chest, on which is written, "Please don't discover me!"[28] This image disrupts the innocuous use of the term "discovery," charging it with a legacy of violence and trauma. Here, Gómez-Peña draws in the white gaze, troubles it, and redirects it in a way to consider the history upon which it was founded.

Of course, I should note that Gómez-Peña is not alone in this endeavor. La Pocha Nostra is a international interdisciplinary artist collective of which Gómez-Peña was a founding artistic director. In their performances and workshops, La Pocha members engage in nonhierarchical collective image creation and multisensory experiences. These images, characters, experiences do not emerge from a solitary conscious mind. Rather, from intuitive, organic, and collaborative efforts, the unimaginable is imagined into being. Gómez-Peña's gringostroika and La Pocha Nostra's pedagogical and artistic practices illustrate that we do not have to accept the terrain of the sensible as it is. We do not need to accept contemporary racial politics as they are. Radical imagination is required. While a more just and free world may not be forged of radical imagination alone, such imaginative acts are nonetheless essential.

If we imagine the project of gringostroika beyond Gómez-Peña, we may find countless examples enacted by scholars, activists, artists, and others living their daily lives. Perhaps grouping these activities under the term "gringostroika" could link them in a counterdiscursive and ideological network that seeks the undoing of whiteness on the border. This frame allows us to flesh out the politics of and learn from a wide set of resistances. One final example is in order. During the parade honoring the San Francisco Giants for their 2012 World Series championship, pitcher Sergio Romo was the only member of the team to get out of his car, walk the street, and celebrate with the fans. The Mexican American player, however, made headlines because he wore a shirt that simply stated "I just look illegal."[29] Romo's rhetorical, political, and pedagogical act is particularly significant when one considers the historical context. In the two years prior, Arizona and other states had begun a spate of anti-immigrant and anti-Latina/o legislation, and the following year white supremacists would openly criticize eleven-year-old San Antonio, Texas, mariachi singer Sebastian de la Cruz for singing the U.S. national anthem prior to an NBA championship game. While some may grimace at Romo's shirt's surface equation of appearance and citizenship, I would contend that Romo and his shirt made legible and troubled the central logic of various states' "show me your papers" laws that required law enforcement to detain those whom they suspected of being undocumented. Indeed, in the lead-up to SB 1070's signing, activists warned that it would lead to an increase in anti-Latina/o racial profiling, and Arizona Governor Jan Brewer acknowledged in a press conference that she did not know what an "illegal immigrant" looks like, a comment that made explicit the potential linkages between phenotype, citizenship, and policing. Moreover, Romo's actions bring the enthymeme to the foreground because to appreciate the humor of his shirt one must recognize the commonplace equation of whiteness and Americanness. Simply put, Romo's agitprop celebration is humorous, but it is also a humor that exposes the daily hurt that white supremacy wields. Here, one is tempted to imagine a complementary example. What happens when white allies begin to don shirts that read "Do I look undocumented?" Such shirts were popular with some Latina/o youth immigration activists and work to question the assumed equation of race and citizenship. However, worn by white bodies such shirts may bring about the enthymeme in a different way. Likely the answer would be "no," disrupting the myth of color blindness and making strikingly visible the disturbing whiteness of citizenship. Of course, I am not so naïve as to believe that donning T-shirts will change the world. Rather, through the examples of Romo and Gómez-Peña, enthymemes and gringostroika, I am gesturing toward discursive and political practices that model efforts to disrupt white supremacy and anti-Mexican racialization. Critically, the fight against white supremacy is not solely the terrain of people of color. White folks have "skin in the game" as well.[30] While the struggle must be multifaceted, it must begin by disrupting the naturalized flow of racial thought, speaking the unspoken, drawing new terrain into the sensible. Learning from these efforts, placing them in conversation, and pairing them with a wide range of other symbolic and material strategies will be essential in the struggle for hegemony.

Whiteness on the border has a long-enduring history. But this intersection of national and racial projects has not taken root without resistance. Nor does it need to stretch endlessly into the future. There are other possibilities. Drawing upon Gómez-Peña, I imagine the coming gringostroika, a thaw, a collapse. Some will retrench into old ways—after all, how does whiteness fashion itself without its constituent Others? But others will tell new stories, fashion new possibilities from the past, in the present, and into the future.

NOTES

PREFACE

1 Clark, "White Professor Teaches 'Problem of Whiteness' Course at Arizona State."
2 "Trouble with Schools."
3 In the summer of 2015, the National Youth Front underwent a leadership change and received a cease-and-desist letter because their name was too similar to another youth organization. The NYF is currently organizing under the moniker of The Dispossessed, a rhetorical invocation of their claims of white victimhood.
4 Lipsitz, *American Studies in a Moment of Danger*, 29.

INTRODUCTION

1 Rocco, "Transforming Citizenship."
2 Vega, *Latino Heartland*.
3 Rosas, "Thickening Borderlands."
4 Fowler, "Señorita Más Fina."
5 Dyer, *White*, 10.
6 For a discussion of abolition and whiteness, see Roediger, *Towards the Abolition of Whiteness*; Olson, *Abolition of White Democracy*; Garner, *Whiteness*.
7 Garner, *Whiteness*, 66; Frankenberg, *White Women, Race Matters*, 56–59, 62–63, 66–67.
8 Du Bois, *Black Reconstruction*; Baldwin, *Price of the Ticket*, xi–xx.
9 Indeed, the "naturalness" and invisibility of the system speaks to how it functions as a form of hegemony and achieves consent.
10 McKinney, *Being White*, 1–5.
11 The use of "common sense" to describe this form of racial hegemony comes from Omi and Winant's discussion of a lack of coherent understanding as what counts as race and racism. Omi and Winant, *Racial Formation*, 70.
12 Franklin, *Color Line*.
13 Roediger, "Color of Whiteness Studies."
14 McIntosh, "White Privilege," 291.
15 Morrison, *Playing in the Dark*.
16 Roediger, *Wages of Whiteness*.
17 Frankenberg, *White Women, Race Matters*. The concept of unwitnessing comes from Lopenzina, *Red Ink*, 5.
18 Ignatiev, *How the Irish Became White*.

19 Dyer, *White.*
20 Lipsitz, *Possessive Investment in Whiteness.*
21 Mills, *Racial Contract.*
22 Hartigan, *Racial Situations.*
23 McKinney, *Being White.*
24 Thandeka, *Learning to Be White.*
25 Olson, *Abolition of White Democracy.*
26 Hirsch, *Cultural Literacy.*
27 Frankenberg, *White Women, Race Matters,* 228–29; Dyer, *White,* 42–45; Thandeka, *Learning to Be White,* 3; McIntosh, "White Privilege," 1.
28 Mills, *Racial Contract,* 18, emphasis original.
29 Dyer, *White,* 10; Thandeka, *Learning to Be White,* 3–4.
30 Frankenberg, *White Women, Race Matters,* 60.
31 Heron, "Whitey on the Moon."
32 Notably, the black/white binary takes on different significance in the United Kingdom. There, various communities of color are encapsulated in the term "black," creating similar and distinct problems for the field.
33 Perea, "Black/White Binary Paradigm of Race," 1229–31.
34 Gómez, *Manifest Destinies,* 88–89, 105–9.
35 Brilliant, *Color of America Has Changed;* Behnken, *Fighting Their Own Battles;* Folely, *Quest for Equality.*
36 Organized by Ted Hayes, the Crispus Attucks Brigade is an anti-Latina/o organization that wraps itself in U.S. nationalist discourses and civil rights movement rhetoric. See http://tedhayes.us/uscab/.
37 Omi and Winant refer to this as the "ethnic model" of understanding race. Omi and Winant, *Racial Formation,* 14–23.
38 That is, as Raymond Rocco and Mae Ngai have each described, Mexican-descent peoples have long been depicted as "perpetually foreign" and "alien citizens." Thus, this ethnic-immigrant model marks Latinas/os as foreign as it holds out an unattainable lure. Rocco, "Transforming Citizenship"; Ngai, *Impossible Subjects,* 2.
39 Haney López, "Retaining Race," 292.
40 Jiménez, *Replenished Ethnicity.*
41 Park, "Between a Myth and a Dream"; Dávila, *Latinos Inc.*
42 While this has certainly been a trend in the field, Dylan Rodriguez's *Suspended Apocalypse* and its examination Filipinos' relationship to white supremacy suggests that this is changing as scholars interrogate the common elements as well as the historical particularities of white supremacy.
43 Smith, "Heteropatriarchy and the Three Pillars of White Supremacy," 70, emphasis original.
44 For linkages between prisons, slavery, and capitalism, see Blackmon, *Slavery by Another Name;* Gilmore, *Golden Gulag.*
45 Abani, "Cost of Change."
46 Smith, "Heteropatriarchy and the Three Pillars of White Supremacy," 69.

47 Ibid., 68–69.

48 Indeed, other communities have experienced multiple pillars/forms of white supremacy as well. The flexibility and specificity of Smith's model are what I find so useful.

49 Smith, "Heteropatriarchy and the Three Pillars of White Supremacy," 67.

50 Turner, *Barbarous Mexico*.

51 Pitt, *Decline of the Californios*, 83–119.

52 May, *Manifest Destiny's Underworld*.

53 Please note that I am not contending that Chicanas/os have the same relationship to indigeneity and land as U.S. Natives. Rather, there is a complex history at play as Nicole Guidotti-Hernández has so clearly demonstrated. However, this aspect of Indigenous heritage and claims to land cannot simply be waved away either. Guidotti-Hernández, *Unspeakable Violence*, 81–132.

54 For a discussion of the complex, multiracial history of Mexican-descent people, see Menchaca, *Recovering History, Constructing Race*.

55 For a discussion of the "Spanish myth"/"fantasy heritage," see McWilliams, *North from Mexico*, 43–53; Nieto-Phillips, *Language of Blood*.

56 Almaguer, *Racial Fault Lines*, 46.

57 Notably, hypodescent did not necessarily apply to Mexican Americans in the same way it did to African Americans. The claim to Spanish ancestry, along with the legal guarantees of the Treaty of Guadalupe Hidalgo, allowed mestizos to claim white legal standing. Gómez, *Manifest Destinies*, 142–44.

58 Menchaca, *Recovering History, Constructing Race*, 62–66; Cope, *Limits of Racial Domination*, 4.

59 Indeed, Bonilla-Silva contends that the future of the United States may be a form of Latin American racial stratification, and he convincingly argues that such a system will be more difficult to contest. Bonilla-Silva, *Racism without Racists*, 177–206.

60 Haney López, "Retaining Race."

61 Almaguer, *Racial Fault Lines*, 46.

62 Omi and Winant, *Racial Formation*, 21–22; Haney López, "Retaining Race," 292.

63 Haney López, "Retaining Race," 283.

64 Ibid., 292.

65 Gómez, *Manifest Destinies*, 87–90, 93.

66 García, *White but Not Equal*, 3, 7.

67 Ibid.

68 Behnken, *Fighting Their Own Battles*, 7–9.

69 Chabram-Dernersesian, "On the Social Construction of Whiteness," 114–30.

70 Gonzales, *I Am Joaquín*, 52, 100.

71 Bebout, *Mythohistorical Interventions*, 5.

72 Acuña, *Occupied America*, 1.

73 Haney López, *White by Law*, 61.

74 Olivas, *Colored Men and Hombres Aquí*; García, *White but Not Equal*.

75 Chabram-Dernersesian, "On the Social Construction of Whiteness," 112.

76 Ibid., 130.

77 With the rise in anti-Latina/o and anti-immigrant politics, there has been a corresponding rise in Latina/o activism. Thus, perhaps the depoliticization Torres noted will not be an ongoing trend. That being said, Cherríe Moraga has pondered the same demise of Chicana/o politicization with the caveat that with each immigrant, and corresponding experiences of inequality, there arrives the potential for Chicana/o politicization. Torres, "Race, Place and Chicana/o Politics"; Moraga, *Last Generation*, 8, 148, 155.

78 While the Mexican Problem discourse is often associated with social science scholarship of the early twentieth century onward, its roots may more accurately be traced back to the early nineteenth century as Anglo-American settlers moved west and came into contact with inhabitants of colonial New Spain and Mexico. De León, *They Called Them Greasers*, 1–13.

79 McWilliams, *North from Mexico*, 188.

80 To a question about the Negro Problem, Richard Wright responded that "there isn't any Negro Problem; there is only a white problem." Notably, George Lipsitz uses this moment as a point of departure in his theorization of whiteness. I seek to extend such a dynamic to ask how the "Mexican Problem" might illustrate other dynamics of whiteness. Lipsitz, *Possessive Investment in Whiteness*, 1.

81 Anzaldúa, *Borderlands/La Frontera*, 108.

82 Garner, *Whiteness*, 80–98.

83 Cohn, "More Hispanics Declaring Themselves White."

84 Notably, other Latina/o groups have also been scripted as "problems." For example, see Chavez, *Out of the Barrio*, 139–60.

85 Dávila, *Latino Spin*, 13.

86 Julito, "1.2 Million Latinos."

87 Indeed, Rebecca St. John's *Line in the Sand* does an excellent job exploring how the seemingly natural geopolitical border was constructed.

88 Lugo, "Theorizing Border Inspections."

89 Olson, *Abolition of White Democracy*, xx.

90 Rocco, "Transforming Citizenship"; Ngai, *Impossible Subjects*, 2.

91 Jacobson, *New Nativism*, 36–37.

92 Interestingly this blonde love interest is the mythohistorical "Yellow Rose of Texas" Emily Morgan. In common Texas legend, Morgan is recognized as mulatta. However, either because of a lack of understanding of the story or because of the potential race politics at the time, *Martyrs* whitewashes Morgan's racial standing.

93 Rodríguez, "Writing Boundaries on Bodies."

94 González, "Ghost of John Wayne."

95 A special thanks to Susan Curtis for reminding me about the Frito Bandito and telling me about the Los Bandidos restaurant. Alas, the examples of anti-Mexican white supremacy are as forgettable as they are abundant.

96 Mills, *Racial Contract*, 18; Feagin, *White Racial Frame*, 9–18.

CHAPTER 1. WHAT DID THEY CALL THEM AFTER THEY CALLED
THEM "GREASERS"?

1 Rodriguez, *Brown*, 30.
2 De León, *They Called Them Greasers*, 105–6.
3 Ibid., 106, emphasis mine.
4 Omi and Winant, *Racial Formation*, 2. Roediger, "White Looks," 44.
5 Winant, *New Politics of Race*, 15–18.
6 "Hate Crimes."
7 "Teen Survivor of Hate Crime Attack."; "Teen Who Survived Brutal Attack."
8 I don't use the term "postracial lynching" lightly. Rather, I am trying to invoke two historical elements that have historically been central to U.S. lynching. First, the element of torture is clearly present in the case of Ritcheson. Second, there is a communal element here as well. However, instead of the act of lynching consecrating the national or local community as in years past, in the postracial era it is the collective rejection of explicit white supremacy and violence that forges the community and its understanding of self. Notably, this also serves the needs of white supremacy in that the rejection of explicit white racist violence without action against overt and covert forms of white supremacy leaves the racial order in place and reinstantiates notions of white innocence and purity, charging them anew for the post-break era.
9 Melamed, *Represent and Destroy*. Indeed, the significance of Melamed's work is evidenced through her effort to make explicit racial violence and the ways in which it is obscured and legitimated by official antiracisms such as those found in institution-conforming multicultural literature classrooms.
10 In recent years, it has become quite rare for professional historians or historically minded cultural critics to write sweeping histories that cover many decades, let alone centuries. As such, many of the works of scholarship that I am drawing upon engage other scholars who are working within their historical context. However, few make connections between their work and the scholarship of others working in different time periods. When those connections are made explicit, they are often fleeting.
11 Nericcio uses quotation marks (e.g., "Mexican") to signal the constructed ethnoracial body in the U.S. white imagination. I have not followed the same practice.
12 Of course, these years were also critical to the birth of the Hollywood film industry. Nericcio, *Tex{t}-Mex*, 27.
13 Streeby, *American Sensations*, xi.
14 Bender, "Wholes and Parts."
15 Burke, *Philosophy of Literary Form*, 110.
16 Here, I am signifying upon George Frederickson classic study *The Black Image in the White Mind* to signal a similar project within the field of Chicana/o studies. Also, while de León's project surely sets the stage for many others to follow, one

must also recognize how critical passages from Américo Paredes's *With His Pistol in His Hand* do similar work. Frederickson, *Black Image*; Paredes, *With His Pistol in His Hand*, 16.

17 Indeed, while he does not refer to them as tropes per se, de León does thematically organize several chapters into discrete trends for representing Mexicans.

18 De León, *They Called Them Greasers*, 1.

19 Ibid., 8, 64–66.

20 Ibid., 17.

21 Ibid., 75, 90.

22 Ibid., 24.

23 As noted in the introduction, colonial New Spain and Mexico had an elaborate system of racial hierarchy prior to the U.S. conquest. Therefore, it is untenable to suggest that the United States introduced white supremacy. Rather, the United States introduced a specific form of white supremacy in which Anglo-Americans were positioned at the top. Importantly, this need not have been the case. U.S. whites could have formed an interethnic white supremacy with U.S. whites and elite (white) Mexicans sharing an elite position. While Mexican elites often retained higher position than lower-class and darker Mexicans, the figure of the Mexican Other fostered their position as neither truly white nor truly American.

24 In part, Streeby's work was groundbreaking because it was one of the earliest works to investigate nineteenth-century popular fiction in terms of its contributions to a nationalist project.

25 While *American Sensations* does not cite de León, Streeby may very well have been aware of *They Called Them Greasers*. This absence of a citation suggests that neither the existence of nor an active construction of this scholarly tradition has been of concern to the scholars that I am discussing here. Importantly, this citational absence is repeated across these texts, as very few refer to one another and none build a sustained dialogue about the transhistorical aspects of the Mexican Other.

26 For some, the Spanish-Mexican elite were an exploitive class like the wealthy elites of the United States. For others, this took the shape of locating the root of Mexican debt peonage in the degeneration of race mixing. Streeby, *American Sensations*, 63, 6, 192–93.

27 Ibid., 58, 60, 255.

28 Ibid., 21, 64, 84–86, 137.

29 Ibid., 39.

30 Ibid., 65, 96, 168.

31 Streeby's analysis of the Mexican Other substantiates several of her key insights, which contribute greatly to this scholarly tradition. Notably, Streeby writes against the tradition that has treated the late nineteenth-century U.S. borders as natural. Rather, Streeby illustrates and disrupts the false dichotomy between foreign and domestic wars (i.e., the Texas Revolution, the U.S.-Mexico War, and the U.S. Civil War). In doing so, Streeby shows how the U.S. racial project can be made legible

through both analysis of imperial expansion and national, racial consolidation. Ibid., 8–10, 56, 58, 168–69, 290.

32 Ibid., 55.

33 Of course, this does not mean that the United States had foregone its interest in military expansion altogether. Indeed, the United States gained control of or influence over the Philippines, Puerto Rico, and Cuba through the 1898 Spanish-American War.

34 Ruiz, *Americans in the Treasure House*, 2.

35 Of course, Mexico was the "little" sister not just because of its more recent date of independence but also because the United States had made it "littler" through two wars.

36 Ruiz's chapters on representations of Diaz's paternalism and mestizaje suggest ways in which Anglo-Americans sought to mediate previous imaginings of the greaser trope and of Indian racialization. Ruiz, *Americans in the Treasure House*, 66, 166.

37 Ibid., 49–51.

38 Ibid., 19–21, 58–62, 132–36.

39 While de León's study overlaps chronologically with a few decades of the Porfiriato, it is important to note that the political exigencies in Texas differed greatly from those of Mexico. While the United States was seeking economic expansion in Mexico, it was fighting a race war in South Texas in the late nineteenth and early twentieth centuries.

40 Mills, *Racial Contract*, 12, 49–50.

41 Ruiz, *Americans in the Treasure House*, 142–43.

42 Mills, *Racial Contract*, 11.

43 Ruiz, *Americans in the Treasure House*, 179–215.

44 Nericcio, *Tex{t}-Mex*, 125–33. Arguably, this move could be linked to Ruiz's articulation of "Porfirian nostalgia." Ruiz argues that after the Porfiriato, there was a "public desire on the part of some Americans to return to the economic, political, and cultural relations created by the long rule of Díaz." This nostalgia can be traced through the upsurge of explicitly pejorative manifestations of the Mexican Other that rendered Mexico and Mexicans as unfit for democracy and modernization. Ruiz, *Americans in the Treasure House*, 199.

45 Nericcio, *Tex{t}-Mex*, 128.

46 Ibid., 34.

47 Ibid., 43.

48 Ibid., 137.

49 Feagin, *White Racial Frame*, 93.

50 Nericcio, *Tex{t}-Mex Gallery*.

51 Alarcón, *Aztec Palimpsest*, 40.

52 Ibid., 95–148. Moreover, Alarcón reveals how Mexicans have used the expectations of Anglo-American Others vis-à-vis the Infernal Paradise trope for their own tactical purposes. Ibid., 74.

53 One may also consider Richard Rodriguez's *Brown* and the way that text embraces neoliberal postracialism. Whether engaging Acosta, Rodriguez, or other Mexican American cultural workers, treating whiteness as an ideology and discursive practice avoids the troubling pitfalls of racial essentialism. For Acosta and Rodriguez, like their Anglo-American counterparts, the Mexican Other functions as a discursive tool for forging an ideological Self. Acosta, *Autobiography of a Brown Buffalo*; Acosta, *Revolt of the Cockroach People*; Rodriguez, *Brown*.

54 Rocco, "Transforming Citizenship"; Ngai, *Impossible Subjects*; Jacobson, *New Nativism*, 48.

55 Chavez, *Latino Threat*, 2–3.

56 Ibid., 3.

57 Ibid., 31.

58 During the nineteenth century, identity on Mexico's northern frontier was more complicated than a strong, rigid nationalism. Many Mexican frontier residents identified by region (e.g., Tejanos, Nuevomexicanos, and Californianos) rather than by nationality. Mexican nationalist identity emerged in the region later in response to three potential factors: (1) Anglo-American oppression, (2) the influx of immigrants after the Mexican Revolution, (3) Mexico's nationalist efforts in the United States from the early twentieth century.

59 Chavez, *Latino Threat*, 42, 27.

60 Joel Olson contends that whiteness and citizenship are mutually constitutive in the United States. He does this by considering the role of African Americans as anticitizens within U.S. history. Here, Mexican-descent peoples fulfill a similar role. However, they are also easily conflated as foreign, something not as available to contemporary discourses on African Americans.

61 Nericcio, *Tex{t}-Mex*, 137. George Yancy also notes that white supremacist ideology shapes the experiences of people of color as they confront images of themselves in the white racial imagination. Yancy describes how the circulation of such images causes him to be defined prior to interaction with other people. Yancy, *Look, a White!*, 39.

62 Drawing on Gramsci for a discussion of Anglo and Mexican conflicts in South Texas, Limón suggests that a war of maneuver was underwritten and followed by a war of position. Limón, *Dancing with the Devil*, 15.

63 One may recognize that Gramsci's war of position engages in what Mills has described as the practice of rendering racialized Others as subpersons.

64 Cervantes, "Poem for the Young White Man," 4.

65 Ibid., 5.

66 Gates, *Signifying Monkey*; Baker, *Blues, Ideology, and Afro-American Literature*.

67 If whiteness is recognized as an ideological positioning, it is critical to acknowledge that some people of color may identify with the logics, rhetorical maneuvers, and political impulses of white supremacy. Here, I use "white-identified" to underscore the ways in which people of color may participate in white supremacy, for it is not uncommon to find examples of members of other racialized com-

munities dressing up in blackface or participating in these moments of racial costuming. Lipsitz, *Possessive Investment in Whiteness*, 149.

68 Importantly, what is recognized as happening in their lifetimes may also be quite limited. Whiteness relies not merely upon a historical amnesia but also a blindness to the lives and experiences of others. See the discussion of HB 2281 in chapter 2.

69 As Bruce Dain has so eloquently explored, the formation of race and white supremacy was intricately connected to the development of social and scientific taxonomies. Perhaps, developing a taxonomy of racist expressions is a required step in making legible and undoing the taxonomies that white supremacy has long deployed. Dain, *Hideous Monster of the Mind*, 1–39.

70 An important component of differential racialization, Mexicans were not rendered a "people without history," as Hegel suggested of Africa and Africans. Rather, the splendor of ancient Mexico is often used to reinforce a notion of a people without modernity. One might also consider how U.S. renderings of Indigenous people in Mexico's past also function to erase contemporary and historic Indigenous civilizations that claim lands now within the United States.

71 Dana, *Two Years before the Mast*, 152–57.

72 Alarcón, *Aztec Palimpsest*, 47.

73 Gutiérrez, "Aztlán, Montezuma, and New Mexico," 180. Indeed, at the risk of challenging the thesis of exceptionalist renderings of New Mexico, one might consider that the discourse of the Land of Enchantment and the Spanish myth plays into and works against many elements of the Infernal Paradise. Moreover, one must ask if these New Mexican rhetorical maneuvers would have risen to such prominence if not for a long history of anti-Mexican renderings typified via the Infernal Paradise.

74 Keith, "Stays in Mexico."

75 Slotkin notes many films that make the southward journey into Mexico. For a literary example, one may consider Kerouac's *On the Road*. Slotkin, *Gunfighter Nation*.

76 As Alarcón demonstrated, there is also a history Mexican Americans deploying this trope. For examples, see note 53 in this chapter.

77 "Juala del Oro (Cage of Gold)" is a corrido about Mexican immigration to the United States, a man's desire to return home, and his son's desire to stay. This song works against the simplistic understanding of immigration to the United States that is fostered solely by the American Dream and American exceptionalism.

78 De León, *They Called Them Greasers*, 65.

79 Obviously this is not to deny the horrific violence endured by many Mexicans under the Porfiriato. Rather, I am suggesting that Turner's readers may have seen these abuses as consistent with pre-Porfirian Mexico. Moreover, such framing may have blinded them from horrific practices in the United States.

80 Nericcio rightly notes that this rape scene actually works to construct a Mexican American sexual deviancy against the film's fashioning of an asexual Mexican in the character of Mike Vargas. That being said, read against a longer lineage be-

yond this film, these sexually aggressive pachuco youth find kinship in the moral degeneracy of Mexicans described by de León and others. Nericcio, *Tex{t}-Mex*, 65–66.

81 Mazón, *Zoot Suit Riots*, 22.

82 Frankenberg, *White Women, Race Matters*, 60.

83 Paredes, *With His Pistol in His Hand*, 16–23.

84 While examples are legion, *The Magnificent Seven* might be particularly useful to consider. Not only does the film depict the chaos and outlawry south of the border, it also forges white masculinity and benevolence as a suitable response, mapping U.S. racial logics onto the original premise of Kurosawa's *Seven Samurai*.

85 Streeby, *American Sensations*, 21. Importantly, the positioning of Mexicans (particularly the elite) within the white American family was not solely the concern of nineteenth-century or Anglo-American literature. Jovita González and Eve Raleigh's *Caballero* also engages this racial dynamic. For a strong discussion of this, see Limón, "Mexicans, Foundational Fictions, and the United States."

86 Of course, just because this trope doesn't figure Mexicanas as specifically unfit for democracy does not mean that it doesn't depict them as subpersons. Rather, the act of tropification, which flattens out complex humans into mere types, is itself a way of making them subpersons.

87 De León, *They Called Them Greasers*, 39–48.

88 Some may question the inclusion of the siesta narrative within this trope, arguing that historically factual events should not be included in deployments of white supremacist renderings of the Mexican Other. However, I would contend that the Battle of San Jacinto and the siesta are not simply events but also stories and images that are told over and over in schools and popular culture. Intentionally or unintentionally, these narratives reinforce white supremacy in the vein in which Nericcio describes.

89 De León, *They Called Them Greasers*, 49, 62.

90 Gamio, *Mexican Immigration to the United States*; Paz, *Labyrinth of Solitude*, 9–28.

91 Streeby, *American Sensations*, 105.

92 Vega, *Latino Heartland*.

93 Streeby, *American Sensations*, 107.

94 Ibid., 168.

95 Jiménez, *Replenished Ethnicity*.

96 In the subtitle to *Tex{t}-Mex*, Nericcio describes these renderings of Mexicans as "seductive hallucinations."

97 Hage argues that both contemporary Australian multiculturalism and white racism depend upon and reinforce a white national fantasy. Arguably a similar dynamic may be found in U.S. manifestations of whiteness on the border that may appear explicitly racist or, at the surface level, benevolent and romantic. Hage, *White Nation*, 18–19.

98 While Winant describes the racial break as a global phenomenon, this project largely examines white supremacy as it functions within and through the United

States. Clearly, however, white supremacy has been a long-enduring global phenomenon.

CHAPTER 2. "THEY ARE COMING TO CONQUER US!"

1 During the Mexican Revolution, approximately 10 percent of Mexico's population migrated to the United States. Because of restrictive housing, racialized wage scales, segregated businesses, and fears of white violence, Mexican immigrants and Mexican Americans settled into ethnic enclaves in the United States. Importantly, during the 1930s, as the United States engaged in Americanization programs to foster assimilation, the Mexican government also sponsored programs for its citizens (and their descendants) living in the United States to maintain their national culture. Sánchez, *Becoming Mexican American*, 87–128.

2 Bebout, *Mythohistorical Interventions*, 71–104.

3 Pérez-Torres, "Refiguring Aztlán," 234.

4 According to Rudolfo Anaya, "Aztlán," 230, Aztlán and the unveiling of "El Plan Espiritual de Aztlán" at the 1969 Denver Youth Conference functioned as a naming ceremony for the Chicano community. Thus, it is unsurprising that some efforts embraced both the political and cultural visions. Ultimately, the sometimes radical rhetoric of Aztlán enveloped the disparate, often reformist goals and strategies of the movement, forging a temporary, unifying vision.

5 Since its embrace as a unifying vision of el movimiento, Aztlán has come under steady, significant critique by Chicana/o cultural workers. For instance, nearly twenty-five years after the drafting of "El Plan Espiritual de Aztlán," Cherríe Moraga's *Last Generation* reimagined a queer Aztlán, mapping the concept of colonized territory onto the colonized queer body. In the dawning of the twenty-first century, Aztlán still maintains a spiritual, psychological importance. Chicana/o cultural workers continue to refer to Aztlán to uncover and inscribe new meanings. Scholars continue to use Aztlán in their discussions of the U.S. Southwest risk adding to the fodder of nativist cultural workers. For instance, in his recent *Mexicano Political Experience in Occupied Aztlán*, Armando Navarro continues to use Aztlán to name the geographic territory ceded to the United States in 1848 (673–707). In doing so, Navarro inadvertently reinforces the nativist fears of an ongoing reconquista. Navarro's work offers a broad-ranging political history of Chicanas/os in the Southwest, examining the ways in which the U.S. Southwest remains a colonized and occupied territory. In his epilogue, Navarro argues that it is liberal capitalism, not a master plot by the Mexican government, that is driving immigration to the United States. However, without offering any evidence, Navarro contends that immigrants as well as Mexicano activists feel that Aztlán belongs to them and they are merely returning home. Navarro's reliance on Aztlán mars his important critique of liberal capitalism and racial hegemony. Perhaps not unsurprisingly, similar Chicano deployments of Aztlán have been used by nativists to claim legitimacy regarding the coming reconquista.

6 Corwin and McCain, "Wetbackism since 1964."

7 Coleman, "Terry Coleman on the Border."

8 Djurdjevic, "When Cultures Collide." While examples of the nativist Aztlán abound via a simple LexisNexis search, the writings of Francis and Webb typify the rhetorical strategies deployed across the genre. Francis, "Poking the Embers of Racial Conflict"; Webb, "How One Citizen Is Feeling about Our Current Immigration Policies."

9 For examples of the nativist Aztlán online, see youtube.com, vadare.com, and illegalaliens.us.

10 Mariscal, "Smearing of Bustamante."

11 Santa Ana, "Like an Animal I Was Treated"; Santa Ana, *Brown Tide Rising*; Inda, "Foreign Bodies"; Cacho, "'People of California Are Suffering'"; Calavita, "New Politics of Immigration"; Chavez, *Latino Threat*.

12 Chavez, *Latino Threat*, 177. Critical responses to this Aztlán-as-reconquista narrative have been more prevalent in the netroots of Chicana/o studies than in traditional academic settings. For instance, Jorge Mariscal's response to the campaign against Bustamante was published online ("Smearing of Bustamante"). Moreover, Edmundo Rocha has used his blogs as a platform to respond to the Aztlán-reconquista narrative. Rocha, "Reconquista: A Nativist Creation" (2006, 2008).

13 Perea, *Immigrants Out!*, 1.

14 Higham, *Strangers in the Land*; Higham "Instead of a Sequel."

15 For a further discussion of political and racial nativism, see Johnson's *"Huddled Masses" Myth*.

16 Proposition 187 was a 1994 California ballot initiative that stripped undocumented immigrants from receiving public education and other social services; it was ruled unconstitutional. HR 4437 was the 2005 federal bill that sought, among other things, to build a seven-hundred-mile wall between the United States and Mexico as well as require federal authorities to take custody of any undocumented immigrants caught by local authorities. HR 4437 did not pass into law. SB 1070 was passed and signed into law in 2010 by Arizona Governor Jan Brewer. This law required police to detain any person suspected of being undocumented. Parts of the law have been ruled unconstitutional.

17 Galindo and Vigil, "Are Anti-immigrant Statements Racist or Nativist?," 420.

18 Galindo and Vigil rightly contend that the media fail to adequately confront anti-immigrant discourse and policies because they lack a historical understanding of the legacy of U.S. nativism. Moreover, the reliance on a black/white dichotomy fosters a blind spot that elides the racial experiences and treatments of Latinas/os. For instance, the exclusion of bilingual (English-Spanish) speakers from a jury will have a disparate impact on Latinas/os. However, such an effort cannot be stopped because the decision does not explicitly discriminate based on race. Ibid.

19 Muller, "Nativism in the Mid-1990s," 109, 116; Chavez, "Immigration Reform and Nativism," 66–67; Santa Ana, *Brown Tide Rising*, 5; Calavita, "New Politics of Immigration"; Williams, "Hydra of Jim Crow," 9; Galindo and Vigil, "Are Anti-immigrant Statements Racist or Nativist?," 424.

20 Lowe, *Immigrant Acts*; Noble, *Death of a Nation*.

21 Roediger, "White Looks," 44.

22 HoSang, *Racial Propositions*.

23 Johnson, *"Huddled Masses" Myth*, 12.

24 Mills, *Racial Contract*, 98–99.

25 Rogin, *Ronald Reagan, the Movie*, xv–xvii.

26 While Streeby noted that nativists have marshaled the spectral threat of national corruption and invasion to argue against imperial expansion, here we also see how it can be deployed to expand national boundaries and colonize lands.

27 Chavez, "Immigration Reform and Nativism," 63; Chavez, *Latino Threat*, 36.

28 Buchanan, *State of Emergency*, 109, 105.

29 Ibid., 107.

30 Ibid., 128, emphasis mine.

31 Ibid., 138.

32 Benedict Anderson, James Baldwin, and others have explored the relationship between amnesia and the construction of whiteness. Anderson argues that the U.S. Civil War needed to be emplotted as a struggle of brother against brother and, in so doing, elided the agency and experiences of African Americans. Baldwin, in his introduction to *Price of the Ticket*, argues that forgetting was part and parcel of the process of becoming white. Anderson, *Imagined Communities*, 201; Baldwin, *Price of the Ticket*, xix–xx.

33 Mills, *Racial Contract*, 49. See also Vizenor, *Manifest Manners*.

34 Rosaldo, *Culture and Truth*, 68–90.

35 Buchanan, *State of Emergency*, 94.

36 Ibid., 105, 93.

37 Mills, *Racial Contract*, 49.

38 Buchanan, *State of Emergency*, 101–4.

39 Rogin, *Ronald Reagan, the Movie*.

40 Buchanan, *State of Emergency*, 95.

41 Williams, *Alchemy of Race and Rights*, 64.

42 Buchanan, *State of Emergency*, 125.

43 Ibid., 138–63.

44 Huntington, *Clash of Civilizations*.

45 Buchanan, *State of Emergency*, 135.

46 De Genova, *Working the Boundaries*, 65–66.

47 Lipsitz, *Possessive Investment in Whiteness*, 50.

48 In 2013, the nativist Aztlán also made its way into the second episode of the police procedural *Chase*, which aired on NBC. In the episode, the team of U.S. marshals hunt down Eduardo "El Lobo" Lopez as he reclaims his possessions that were seized when he went to prison. Naturally, he uses the Aztlán-reconquista narrative and his understanding of the Treaty of Guadalupe Hidalgo to justify his actions.

49 *Flagstaff Republican Women Newsletter*, 3.

50 Ibid.

51 In 2010, Arendt also ran for a seat on the City Council of Flagstaff, Arizona. He did not win.

52 Arendt, *Reclaiming Aztlan*, 33.

53 Ibid., 348.

54 Williams, *Alchemy of Race and Rights*, 28.

55 Haney López, *White by Law*, 14–15; Feagin, "Old Poison in New Bottles," 14.

56 Note how this deployment of the American immigrant success story occludes the role of neoliberalism and globalization.

57 The only example of a nonwhite positive immigration model is that of a Jamaican immigrant who opens a restaurant and proves the ideals of capitalism. Of course, the character is only mentioned and never actually enters the text. Moreover, this figure becomes a marker of soft multiculturalism wherein food (exotic salads), drink (Red Stripe), and culture (steel drum night) become stand-ins for a more engaging form of diversity. Arguably, this exception is one that very much proves the rule. Arendt, *Reclaiming Aztlan*, 262.

58 For an example of these scholarly connections, see the December 2010 issue of *American Quarterly* (62.4).

59 Here, Arendt was in part likely appropriating the discourse of other conservative cultural workers who have taken anti-Mexican and anti-Palestinian views, and who sometimes are themselves responding to the fringe website La Voz de Aztlán.

60 Arendt, *Reclaiming Aztlan*, 214.

61 Ibid., 61.

62 Ibid., 206, emphasis mine.

63 Ibid., 129, emphasis mine.

64 Ibid.

65 I would like to thank Charles Park for suggesting the term "outmanned" to describe the competitive nature of hegemonic white masculinity.

66 Arendt, *Reclaiming Aztlan*, 82.

67 Ibid., 173.

68 This dystopian connection to science fiction is far from isolated to Arendt's novel. Under the pseudonym Andrew Macdonald, William Luther Pierce wrote the infamous *The Turner Diaries*, which uses a future narration set in 2099 to tell of a brutal race war at the end of the twentieth century. Pierce is also the founder of the white supremacist/nationalist organization National Alliance.

69 *Flagstaff Republican Women Newsletter*, 3, emphasis mine.

70 Around this time, Absolut was purchased by French-owned Pernod. Unsurprisingly, the foreign ownership became a specific target of conservative cultural workers.

71 "Skyy Tastelessly."

72 Usborne, "Storm in a Shot Glass."

73 Uncooperative Blogger, "Drink Absolut Vodka."

74 Carl, "Absolut Stupidity."

75 *Lou Dobbs Tonight*, CNN, April 7, 2008.

76 *Glenn Beck*, CNN Headline News, April 7, 2008.

77 For examples of conservative deployments of historical amnesia and white victim-hood, see Carl, "Absolut Stupidity," and Uncooperative Blogger, "Drink Absolut Vodka."

78 Johnson, *"Huddled Masses" Myth*, 12.

79 This is far from suggesting that Chicanas/os have not been targeted for expulsion and oppression. Indeed, twentieth-century repatriation efforts that deported U.S.-born Mexican Americans illustrate the tentative nature of juridical citizenship. A cursory survey of Mexican American history demonstrates the myriad ways Mexican Americans have been marginalized in the United States. Rather, through Johnson, I am asserting that juridical citizenship has historically afforded Mexican Americans more avenues for resistance than Mexican immigrants.

80 Miller, "Bustamante Foes"; "California Candidate."

81 Notably, the Sothern Poverty Law Center lists La Voz de Aztlán as a hate group. Because La Voz deploys the Aztlán narrative and the website has a link to "The Spiritual Plan of Aztlán," Buchanan and others have used the group as a rhetorical straw man, tainting progressive activism and reframing it as part and parcel of a pro-Mexican/Chicano antiwhite, anti-Semitic hate group. These efforts contend that La Voz is part of the Chicana/o mainstream, and not a small, isolated organization. Southern Poverty Law Center, "Ethnic Nationalism."

82 Richardson, "Chicano Group Denied Funding"; Beamish, "Latino Organization."

83 Cammarota, "Generational Battle for Curriculum."

84 Clark and Reed, "Future We Wish to See," 38; Cacho, "But Some of Us Are Wise," 29–31; Winkler-Morey, "War on History," 51–52.

85 Arguably, some models of ethnic studies, particularly those emerging out of the 1970s, did call for a form of ethnic solidarity. However, even "El Plan de Santa Barbara," a formative text in the field of Chicana/o studies in its call for culturally relevant curricula, recognized the need for white allies in educational settings. Also of note, at first TUSD and MAS supporters contended that the bill did not implicate MAS because MAS classes did not teach revolution or meet the other criteria. This initial response suggests that TUSD and MAS supporters underestimated the way in which nativist fears have worked their way into the everyday logics of whiteness.

86 Notably, she is given much more space than any other individual interviewed by the audit team. Cambium Learning, "Curriculum Audit," 100.

87 Ibid.

88 Ibid.

89 Mills, "White Lies and the Making of the World"; Mills, *Racial Contract*, 18.

90 It is important to remember that the policing of the border does not simply occur near the imagined geopolitical line between the United States and Mexico. Rather, as Rosas contended, the border has thickened and its policing occurs throughout the United States. Rosas, "Thickening Borderlands."

91 Colleagues have told me that it is a good thing that no one listens to these conservative cultural workers. In those moments, it may be good to consider the average print run and readership of a scholarly monograph and compare them to those of the best-sellers of Buchanan, Dobbs, Beck, and other less "serious" thinkers. Indeed, this underscores the need for academics to hone their skills as public intellectuals.

92 Baker-Cristales, "Mediated Resistance," 63.

93 Ibid., 78.

94 Lipsitz, *American Studies in a Moment of Danger*, 56.

95 Perhaps Renato Rosaldo's innovative model of Latino Cultural Citizenship, wherein Latinas/os claim civic belonging through cultural practices of difference, may hold possibilities as a counterforce to the nativist Aztlán and other exclusionary models of ethnic nationalism. Flores and Benmayor, *Latino Cultural Citizenship*.

CHAPTER 3. WITH FRIENDS LIKE THESE

1 "Southwest Border Unaccompanied Alien Children."

2 Moreno, "Bill Maher Bashes Republicans."

3 "In Quest to Mock Immigration Racism of Tea Party."

4 Dyer, *White*, 67.

5 Mills, *Racial Contract*.

6 Sánchez, *Becoming Mexican American*, 87–107.

7 In an earlier draft of this chapter, I described this dynamic as white benevolence. For me, "benevolence" is a useful term because it signals the shared origins between colonialism and white supremacy. In recent years, "saviorism" has been deployed more widely by online cultural critics and academics. While I feel that a number of terms are useful in describing this dynamic, I have foregrounded the use of "saviorism" and deployed apt synonyms throughout.

8 Streeby, *American Sensations*, 107.

9 The myth of U.S. historical acceptance of immigrants is epitomized by Emma Lazarus's "The New Colossus," which is etched onto the Statue of Liberty and in part reads "Give me your tired, your poor, / Your huddled masses yearning to breathe free." However, as Kevin Johnson demonstrates, the United States has been marked by not just a history of immigrant embrace but also one of immigrant exclusion. Lazarus, "New Colossus"; Johnson, *"Huddled Masses" Myth*.

10 This is not to say that to say that depictions and rejections of racialized Others are not readily deployed in the contemporary era. Rather, I am noting a shift in prevalence and not a clean break in the strategies of white supremacy.

11 A note on names and terminology: because characters' names vary between the two versions of *Giant*, I have chosen to use the names from the film to foster consistency.

12 This romantic image of transformation is the one the film attempts to depict. Arguably, Bick would probably continue to exploit his workers because this is a fairly hollow resolution.

13 In his second novel, Alex Espinoza offers an interesting revision of this scene where the phenotypically white Mexican protagonist witnesses a brown-skinned Mexican being kicked out of a diner in Southern California. The protagonist does nothing to intervene. In contrast to Bick's resolution and apparent rejection of bigotry, Espinoza's scene exposes a complicity with white supremacy through the character's act of passing and remaining silent. For a reading of Villanueva's and Urrea's revisions of this scene, see Bebout, "Troubling White Benevolence." Espinoza, *Five Acts of Diego Leon*; Villanueva, *Scene from the Movie GIANT*; Urrea, *In Search of Snow*.

14 Galan, *Children of* Giant.

15 Baxter, "*Giant* Helps America Recognize the Cost of Discrimination," 161; Shapiro, "Edna Ferber, Jewish American Feminist," 52; Watts, "Edna Ferber, Jewish American Writer," 43.

16 Graham, *Cowboys and Cadillacs*, 60; Hendler, *Best-Sellers and Their Film Adaptations*, 125–32; Watts, "Edna Ferber, Jewish American Writer," 43.

17 Baxter, "*Giant* Helps American Recognize the Cost of Discrimination," 171.

18 Graham, *Cowboys and Cadillacs*, 60.

19 Pérez-Torres, *Mestizaje*, 53.

20 Limón, *American Encounters*, 123.

21 Indeed, while not the core of his argument, Rafael Pérez-Torres does gesture toward an examination of whiteness in this scene.

22 Graham, *Cowboys and Cadillacs*, 59–60.

23 Nichols, "Talk with Edna Ferber," 30.

24 In the film, the diner scene takes place *after* Jett Rink's celebration and the confrontations between Rink and the Benedicts.

25 Ferber, *Giant*, 394.

26 Ibid.

27 Ibid., 395.

28 Ibid., 396.

29 Ibid., 401.

30 Ibid.

31 Ibid., 401–2.

32 Hendler, *Best-Sellers and Their Film Adaptations*, 124.

33 Ferber, *Giant*, 51.

34 Of course, this distinction between exploitation and benevolence is really a distinction of degree and not of kind. As this chapter exposes the supremacist logics of saviorism, it should be evident that exploitation and benevolence are quite clearly linked in many instances.

35 Despite the erasure of many forms of Mexican American activism, the narrative does provide small hints of a growing political consciousness, particularly evident in Angel's assertion that he is "Latin American." This moment suggests an incorporation of the discourse and concerns of Mexican American activists epitomized by LULAC and the American GI Forum. At the same time, *Giant* does

not interrogate Latina/o-led activism as much as the racial injustices that spur that activism. Ferber, *Giant*, 370.

36 Notably, Limón lauds the film's inclusion of Dr. Guerra/Dr. García. However, his inclusion is relatively minor, and as Pérez-Torres notes, he is quickly replaced by Jordan.

37 Ferber, *Giant*, 390.

38 Ibid.

39 LULAC was formed in 1929, and the American GI Forum was established in 1948. Both originated in Corpus Christi, Texas. Moreover, *Romo v. Laird* (1925) and *Mendez v. Westminster* (1947) were two early school desegregation cases. Recently, there has been tremendous scholarship published on early twentieth-century Mexican American activism. See Zamora, *Claiming Rights and Righting Wrongs*; Orozco, *No Mexicans, Women or Dogs Allowed*.

40 Ferber, *Giant*, 394.

41 While Leslie may be protected by race and class privilege, she is continuously exposed to injustice through patriarchy. Campbell, "'Written with a Hard and Ruthless Purpose,'" 39.

42 Ferber, *Giant*, 396.

43 Ibid., 395.

44 Ibid.

45 García, *White but Not Equal*; Gómez, *Manifest Destinies*.

46 Hendler, *Best-Sellers and Their Film Adaptations*, 120.

47 In his influential *White*, Dyer warns that the emphasis on extreme whiteness coexists with and is a distraction from ordinary whiteness. Here, the extreme may be the bigotry embodied in Sarge, while Bick can occupy a position of extreme goodness that reinstantiates the supremacy of everyday whiteness. Dyer, *White*, 222–23.

48 Graham, *Cowboys and Cadillacs*, 60.

49 This use of "papoose" evidences what Jane Hill refers to as the everyday language of white supremacy wherein people of color have been ascribed nonhuman taxonomic descriptors: "For Africans these were 'buck, wench (among other terms), pickaninny,' and for American Indians 'buck, squaw, papoose.' The unmarked English words 'man, woman, child' were used for Whites." Hill, *Everyday Language of White Racism*, 59.

50 Hendler, *Best-Sellers and Their Film Adaptations*, 139.

51 Dyer, *White*, 184.

52 Baxter, "*Giant* Helps America Recognize the Cost of Discrimination," 170; Hendler, *Best-Sellers and Their Film Adaptations*, 135.

53 Pérez-Torres, *Mestizaje*, 58.

54 Treviño, "Latino Portrayals," 4.

55 De León, *They Called Them Greasers*, 24–35.

56 Hendler, *Best-Sellers and Their Film Adaptations*, 135.

57 George Lipsitz makes an argument similar to this regarding the film *Lean on Me*. He contends that the movie and others like it feed fantasies of racial violence and

narratives of white supremacy without addressing the structural issues of racism. Lipsitz, *Possessive Investment in Whiteness*, 140–47.

58 Indeed, José Limón's *American Encounters* and Villanueva's *A Scene from the Movie GIANT* epitomize the disparate views of the film's racial logics. While both Limón and Villanueva watched the film initially from segregated theaters in Texas, Villanueva actively troubles the film's easy conclusion while Limón embraces the film as revolutionary for its time. Villanueva, *Scene from the Movie GIANT*; Limón, *American Encounters*, 119–24.

59 I learned about this incident from Michael Olivas's "'Trial of the Century' That Never Was" where he cites a now defunct online oral history of Dr. García once found at Justiceformypeople.org. Olivas, "'Trial of the Century' That Never Was," 1401n37.

60 Again I would like to thank Michael Olivas for introducing me to the case of Macario García. My retelling of the events relies upon Olivas's fact pattern of the case. Olivas, "'Trial of the Century' That Never Was," 1392–94.

61 Perales, *Are We Good Neighbors?*, 156–57.

62 Olivas, "'Trial of the Century' That Never Was," 1395.

63 Drawn from the September 27, 1945, article in the *Texas Coaster* as quoted in Olivas, "'Trial of the Century' That Never Was," 1393–94. This is contradicted by García's affidavit found in Perales, *Are We Good Neighbors?*, 156–57.

64 Drawn from the September 27, 1945, article in the *Texas Coaster* as quoted in Olivas, "'Trial of the Century' That Never Was," 1394.

65 Ibid., 1394.

66 Ibid.

67 Ibid.

68 Ibid.

69 Ibid., 1395n11.

70 Jodi Melamed contends that the years after World War II marked the rise of racial liberalism, wherein "the liberal race paradigm recognizes racial inequality as a problem, and it secures a liberal symbolic framework for race reform centered in abstract equality, market individualism, and inclusive civic nationalism. Antiracism becomes a nationally recognized social value and, for the first time, gets absorbed into U.S. governmentality. Importantly, postwar liberal racial formation sutures an 'official antiracism' to U.S. nationalism, itself bearing the agency for transnational capitalism" (2). Thus, the Macario García incident and the contestation over the meaning of race and racism in the United States fall within the larger national-racial project. One may find common ground between this case and Derrick Bell's reading of *Brown v. Board*. Bell argued, and was later proven correct, that the shift in the U.S. Supreme Court's attitude toward formal racial inequality was spurred in part by the interest of the United States not to appear racially oppressive to a global audience during the Cold War. That is, it would be difficult to win hearts and minds of third world peoples if the United States explicitly evidenced violence toward people of color at home. One can locate

the desire to foster beliefs in whitely, American goodness in the debate over the Macario García incident, which predated *Brown v. Board* by nine years. Melamed, "Spirit of Neoliberalism"; Bell, "Serving Two Masters"; Bell, "*Brown v. Board of Education* and the Interest Convergence Dilemma."

71 The September 27, 1945, article in the *Texas Coaster* as quoted in Olivas, "'Trial of the Century' That Never Was," 1394.

72 Perales, *Are We Good Neighbors?*, 156–57.

73 Martinot, *Machinery of Whiteness*, 66–75, 101, 107–11.

74 Ibid., 106–28.

75 Corkin, *Cowboys as Cold Warriors*, 179.

76 "Mexico Censors Brynner," 12; Schumach, "Producer Scores Mexican Censor," 25.

77 Notably this agency is also subordinated elsewhere in the movie. While the Mexicans are willing to fight, they must be armed and trained by the Americans. At one point the training is transformed into paternalizing humor. When one of the villagers is unable to hit a target with a rifle, his white instructor tells the Mexican to just wield the gun like a club. This encounter strikes at comic relief, but its laughter is rooted in the villager's inability to shoot straight and to wield the weapon appropriately. Despite this agency, *The Magnificent Seven* still deploys a paternalism reminiscent of *Giant*.

78 Critically, the U.S. culture industry has not ended this tradition of characters of color being played by white actors. Consider the 2012 film *Argo*, in which Ben Affleck played the lead role of the historical Mexican American figure Tony Mendez, or the 2015 film *Aloha*, for which Emma Stone was cast to play mixed-race Chinese/native Hawaiian/white Allison Ng. Today, however, Hollywood is reticent to put its white actors in brownface, and in the case of *Aloha* there was some public outcry. One should also note the interesting racial history of Bronson's career. While he played a half Mexican hero in *The Magnificent Seven*, he has also played Indian on film and enacted white fantasies of violence on urban youth of color in his *Death Wish* series.

79 Stinson, "'Magnificent Seven' Magnificent Western," C15; Scheuer, "Swords of Bushido Become Guns in 'Magnificent Seven,'" B3.

80 The goodness of the seven is also established through their treatment of the villagers. Initially, the men of the village send the women into hiding out of fear that the seven gunslingers might rape them. When the heroes discover this, Chris jokes that they might rape the women but they would have appreciated the benefit of the doubt. This humorous moment both gestures to the threat of sexual violence and solidifies the U.S. whites as chivalrous heroes. Moreover, after the seven learn that the villagers are going hungry while the gunmen eat, the white heroes are shown serving food to the villagers.

81 Usually scholars locate the rise of the revisionist Western with later films. However, I believe that many of the elements of the revisionist Western (e.g., questioning the social order, interrogation of inequality, and not-quite-stock characters in the protagonists) are evidenced in these films.

82 Corkin, *Cowboys as Cold Warriors*, 180.

83 Here one might suggest that the evolution of the Western genre shares a similar trajectory to broader discourses and ideologies of white supremacy, for across the mid-twentieth century, the Western shifted from a simplified good/bad dichotomy to more complex iterations that often ultimately reinforced the social order.

84 While all of the seven gunmen undergo some transformation, these changes are less notable in characters who receive less development.

85 Alarcón, *Aztec Palimpsest*, 40.

86 I would be remiss if I did not point out that Chico simply translates to "boy." Here one must question whether this is his actual name or if it simply reinforces a type of infantilization on the one Mexican member of the seven.

87 Kennedy, *The Return of the Seven*.

88 Here I am troping upon former Mexican President Porfirio Díaz, who is attributed with coining the phrase "¡Pobre México! ¡Tan lejos de Dios y tan cerca de los Estados Unidos!" (Poor Mexico, so far from God and so close to the United States!).

89 Brooks, *The Professionals*.

90 "April Starts Off Busy."

91 "Laredo Border Patrol Sector Agents."

92 For my analysis of the Border Patrol rescue narrative, I sampled and examined press releases from 2013 to 2015. Between January 1, 2013, and June 1, 2015, CBP issued over 3,300 media releases covering a variety of subjects. Over 350 (or 10 percent) of those releases mentioned some form of rescue.

93 In a discussion of cultural memory and minstrelsy, Cedric Robinson has made a similar argument about the force of images repeated over time to become naturalized and racially armed without intent. Robinson, *Forgeries of Memory and Meaning*, 189.

94 "Joint CBP Efforts in El Paso"; "Border Patrol Rescues Three Individuals"; "CBP Office of Air and Marine."

95 "Joint Efforts Save Another Life."

96 "Temperatures, Dangers on Rise in Arizona."

97 "Rio Grande Valley Border Patrol Agents Rescue Immigrants."

98 "Alleged Human Smuggling Attempt."

99 "Rio Grande Valley Border Patrol Agents Rescue 35 People at Falfurrias Checkpoint"; "Border Patrol Rescues 49 People within 24 Hours"; "Rio Grande Valley Sector Border Patrol Agents"; "Border Patrol Agents Halt Human Smuggling Attempts."

100 "Border Patrol Agents Rescue Illegal Immigrants."

101 "Del Rio Border Patrol Agents Rescue Drowning Victim."

102 "CBP Rescues Hitchhiking Baby Squirrel."

103 "Human Trafficking."

104 This useful phrase is actually repeated verbatim in at least two of the press releases, perhaps indicating the rote nature of this genre and the narrative it

constructs. "Joint Border Patrol, Office of Air and Marine Effort Saves Man's Life"; "Border Patrol Agents in Texas Save 4; Find Remains."

105 "Rio Grande Valley Agents Rescue 36 Illegal Immigrants; Pregnant Woman."

106 Importantly, the U.S. military is used to deliver humanitarian aid for both manmade (e.g., refugee crises and the destruction caused through warfare) and natural disasters (e.g., earthquakes, tsunamis).

107 This is arguably the same for international cases of humanitarian aid as well, for the U.S. public is as much the rhetorical audience as international victims are the recipients of aid.

108 Shemak, *Asylum Speakers*, 88–130.

109 Ibid., 89, 94–96.

110 For sample discussions of the economic impact of NAFTA and the effects of Operation Gatekeeper, see Urrea, *Devil's Highway*, 45–47, 58–59.

111 Ibid., 43–53, 23.

112 Ibid., 18.

113 "Border Patrol Rescues Three Individuals"; "Border Patrol Agents Assist Citizens"; "Border Patrol Rescues Two Migrants from Desert."

114 Urrea, *Devil's Highway*, 59–60.

115 Ibid., 17.

116 Ionide, "Alchemy of Race and Affect," 154.

117 Ibid., 155.

118 McKenzie, "No More 'Allies.'"

119 Shih, "What Happened to White Privilege?"

CHAPTER 4. DEEP IN THE HEART OF WHITENESS

1 Buffett, "Margaritaville."

2 Perhaps unsurprisingly, there is a strong tradition in country music of not just traveling to Mexico but also engaging in drunken revelry while there. For an example, see Max Stalling's "Drunk in Mexico."

3 These are but two examples. One could also consider representations of Mexicanas in *A Fistful of Dollars* or *The Magnificent Seven*. Vidor, *Duel in the Sun*; Peckinpah, *The Wild Bunch*; Leone, *A Fistful of Dollars*; Sturges, *The Magnificent Seven*.

4 In *Manifest Manners*, Vizenor explores how representations and simulations of Native peoples can work to enable the discursive and imaginative components of colonization. In particular, I find Vizenor's repetition of "This portrait is not an Indian" to be a key point of departure for my own thinking. Vizenor initially deploys this phrase as a way of distinguishing between Andy Warhol's portrait of Russell Means and Russell Means himself. Vizenor reiterates the phrase throughout the chapter to challenge how various representations and simulations cannot and should not be confused with a constructed-as-authentic indigeneity signified through the term "Indian." Through Vizenor, I find a model for how racialized simulations of an "authentic" Other are fashioned. In stating "this is *not* a Mexi-

cana," I draw upon Vizenor to illustrate the discursive and cultural work of these tropes. Emerging out of the white imagination (what Vizenor might call a place of manifest manners), these simulations can be readily confused with reality. Vizenor, *Manifest Manners*, 18.

5 There is also a rich history of U.S. cinema putting white male actors in brownface. In cases of men and women dressing in brownface or racial costuming, one can see that the racial discourses and social meanings affix to the body along with the makeup or clothing.

6 I have changed the names of these individuals to ensure anonymity. Moreover, the purpose of this anecdote is to focus less on the individuals and more on the discursive maneuvers deployed.

7 Emphasis mine.

8 Drew Lopenzina describes "unwitnessing" as "not simply the conscious act of turning a blind eye. Nor is it the result, necessarily, of ignorance or an utter failure of imagination. *Unwitnessing* is the largely passive decision to maintain a particular narrative structure by keeping undesirable aspects of cultural memory repressed or inactive." Lopenzina, *Red Ink*, 9.

9 Nor should Jeff be simply written off as the caricature of an unredeemable bigot. As Patricia Williams so astutely argues, life and people are complicated. I have known Jeff for many years, and while I find these comments and attitudes repugnant, I must also acknowledge that he does genuinely care for nonwhite members of my family. The effort here is not to demonize Jeff or to provide him a get-out-of-racism-free card because of his ability to love. Rather, I seek to put pressure on the ability of these seemingly incompatible aspects to exist in tandem. Williams, *Alchemy of Race and Rights*, 10.

10 Chin and Chan, "Racist Love."

11 Lipsitz, *Possessive Investment in Whiteness*, 118.

12 As Morrison and others have noted, a romantic obsession with liberal individualism has long been a part of the ideological foundation for U.S. white supremacy. In his analysis, Lipsitz also points to how cleaving the objects of white desire from collective treatment and casting them as individuals allows for white supremacy to remove white people from culpability or claims of collective benefit. Morrison, *Playing in the Dark*, 44; Lipsitz, *Possessive Investment in Whiteness*, 120.

13 Said, *Orientalism*, 6.

14 Hyam, *Empire and Sexuality*.

15 McClintock, *Imperial Leather*, 15.

16 For example, see McClintock's chapter "No Longer in a Future Heaven" for a discussion of how gender, time, and historical memory are deployed by nationalist projects. Ibid., 352–89.

17 Hooks, "Eating the Other," 24.

18 Ibid., 23.

19 Alarcón, *Aztec Palimpsest*, xiv.

20 Said, *Orientalism*, 5–8.

21 The borders between musical genres are far from rigid. These musicians may also be classified as Alt (i.e., Alternative) country or Red Dirt music, signaling an Oklahoma/North Texas regional influence. For the sake of consistency and because it is a fairly well-recognized musical tradition, I use "Texas country" throughout this chapter.

22 Here we may redeploy Anderson's concept of the nation as an imagined community. Rather than an emphasis strictly on print culture, I would contend that radio and other discursive locations also foster an imagined community not just through "homogenous empty time" but through discourse and ideology. Moreover, these racial tropes particularly function to imagine community through who belongs, who does not belong, and how one does or does not belong in the nation imagined. Anderson, *Imagined Communities*, 24, 37–46.

23 Zac Brown Band, "Toes." For some, the reference to "islands" may initially signal the Caribbean rather than Mexico. One may contend that the reference to "pesos" indicates a likelihood of Mexico and that Mexico too has islands. However, I think the deployment of "pesos" and "islands" more likely suggests some form of fungibility of Latinidad in the U.S. white racial imagination. Zac Brown Band is from Georgia and closer to the Caribbean, but they engage in a musical tradition deeply influenced by Texas and the U.S.-Mexico border. In this way, we see how all Latinas/os may be pulled into and ascribed meaning through whiteness on the border as racial scripts are not sticklers for accuracy.

24 Limón, *American Encounters*, 113–27.

25 Ibid., 111–13.

26 Ibid., 124.

27 Earlier in his chapter Limón also articulates his experience of watching *Giant* in a segregated theater and mentions that Tino Villanueva also wrote a collection of poetry based on a similar experience (119). What Limón elides is the way in which Villanueva problematizes the white benevolence and racial dynamics of *Giant*, exposing how white supremacy works in less direct ways. For greater discussion of Villanueva's poetry, see Bebout, "Troubling White Benevolence"; Limón, *American Encounters*, 124–25; Villanueva, *Scene from the Movie GIANT*.

28 Limón, *American Encounters*, 129.

29 In his *Dancing with the Devil*, Limón deploys Gramsci's model of "war of maneuver" and "war of position" to describe the relationships between Anglos and Tejanos in South Texas. In *American Encounters*, he engages these terms again, but to articulate that ambivalences found in 1950s texts like *High Noon* are "tactical victories" for Mexican Americans. In contrast, I would suggest that these may be seen as victories for Mexican Americans, but they allow for a long-term (i.e., strategic) victory for white supremacy as it functions through a "war of position." Limón, *Dancing with the Devil*, 15, 25; Limón, *American Encounters*, 117.

30 Snow, *Award Winners* (1971) and Weller, *The Promised Land* (1972).

31 Haggard and Nelson, "Seashores of Old Mexico."

32 Strait, "Seashores of Old Mexico."

33 Those familiar with the song may note that the singer is not explicitly racialized as white. However, that invisibility and unmarkedness is exactly how whiteness works. For an insightful examination of this, see Chambers, "Unexamined."

34 The song adds an "s" to the name of the city, making it Manzanillos. However, that is likely just an error on Haggard's part.

35 Haggard and Nelson, "Seashores of Old Mexico."

36 Ibid.

37 De León, *They Called Them Greasers*, 39–48.

38 Mulvey, "Visual Pleasure and Narrative Cinema."

39 Yancy, *Look, A White!*, 2–3, 109–10.

40 Bebout, "Washing Education White."

41 Haggard and Nelson, "Seashores of Old Mexico."

42 Browne, "Race," 9.

43 Rich, "Compulsory Heterosexuality and Lesbian Existence."

44 In a strange way, this tradition within the U.S. white racial imagination bears striking similarity to the nationalist and patriarchal deployments of la Malinche. Also known as Doña Marina and Malintzin, la Malinche is the name ascribed to the translator and sexual consort of Hernán Cortés. Within nationalist and patriarchal rhetoric, she is often described as a traitor to her people. Indeed, during the Chicano movement Chicana feminists would be policed by this term. That is, those who were seen as affiliating with ideas of whiteness were scripted as Malinches, sellouts, and traitors. While it is doubtful that country music is tapped into the patriarchal anxieties of Greater Mexico, this similarity illustrates how women's bodies are used to discursively manifest racial and national power.

45 Thanks to María DeGuzmán for pointing out the similarities here. We should also note that the subtlety of this tropic move is important as it exposes a power of whiteness. That is, the video's protagonist has no danger of being scripted as a lazy and sleeping fellow. He is white, is seen as an individual, and will not have negative characteristics ascribed to his race.

46 Schaeffer, *Love and Empire*, 66–67.

47 Du Bois, *Black Reconstruction*, 700–701; Roediger, *Wages of Whiteness*, 12–13.

48 Notably, Alverson pronounces this line with the stereotypical "spiggoty English." Juan Vidal has argued that this pronunciation of "speak the English" as "spiggoty English" emerged from U.S. encounters in Panama and is the origin for the anti-Latina/o term "spic." While this is likely an unintentional connection for Alverson, the discursive and ideological connections are revealing. Vidal, "Spic-O-Rama"; Alverson, "Una Más Cerveza."

49 Alverson, "Una Más Cerveza."

50 Ibid.

51 Stalling, "Drunk in Mexico."

52 Here one must note how the phrase "My latino lolita" demonstrates both the hypersexualized excess of this trope and how Mexico occupies a space of sexual lawlessness in the U.S. imagination. Moreover, this moment elucidates some deeply

troubling aspects of the ways in which U.S. white masculinity can be imagined. Fowler, "Señorita Más Fina."

53 Ibid.
54 Keen, *West Textures*; Strait, *One Step at a Time.*
55 Keen, "Maria."
56 Ibid.
57 Alarcón, *Aztec Palimpsest*, 40.
58 Keen, "Maria."
59 Said, *Orientalism*, 53–60; Mills, *Racial Contract*, 41–53.
60 Keen, *West Textures.*
61 Bonilla-Silva, *Racism without Racists*, 26.
62 Cofer, "Myth of the Latin Woman," 148, 151–52.
63 Notably, both de León and Ruiz recognize that the explicit white supremacy of the earlier era produced a contradictory impulse where Mexicanas were rendered desirable and not desirable (i.e., forbidden or unattractive). Arguably, the post-break era sees a rise in desirable and desiring Mexicana. However, this is not to say that Mexicanas are always cast as such. Consider that that nativist discourse surrounding anchor babies and Mexican fertility forms an oppositional pole in the construction of Mexicanas as desirable. Moreover, referring to the Porfiriato, Ruiz suggests that U.S. white men found Mexicanas desirable in part "because they posed not no threat to American manhood, which many politicians and cultural workers understood to be threatened in the late nineteenth century" (61). I would extend Ruiz's analysis, arguing instead that beyond posing no threat, Mexicanas and their construction as desirable and desiring actively shored up white masculinity. De León, *They Called Them Greasers*, 39–48; Ruiz, *Americans in the Treasure House*, 21, 61, 136.
64 These websites specializing in international matchmaking occupy a similar role to historical mail-order bride services. The ones that I mention have pages that specialize in and articulate a market for Mexican and Latin American women. However, a quick search will also identify similar sites catering to those in search of Russian or Eastern European brides.
65 Emphasis mine.
66 Thompson, *Cowboy Cupid*, 6.
67 Ohayon, *Cowboy del Amor.*
68 Thompson, *Cowboy Cupid*, 9.
69 See amolatino.com and rosebrides.com.
70 Campbell, "Cultural Seduction," 261–62, 272, 275.
71 Ibid.; Schaeffer, *Love and Empire*, 4, 20, 60.
72 Campbell, "Cultural Seduction," 270; Schaeffer, *Love and Empire*, 78–92.
73 Campbell, "Cultural Seduction," 273.
74 Thompson, *Cowboy Cupid*, 40.
75 Ibid., 42.
76 Ibid., 43.
77 Ibid., 43.

78 Again we are reminded of Gerald Vizenor's "'This portrait is not an Indian" from *Manifest Manners*. These websites are depicting not Mexicanas but simulations, discursive tropes that emerge from and activate the U.S. white imagination. For a greater discussion of Vizenor, see note 4 of this chapter.

79 Campbell, "Cultural Seduction," 277.

80 Thompson, *Cowboy Cupid*, 6.

81 Schaeffer, *Love and Empire*, 78–92.

82 Lipsitz, *Possessive Investment in Whiteness*, 50.

83 Thompson, *Cowboy Cupid*, 20.

84 Ibid., 22.

85 Kaplan, "Manifest Domesticity."

86 This scripting of Mexican women as more traditional than U.S. women is not limited to U.S. whites. As Gordillo notes, some Mexican-descent men in the United States also describe women from Mexico as more "attractive" because they are more "traditional" than Chicanas and Mexican immigrant women who have spent time in the United States. This connection between U.S. white and Mexican-descent men looking south for attractive and traditional partners suggests an interesting nexus of the logics of white supremacy, heteropatriarchy, and national imaginations. Gordillo, *Mexican Women and the Other Side of Immigration*, 60.

87 Schaeffer, *Love and Empire*, 4.

88 Thompson, *Cowboy Cupid*, 28.

89 Ibid.

90 Haney López, *White by Law*, 18.

91 Bebout, "Postracial Mestizaje."

92 Indeed, many critics note how whiteness is ascribed connotations of virtue, goodness, purity, and morality. Feagin, *White Racial Frame*, 56, 68, 90, 126; Dyer, *White*, 17, 63.

93 Melamed, *Represent and Destroy*, 169.

94 As an introduction to the story, Thompson recalls beating his Mexican house-mates in a game of poker. Afterward, with the help of a translating friend, Thompson tells the Mexicanos that "if they messed with me or my money, I'd shoot their eyeballs out." This brief vignette proves interesting in that it elicits the trope of Mexicans as thieves, suggests that the white cowboys outsmarted (i.e., outplayed) and outmanned the Mexicanos, and foreshadows the future dehumanization of these men through the dog food incident. Thompson, *Cowboy Cupid*, 45.

95 Thompson, *Cowboy Cupid*, 46.

96 "Strategic color blindness" is a rhetorical tactic in which colorblind discourses are deployed in order to conceal white supremacy and racially disparate impacts. Bebout, "Washing Education White"; Thompson, *Cowboy Cupid*, 47–48.

97 Thompson, *Cowboy Cupid*, 49.

98 Toward the end of the anecdote, Thompson notes that men from the association that coordinated Mexican workers investigated the incident. Here, one must wonder if Thompson's Mexican housemates were braceros. If so, might they have

expected him to cook for them as part of their labor conditions? Moreover, they may have expected him to do so because he was younger than they were. In either case, Thompson's narrative gestures toward and occludes a wealth of possibilities.

99 Ibid., 47, emphasis mine.

100 Ibid., 51.

101 Mills, *Racial Contract*, 53–62; Santa Ana, "Like an Animal I Was Treated."

102 Thompson, *Cowboy Cupid*, 50.

103 The frontstage/backstage dynamic is an interesting inversion of the African American hush harbor tradition where barbershops and other spaces racialized as black allow for more open conversations about race and power. While hush harbors have their roots in slavery, one might suggest that the frontstage/backstage dynamics is particularly rooted in the post-break era when explicitly racist discourse must be hidden from mixed audiences. Feagin, *White Racial Frame*, 123–38; Nunley, *Keepin' It Hushed*.

104 Ladenburg, "Illuminating Whiteness and Racial Prejudice."

105 Thompson, *Cowboy Cupid*, 51.

106 Levine, "Whoa, Nelly."

107 O'Brien, "Palm Springs Film Festival."

108 Ibid.

109 This image of Bush and cowboy masculinity traveled far during his presidency. In 2006, when Sujey and I visited Istanbul, Turkey, for a conference, we found ourselves engaged in a memorable conversation in a local shop. The proprietor asked us where in the United States we were from. While we were both completing our PhDs in the Midwest, I answered that we were both from Texas. In response, the proprietor smiled, said "oh, George Bush," and put his hands to his sides and pretended to draw pistols and shoot "pow pow." Turner, *Frontier in American History*, 18, 30.

110 Ibid., 2.

111 Ibid., 18; Morrison, *Playing in the Dark*, 44.

112 Turner, *Frontier in American History*, 22, 23.

113 Baldwin makes a similar argument when he describes the loss of European ethnic identities as part of the price people paid for their entrance into whiteness. Baldwin, *Price of the Ticket*, xix–xx.

114 For an insightful critique and reimagining of Turner's frontier thesis, see Patricia Nelson Limerick's "Turnerians All."

115 Turner, *Frontier in American History*, 1.

116 Schaeffer, *Love and Empire*, 89–92.

117 Huggins, *Harlem Renaissance*, 298–301.

118 Jameson, "Reification and Utopia," 146–47.

119 McCarthy, *All the Pretty Horses*.

120 Grassley, "Prepared Statement."

121 Here one may see this as yet another triangulation against U.S. feminists. This time, however, immigrant (read: Mexican and Latin American) women are rendered as potential threats in order to hinder domestic violence protections for

all women. Moreover, Representative James Sensenbrenner, who had sponsored the 2005 anti-immigration HB 4437 and Senator Grassley also feared that VAWA would give undue protections to Native women against non-Native abusers. Here, anti-immigrant and anti-Indigenous politics work to organize a logic the sexual-racial hierarchies in the home. Immigrant women and Indigenous women are positioned as lesser citizens undeserving of legal protections from abuse. At the same time, these racialized women as discursive tropes were used to obstruct the bill, a move that could protect white men who batter white women as well.

122 For her meditation on the obstacles between women of color and white women in particular, see Lugones, *Pilgrimages/Peregrinajes*, 65–75.

123 Ibid., 77.

124 Ibid., 78.

125 Ibid., 96.

126 Ibid., 97, emphasis original.

127 Ingram, "Inna from Mexico."

128 Ibid.

129 Ibid.

130 Ibid.

131 Schaeffer, *Love and Empire*, 32, 87–92.

132 Dixie Chicks, "Long Time Gone."

133 Padilla, *My History, Not Yours*, 16, 31.

134 This is, of course, not without complication. In an earlier chapter, Lugones draws on Spelman's "boomerang perception" that is ultimately self-centered: "I look at you and come right back to myself. White children in the U.S. got early training in boomerang perception when they were told by well-meaning white adults that Black people were just like us—never, however, that we were just like Blacks." Here, one must ask if such a move is being made with the Dixie Chicks' video. That is, are viewers asked to think of Mexicans like white southerners, or are they asked to think of themselves being like Mexicans? Lugones, *Pilgrimages/Peregrinajes*, 71; Spelman, *Inessential Woman*, 12.

135 Olson, *Abolition of White Democracy*, 16–17.

136 In an effort to avoid the trap of romance, one must ask if such an excursion embodies the "world" traveling Lugones advocates of the colonialist adventure she warns against. Here it would be useful to consider two aspects that stand out regarding the video for "Long Time Gone." First, there is one scene where a young man "checks out" a member of the Dixie Chicks by looking at her rear. This moment is ripe for analysis when considering race, gender, and the gaze. Second, when discussing the making of the video, one of the Chicks, Martie Maguire, joked, "We tried to pick the seediest place we could find." This is a rich moment, yet the reporting on this comment does not provide context or analysis. Was Maguire attempting to address and subvert stereotypes of Mexico and border towns in particular? Or was she reinforcing those images? That is, was she challenging or reinscribing whiteness on the border? Orr, "'Long Time Gone' Video Arrives."

CONCLUSION

1 Mendoza, *Journey around Our America*.
2 Griffin, "At 50, Still Love or Hate at First Sight."
3 See www.thesouthoftheborder.com.
4 For a discussion of other regional discourses of hospitality and how they can mask racial injustice, see Vega, *Latino Heartland*.
5 Rancière, *Politics of Aesthetics*, 7.
6 Rockhill, "Introduction," xii.
7 Pease, *New American Exceptionalism*, 22.
8 Ibid., 7, 12.
9 Mills, *Racial Contract*, 18, emphasis original.
10 Molina, *How Race Is Made in America*, 6–7, 11, 150.
11 Here, Ruiz de Burton's call for a cross-ethnic alliance of whites mirrors the cross-class alliance of rich and working-class whites described by Joel Olson. Ruiz de Burton, *Squatter and the Don*, 344; Olson, *Abolition of White Democracy*, xxiv, 16–17.
12 Molina, *How Race Is Made in America*, 40; Nieto-Phillips, *Language of Blood*.
13 Behnken, *Fighting Their Own Battles*.
14 García, *White but Not Equal*, 164–86.
15 Ruiz de Burton, *Squatter and the Don*; González and Raleigh, *Caballero*.
16 Saldaña-Portillo, "Who's the Indian in Aztlán?"
17 Bag, *Violence Girl*, 103.
18 Skyhorse, *Madonnas of Echo Park*, 155.
19 Williams, *Alchemy of Race and Rights*, 11; Gordon, *Ghostly Matters*, 3–5.
20 Hall, "Gramsci's Relevance," 16, 25.
21 Ibid., 18, 27.
22 While whiteness strives to achieve invisibility, we must recognize that it cannot maintain this position. Indeed, whiteness is often quite visible to people of color. Indeed, such an observation may complicate Rancière as that which is outside the sensible for some may be hypervisible to others.
23 For example, Thandeka has proposed naming whiteness rather than letting it go unmarked. George Yancy has drawn on Frantz Fanon to invert the gaze and make white behavior legible with the phrase "look, a white!" Thandeka, *Learning to Be White*; Yancy, *Look, a White!*
24 Russell, "Who's Gonna Build Your Wall?"
25 Omi and Winant, *Racial Formation*, 84–88.
26 Interestingly, the term "gringo" evidences a similar slippage to white and American, for it can be deployed to mean both simultaneously.
27 Gómez-Peña, *New World Border*, 1–3.
28 Gómez-Peña, *Warrior for Gringostroika*, 139.
29 Leonard, "'I Just Look Illegal.'"
30 Bebout, "Skin in the Game."

BIBLIOGRAPHY

Abani, Chris. "The Cost of Change." Presentation at Texas A&M University, November 28, 2007.

Acosta, Oscar "Zeta." *Autobiography of a Brown Buffalo.* 1972. Reprint, New York: Vintage, 1989.

———. *Revolt of the Cockroach People.* 1973. Reprint, New York: Vintage, 1989.

Acuña, Rodolfo. *Occupied America: The Chicano's Struggle toward Liberation.* San Francisco: Canfield Press, 1972.

Alarcón, Daniel Cooper. *The Aztec Palimpsest: Mexico in the Modern Imagination.* Tucson: University of Arizona Press, 1997.

Almaguer, Tomás. *Racial Fault Lines: The Historical Origins of White Supremacy in California.* Berkeley: University of California Press, 1994.

Aloha. Directed by Cameron Crowe. Sony Pictures, 2015. DVD.

Alverson, Tommy. "Una Más Cerveza." Tommy Alverson, Willie Nelson, and W. Seth Russell. *Alive and Pickin.* Smith Entertainment, 2003. CD.

Anaya, Rudolfo A. "Aztlán: A Homeland without Boundaries." In Anaya and Lomelí, *Aztlán,* 230–41.

Anaya, Rudolfo A., and Francisco A. Lomelí, ed. *Aztlán: Essays of the Chicano Homeland.* Albuquerque: University of New Mexico Press, 1989.

Anderson, Benedict. *Imagined Communities: Reflections on the Origin and Spread of Nationalism.* Rev. ed. New York: Verso, 1991.

Anzaldúa, Gloria. *Borderlands/La Frontera: The New Mestiza.* 3rd ed. 1987. San Francisco: Aunt Lute, 2007.

Arendt, Dave. *Reclaiming Aztlan.* Baltimore: Publish America, 2007.

Argo. Directed by Ben Affleck. Warner Brothers, 2012. DVD.

Bag, Alice. *Violence Girl: East L.A. Rage to Hollywood Stage, A Chicana Punk Story.* Port Townsend, WA: Feral House, 2011.

Baker, Houston A. *Blues, Ideology, and Afro-American Literature: A Vernacular Theory.* Chicago: University of Chicago Press, 1984.

Baker-Cristales, Beth. "Mediated Resistance: The Construction of Neoliberal Citizenship in the Immigrant Rights Movement." *Latino Studies* 7.1 (2009): 60–82.

Baldwin, James. *The Price of the Ticket: Collected Nonfiction, 1948–1985.* New York: St. Martin's, 1985.

Baxter, Monique James. "*Giant* Helps America Recognize the Cost of Discrimination: A Lesson of World War II." In *Hollywood's West: The American Frontier in Film,*

Television, and History, edited by Peter C. Rollins and John E. O'Connor, 60–172. Lexington: University Press of Kentucky, 2009.

Beamish, Rita. "Latino Organization Unable to Shake Accusations of Racism, Conservative Activists Vow to Dog MEChA." *Boston Globe*, September 5, 2004, 3rd ed., A23.

Bebout, Lee. "Hero Making in El Movimietno: Reies López Tijerina and the Chicano Nationalist Imaginary." *Aztlán: A Journal of Chicano Studies* 32.2 (2007): 93–121.

———. *Mythohistorical Interventions: The Chicano Movement and Its Legacies*. Minneapolis: University of Minnesota Press, 2011.

———. "Postracial Mestizaje: Richard Rodriguez's Racial Imagination in an America Where Everyone Is Beginning to Melt." *American Studies* 54.1 (2015): 89–113.

———. "Skin in the Game: Toward a Theorization of Whiteness in the Classroom." *Pedagogy* 14.2 (2014): 343–54.

———. "Troubling White Benevolence: Four Takes on a Scene from *Giant*." *MELUS* 36.3 (2011): 13–36.

———. "Washing Education White." In *Rhetorics of Whiteness: Postracial Culture, Social Media, and Education*, edited by Tammie Kennedy, Joyce Middleton, and Krista Ratcliffe. Carbondale: Southern Illinois University Press, forthcoming.

Behnken, Brian. *Fighting Their Own Battles: Mexican Americans, African Americans, and the Struggle for Civil Rights in Texas*. Chapel Hill: University of North Carolina Press, 2011.

Bell, Derrick. "*Brown v. Board of Education* and the Interest Convergence Dilemma." In Delgado and Stefancic, *Derrick Bell Reader*, 33–39.

———. "Serving Two Masters." In Delgado and Stefancic, *Derrick Bell Reader*, 99–109.

Bender, Thomas. "Wholes and Parts: The Need for Synthesis in American History." *Journal of American History* 73.1 (1986): 120–36.

Blackmon, Douglas A. *Slavery by Another Name: The Re-enslavement of Black Americans from the Civil War to World War II*. New York: Anchor, 2009.

Bonilla-Silva, Eduardo. *Racism without Racists: Color-Blind Racism and Racial Inequality in Contemporary America*. 3rd ed. New York: Rowman & Littlefield, 2010.

Brilliant, Mark. *The Color of America Has Changed: How Racial Diversity Shaped Civil Rights Reform in California, 1941–1978*. New York: Oxford University Press, 2010.

Browne, Nick. "Race: The Political Unconscious of American Film." *East-West Film Journal* 6 (1992): 5–16.

Buchanan, Patrick J. *The Death of the West: How Dying Populations and Immigrant Invasions Imperil Our Country and Civilization*. New York: St. Martin's Griffin, 2002.

———. *State of Emergency: The Third World Invasion and Conquest of America*. New York: St. Martin's, 2006.

Buffett, Jimmy. "Margaritaville." Jimmy Buffett. *Changes in Latitudes, Changes in Attitudes*. 1977. Geffen, 1987. CD.

Burke, Kenneth. *The Philosophy of Literary Form: Studies in Symbolic Action*. Baton Rouge: Louisiana State University Press, 1967.

Cacho, Lisa Marie. "But Some of Us Are Wise: Academic Illegitimacy and the Affective Value of Ethnic Studies." *Black Scholar* 40.4 (2010): 28–36.

———. "'The People of California Are Suffering': The Ideology of White Injury in Discourses of Immigration." *Cultural Values* 4.4 (2000): 389–418.

Calavita, Kitty. "The New Politics of Immigration: 'Balanced-Budget Conservatism' and the Symbolism of Proposition 187." *Social Problems* 43.3 (1996): 284–305.

"California Candidate Owes Public an Apology." *Dallas Morning News*, September 9, 2003.

Cambium Learning. "Curriculum Audit of the Mexican American Studies Department, Tucson Unified School District." May 2, 2011.

Cammarota, Julio. "The Generational Battle for Curriculum: Figuring Race and Culture on the Border." *Transforming Anthropology* 17.2 (2009): 117–30.

Campbell, Donna. "'Written with a Hard and Ruthless Purpose': Rose Wilder lane, Edna Ferber, and Middlebrow Regional Fiction." In *Middlebrow Moderns: Popular American Women Writers of the 1920s*, edited by Meredith Goldsmith and Lisa Botshon, 25–44. Boston: Northeastern University Press, 2003.

Campbell, Howard. "Cultural Seduction: American Men, Mexican Women, Cross-Border Attraction." *Critique of Anthropology* 27.3 (2007): 261–83.

Carl, A. S. "Absolut Stupidity." *Donklephant*, April 8, 2008.

Cervantes, Lorna Dee. "Poem for the Young White Man Who Asked Me How I, an Intelligent, Well-Read Person, Could Believe in the War between Races." In *Making Face, Making Soul, Haciendo Caras: Creative and Critical Perspectives by Feminists of Color*, edited by Gloria Anzaldua, 4–5. San Francisco: Aunt Lute Books, 1990.

Chabram-Dernersesian, Angie. "On the Social Construction of Whiteness within Selected Chicana/o Discourse." In *Displacing Whiteness: Essays in Social and Cultural Criticism*, edited by Ruth Frankenberg, 107–64. Durham, NC: Duke University Press, 1997.

Chambers, Ross. "The Unexamined." In Hill, *Whiteness*, 187–203.

Chávez, John R. *The Lost Land: The Chicano Image of the Southwest*. Albuquerque: University of New Mexico Press, 1986.

Chavez, Leo. "Immigration Reform and Nativism: The Nationalist Response to the Transnationalist Challenge." In Perea, *Immigrants Out!*, 61–77.

———. *The Latino Threat: Constructing Immigrants, Citizens, and the Nation*. Stanford: Stanford University Press, 2008.

Chavez, Linda. *Out of the Barrio: Toward a New Politics of Hispanic Assimilation*. New York: Basic Books, 1991.

Children of Giant. Directed by Hector Galan. Public Broadcasting Service, 2015. DVD.

Chin, Frank, and Jeffery Paul Chan. "Racist Love." *Chin Talks*, August 3, 2008. http://chintalks.blogspot.com.

Clark, D. Anthony, and Tamilia D. Reed. "A Future We Wish to See: Racialized Communities Studies after White Racial Anxiety and Resentment." *Black Scholar* 40.4 (2010): 37–49.

Clark, Lauren. "White Professor Teaches 'Problem of Whiteness' Course at Arizona State." *Campus Reform*, January 22, 2015. http://campusreform.org.

Cofer, Judith Ortíz. "The Myth of the Latin Woman." In *The Latin Deli: Telling the Lives of Barrio Women*, 148–54. New York: Norton, 1993.

Cohn, Nate. "More Hispanics Declaring Themselves White." *New York Times*, May 21, 2014. www.nytimes.com.

Coleman, Terry. "Terry Coleman on the Border: Learning to Live with el Future Americano/Language Problems for Mexican Immigrants in the U.S." *Guardian*, August 28, 1986.

Cope, R. Douglas. *The Limits of Racial Domination: Plebeian Society in Colonial Mexico City, 1660–1720*. Madison: University of Wisconsin Press, 1994.

Corkin, Stanley. *Cowboys as Cold Warriors: The Western and U.S. History*. Philadelphia: Temple University Press, 2004.

Corwin, Arthur F., and Johnny M. McCain. "Wetbackism since 1964: A Catalogue of Factors." In *Immigrants—and Immigrants: Perspectives on Mexican Labor Migration to the United States*, edited by Arthur F. Corwin, 67–107. Westport, CT: Greenwood, 1978.

Cowboy del Amor. Directed by Michèle Ohayon. 2005. Magnolia Home Entertainment, 2009. DVD.

Creager, Roger. "Long Way to Mexico." Jeremy Elliot and Roger Creager. *Long Way to Mexico*. Dualtone Music Group, 2003. CD.

Dain, Bruce. *A Hideous Monster of the Mind: American Race Theory in the Early Republic*. Cambridge, MA: Harvard University Press, 2003.

Dana, Richard Henry, Jr. *Two Years before the Mast*. 1840. Reprint, New York: Signet Classics, 2009.

Dávila, Arlene. *Latinos Inc.: The Marketing and Making of a People*. Berkeley: University of California Press, 2001.

———. *Latino Spin: Public Image and the Whitewashing of Race*. New York: New York University Press, 2008.

De Genova, Nickolas. *Working the Boundaries: Race, Space, and "Illegality" in Mexican Chicago*. Durham, NC: Duke University Press, 2005.

de León, Arnoldo. *They Called Them Greasers: Anglo Attitudes toward Mexicans in Texas, 1821–1900*. Austin: University of Texas, 1983.

Delgado, Richard, and Jean Stefancic, eds. *The Derrick Bell Reader*. New York: New York University Press, 2005.

Dixie Chicks. "Long Time Gone." Darrell Scott. *Home*. Sony, 2002. CD.

Djurdjevic, Bob. "When Cultures Collide. . . ." *Washington Times*, August 18, 1996, final ed., B5.

Du Bois, W. E. B. *Black Reconstruction in the United States, 1860–1880*. New York: Free Press, 1998.

Duel in the Sun. Directed by King Vidor. 1946. MGM, 2004. DVD.

Dyer, Richard. *White*. New York: Routledge, 1997.

Espinoza, Alex. *The Five Acts of Diego Leon*. New York: Random House, 2013.

Feagin, Joe. "Old Poison in New Bottles: The Deep Roots of Modern Nativism." In Perea, *Immigrants Out!*, 13–43.

———. *The White Racial Frame: Centuries of Racial Framing and Counter-framing.* New York: Routledge, 2009.

Ferber, Edna. *Giant.* 1952. Reprint, New York: HarperCollins, 2000.

A Fistful of Dollars. Directed by Sergio Leone. United Artists, 1964. DVD.

Flagstaff Republican Women Newsletter. June 2008. www.coconinogop.org.

Flores, William, and Rina Benmayor, eds. *Latino Cultural Citizenship: Claiming Identity, Space, and Rights.* New York: Beacon, 1998.

Folely, Neil. *The Quest for Equality: The Failed Promise of Black-Brown Solidarity.* Cambridge, MA: Harvard University Press, 2010.

———. *The White Scourge: Mexicans, Blacks, and Poor Whites in Texas Cotton Culture.* Rev. ed. Berkeley: University of California Press, 1999.

Fowler, Kevin. "Señorita Más Fina." Clay Baker and Kevin Fowler. *High on the Hog.* Tin Roof, 2002. CD.

Francis, Samuel. "Poking the Embers of Racial Conflict." *Washington Times,* July 21, 1995, final ed., A19.

Frankenberg, Ruth. *White Women, Race Matters: The Social Construction of Whiteness.* Minneapolis: University of Minnesota Press, 1993.

Franklin, John Hope. *The Color Line: Legacy for the Twenty-First Century.* Columbia: University of Missouri Press, 1993.

Frederickson, George M. *The Black Image in the White Mind: The Debate on Afro-American Character and Destiny, 1817–1914.* New York: Harper & Row, 1971.

Galindo, René, and Jami Vigil. "Are Anti-immigrant Statements Racist or Nativist? What Difference Does It Make?" *Latino Studies* 4.4 (2006): 419–47.

Gamio, Manuel. *Mexican Immigration to the United States: A Study of Human Migration and Adjustment.* Chicago: University of Chicago Press, 1930.

García, Ignacio M. *White but Not Equal: Mexican Americans, Jury Discrimination, and the Supreme Court.* Tucson: University of Arizona Press, 2009.

Garner, Steve. *Whiteness: An Introduction.* New York: Routledge, 2007.

Gates, Henry Louis, Jr. *The Signifying Monkey: A Theory of Afro-American Literary Criticism.* New York: Oxford University Press, 1988.

Giant. Directed by George Stevens. Warner Brothers, 1956. DVD.

Gilmore, Ruth Wilson. *Golden Gulag: Prisons, Surplus, Crisis and Opposition in Globalizing California.* Berkeley: University of California Press, 2007.

Gómez, Laura E. *Manifest Destinies: The Making of the Mexican American Race.* New York: New York University Press, 2007.

Gómez-Peña, Guillermo. *New World Border: Prophecies, Poems and Loqueras for the End of the Century.* San Francisco: City Lights Books, 1996.

———. *Warrior for Gringostroika: Essays, Performance Texts, and Poetry.* St. Paul, MN: Grey Wolf, 1993.

Gonzales, Rodolpho "Corky." *I Am Joaquín.* New York: Bantam Books, 1972.

González, Jovita, and Eve Raleigh. *Caballero: A Historical Novel.* Edited by José Limón and María Cotera. College Station: Texas A&M University Press, 1996.

González, Ray. "The Ghost of John Wayne." In *The Ghost of John Wayne and Other Stories*, 86–99. Tucson: University of Arizona Press, 2001.

Gordillo, Luz María. *Mexican Women and the Other Side of Immigration: Engendering Transnational Ties*. Austin: University of Texas Press, 2010.

Gordon, Avery. *Ghostly Matters: Haunting and the Sociological Imagination*. Minneapolis: University of Minnesota Press, 1997.

Graham, Don. *Cowboys and Cadillacs: How Hollywood Looks at Texas*. Austin: Texas Monthly Press, 1983.

Grassley, Chuck. "Prepared Statement of Senator Chuck Grassley." February 2, 2012. Stop Abuse and Violent Environments. http://saveservices.org.

Griffin, Anna. "At 50, Still Love or Hate at First Sight." *Charlotte Observer*, March 19, 2000, 1B.

Guidotti-Hernández, Nicole. *Unspeakable Violence: Remapping U.S. and Mexican National Imaginaries*. Durham, NC: Duke University Press, 2011.

Gutiérrez, Ramón A. "Aztlán, Montezuma, and New Mexico: The Political Uses of American Indian Mythology." In Anaya and Lomelí, *Aztlán*, 172–90.

Hage, Ghassan. *White Nation: Fantasies of White Supremacy in a Multicultural Society*. New York: Routledge, 2000.

Haggard, Merle, and Willie Nelson. "The Seashores of Old Mexico." Merle Haggard and Willie Nelson. *The Seashores of Old Mexico*. 1987. SBME Special Markets, 2008.

Hall, Stuart. "Gramsci's Relevance for the Study of Race and Ethnicity." *Journal of Communication Inquiry* 10.2 (1986): 5–27.

Haney López, Ian. "Retaining Race: LatCrit Theory and Mexican American Identity in *Hernandez v. Texas*." *Harvard Latino Law Review* 2 (1997): 279–96.

———. *White by Law: The Legal Construction of Race*. New York: New York University Press, 1996.

Hartigan, John, Jr. *Racial Situations: Class Predicaments of Whiteness in Detroit*. Princeton: Princeton University Press, 1999.

"Hate Crimes: Anti-Latino Hate Crimes Up for Fourth Straight Year." *Intelligence Report*, November 30, 2008. http://splcenter.org.

Hendler, Jane. *Best-Sellers and Their Film Adaptations in Postwar America*. New York: Peter Lang, 2001.

Higham, John. "Instead of a Sequel, or How I Lost My Subject." *Reviews in American History* 28 (2000): 327–39.

———. *Strangers in the Land: Patterns of American Nativism, 1860–1925*. 1955. Reprint, New Brunswick, NJ: Rutgers University Press, 1988.

Hill, Jane E. *The Everyday Language of White Racism*. Malden, MA: Wiley-Blackwell, 2008.

Hill, Mike, ed. *Whiteness: A Critical Reader*. New York: New York University Press, 1997.

Hirsch, E. D., Jr. *Cultural Literacy: What Every American Needs to Know*. New York: Vintage, 1988.

hooks, bell. "Eating the Other." In *Black Looks: Race and Representation*, 21–40. Boston: South End Press, 1992.

HoSang, Daniel Martinez. *Racial Propositions: Ballot Initiatives and the Making of Postwar California*. Berkeley: University of California Press, 2010.

Huggins, Nathan Irvin. *Harlem Renaissance*. New York: Oxford University Press, 1971.

"Human Trafficking." U.S. Customs and Border Protection. http://cbp.gov.

Huntington, Samuel P. *The Clash of Civilizations and the Remaking of the World Order*. New York: Simon & Schuster, 1996.

Hyam, Ronald. *Empire and Sexuality: The British Experience*. New York: Manchester University Press, 1990.

Ignatiev, Noel. *How the Irish Became White*. New York: Routledge, 1995.

"In Quest to Mock Immigration Racism of Tea Party, Bill Maher Gets a Big #No-Mames." *Latino Rebels*, July 29, 2014. http://latinorebels.com.

Inda, Jonathan Xavier. "Foreign Bodies: Migrants, Parasites, and the Pathological Nation." *Discourse* 22.3 (2000): 46–62.

Ingram, Jack. "Inna from Mexico." Jack Ingram and Bruce Robinson. *Hey You*. 1999. Columbia, Nashville, Lucky Dog, 2011. CD.

Ionide, Paula. "The Alchemy of Race and Affect: 'White Innocence' and Public Secrets in the Post–Civil Rights Era." *Kalfou* 1.1 (2014): 151–68.

Jacobson, Robin Dale. *The New Nativism: Proposition 187 and the Debate over Immigration*. Minneapolis: University of Minnesota Press, 2008.

Jameson, Fredric. "Reification and Utopia in Mass Culture." *Social Text* 1 (1979): 130–48.

Jiménez, Tomás R. *Replenished Ethnicity: Mexican Americans, Immigration, and Identity*. Berkeley: University of California Press, 2010.

Johnson, Kevin. *The "Huddled Masses" Myth: Immigration and Civil Rights*. Philadelphia: Temple University Press, 2004.

Julito. "1.2 Million Latinos Tell Census They're Now White, and NYTimes Thinks It's Awesome." *Latino Rebels*, May 21, 2014. http://latinorebels.com.

Kaplan, Amy. "Manifest Domesticity." *American Literature* 70.3 (1998): 581–606.

Keen, Robert Earl. "Maria." Robert Earl Keen. *West Textures*. Sugar Hill, 1989. CD.

———. *West Textures*. Sugar Hill, 1989. CD.

Keith, Toby. "Stays in Mexico." Toby Keith. *Greatest Hits 2*. Dreamworks Nashville, 2004. CD.

Kerouac, Jack. *On the Road*. 1957. Reprint, New York: Penguin, 1999.

Ladenburg, Kenneth. "Illuminating Whiteness and Racial Prejudice through Humor in *It's Always Sunny in Philadelphia*'s 'The Gang Gets Racist.'" *Journal of Popular Culture* 48.5 (2015): 859–77.

Lazarus, Emma. "The New Colossus." In *Emma Lazarus: Selected Poems and Other Writings*, 233. New York: Broadview Press, 2002.

Leonard, Andrew. "'I Just Look Illegal': San Francisco Giants Closer Sergio Romo Gives His Hometown Fans Yet Another Thrill." *Salon*, October 31, 2012. www.salon.com.

Levine, Melissa. "Whoa, Nelly; A Cowboy Matchmaker Rustles Up Mexican Brides. But Who Gets the Happy Ending?" *Dallas Observer*, March 2, 2006.

Limerick, Patricia Nelson. "Turnerians All: The Dream of a Helpful History in an Intelligible World." *American Historical Review* 100.3 (1995): 697–716.

Limón, José E. *American Encounters: Greater Mexico, the United States and the Erotics of Culture.* Boston: Beacon, 1998.

———. *Dancing with the Devil: Society and Cultural Poetics in Mexican American South Texas.* Madison: University of Wisconsin Press, 1994.

———. "Mexicans, Foundational Fictions, and the United States: *Caballero,* a Late Border Romance." *Modern Language Quarterly* 57.2 (1996): 341–53.

Lipsitz, George. *American Studies in a Moment of Danger.* Minneapolis: University of Minnesota Press, 2001.

———. *The Possessive Investment in Whiteness: How White People Profit from Identity Politics.* Rev. ed. Philadelphia: Temple University Press, 2006.

Lopenzina, Drew. *Red Ink: Native Americans Picking Up the Pen in the Colonial Period.* Albany: State University of New York Press, 2012.

Lowe, Lisa. *Immigrant Acts: On Asian American Cultural Politics.* Durham, NC: Duke University Press, 1996.

Lugo, Alejandro. "Theorizing Border Inspections." *Cultural Dynamics* 12.3 (2000): 353–73.

Lugones, María. *Pilgrimages/Peregrinajes: Theorizing Coalition Against Multiple Oppressions.* New York: Rowman & Littlefield, 2003.

Macdonald, Andrew. *The Turner Diaries.* Fort Lee, NJ: Barricade Books, 1978.

The Magnificent Seven. Directed by John Sturges. 1960. MGM, 2001. DVD.

Mariscal, Jorge. "The Smearing of Bustamante: The Far Right and Anti-Mexican Racism." *Counterpunch,* August 30, 2003. www.counterpunch.org.

Martinot, Steve. *The Machinery of Whiteness: Studies in the Structure of Racialization.* Philadelphia: Temple University Press, 2010.

May, Robert E. *Manifest Destiny's Underworld: Filibustering in Antebellum America.* Chapel Hill: University of North Carolina Press, 2002.

Mazón, Mauricio. *The Zoot Suit Riots: The Psychology of Symbolic Annihilation.* Austin: University of Texas Press, 1984.

McCarthy, Cormac. *All the Pretty Horses.* New York: Vintage, 1993.

———. *Cities of the Plain.* New York: Vintage, 1999.

McClintock, Anne. *Imperial Leather: Race, Gender, and Sexuality in the Colonial Contest.* New York: Routledge, 1995.

McIntosh, Peggy. "White Privilege and Male Privilege: A Personal Account of Coming to See Correspondences through Work in Women's Studies." In *Critical White Studies: Looking Behind the Mirror,* edited by Richard Delgado and Jean Stefancic, 291–99. Philadelphia: Temple University Press, 1997.

McKenzie, Mia. "No More 'Allies.'" *Black Girl Dangerous,* September 9, 2013. http://blackgirldangerous.org.

McKinney, Karyn D. *Being White: Stories of Race and Racism.* New York: Routledge, 2005.

McWilliams, Carey. *North from Mexico: The Spanish Speaking People of the United States.* 1949. Reprint, New York: Greenwood, 1968.

Melamed, Jodi. *Represent and Destroy: Rationalizing Violence in the New Racial Capitalism.* Minneapolis: University of Minnesota Press, 2011.

———. "The Spirit of Neoliberalism: From Racial Liberalism to Neoliberal Multiculturalism." *Social Text* 24.4 (2006): 1–24.

Menchaca, Martha. *Recovering History, Constructing Race: The Indian, Black, and White Roots of Mexican Americans.* Austin: University of Texas Press, 2001.

Mendoza, Louis. *A Journey around Our America: A Memoir on Cycling, Immigration, and the Latinoization of the U.S.* Austin: University of Texas Press, 2012.

"Mexican Dating—Hot Latinas at Your Doorstep." International Love Scout. http://internationallovescout.com.

"Mexico Censors Brynner." *Hartford Courant*, February 26, 1960, 12.

Miller, Steve. "Bustamante Foes Cite Ties to 'Klan-Like' Group." *Washington Times*, September 12, 2003, final ed., A1.

Mills, Charles W. *The Racial Contract.* Ithaca, NY: Cornell University Press, 1997.

———. "White Lies and the Making of the World." Presentation at Arizona State University, October 18, 2012.

Molina, Natalia. *How Race Is Made in America: Immigration, Citizenship, and the Historical Power of Racial Scripts.* Berkeley: University of California Press, 2014.

Montejano, David. *Anglos and Mexicans in the Making of Texas, 1836–1986.* Austin: University of Texas Press, 1987.

Moraga, Cherríe. *The Last Generation: Prose and Poetry.* Boston: South End Press, 1993.

Moreno, Carolina. "Bill Maher Bashes Republicans over Border Crisis with Epic Dr. Seuss Parody." *Huffington Post*, July 28, 2014. www.huffingtonpost.com.

Morrison, Toni. *Playing in the Dark: Whiteness and the Literary Imagination.* New York: Random House, 1992.

Muller, Thomas. "Nativism in the Mid-1990s: Why Now?" In Perea, *Immigrants Out!*, 105–18.

Mulvey, Laura. "Changes: Thoughts on Myth, Narrative and Historical Experience." *History Workshop* 23 (1987): 3–19.

———. "Visual Pleasure and Narrative Cinema." *Screen* 16.3 (1975): 6–18.

Navarro, Armando. *Mexicano Political Experience in Occupied Aztlán: Struggles and Change.* Walnut Creek, CA: AltaMira, 2005.

Nericcio, William Anthony. *Tex{t}-Mex Gallery.* http://textmex.blogspot.com.

———. *Tex{t}-Mex: Seductive Hallucinations of the "Mexican" in America.* Austin: University of Texas Press, 2007.

Ngai, Mae M. *Impossible Subjects: Illegal Aliens and the Making of Modern America.* Princeton: Princeton University Press, 2004.

Nichols, Lewis. "Talk with Edna Ferber." *New York Times Book Review*, October 5, 1952, 30.

Nieto-Phillips, John M. *The Language of Blood: The Making of Spanish-American Identity in New Mexico, 1880s–1930s.* Albuquerque: University of New Mexico Press, 2004.

Noble, David. *Death of a Nation: American Culture and the End of Exceptionalism*. Minneapolis: University of Minnesota Press, 2002.

Nora, Amaury. "Reconquista: A Nativist Creation." *Scholars and Rogues*, June 9, 2008. http://scholarsandrogues.com.

Nunley, Vorris. *Keepin' It Hushed: The Barbershop and African American Hush Harbor Rhetoric*. Detroit, MI: Wayne State University Press, 2011.

O'Brien, Pat. "Palm Springs Film Festival/Documentaries/Review: *Cowboy del Amor*." *Press-Enterprise*, January 6, 2006, AA26.

"Oh, the Places You'll Go! . . . And Get Kicked Out Of." *Real Time with Bill Maher*. HBO. July 25, 2014.

Olivas, Michael. *Colored Men and Hombres Aquí: Hernandez v. Texas and the Emergence of Mexican-American Lawyering*. Houston: Arté Publico Press, 2006.

———. "The 'Trial of the Century' That Never Was: Staff Sgt. Macario García, the Congressional Medal of Honor, and the Oasis Café." *Indiana Law Journal* 83.4 (2008): 1391–1403.

Olson, Joel. *The Abolition of White Democracy*. Minneapolis: University of Minnesota Press, 2004.

Omi, Michael, and Howard Winant. *Racial Formation in the United States: From the 1960s to the 1990s*. 2nd ed. New York: Routledge, 1994.

Orozco, Cynthia E. *No Mexicans, Women or Dogs Allowed: The Rise of the Mexican American Civil Rights Movement*. Austin: University of Texas Press, 2009.

Orr, Jay. "'Long Time Gone' Video Arrives." *CMT News*, June 13, 2002. www.cmt.com.

Padilla, Genaro. *My History, Not Yours: The Formation of Mexican American Autobiography*. Madison: University of Wisconsin Press, 1993.

Palmer, Bruce. *"Man over Money": The Southern Populist Critique of American Capitalism*. Chapel Hill: University of North Carolina Press, 1980.

Paredes, Américo. *With His Pistol in His Hand: A Border Ballad and Its Hero*. 1958. Reprint, Austin: University of Texas Press, 2000.

Park, Charles. "Between a Myth and a Dream: The Model Minority Myth, the American Dream, and Asian Americans in Consumer Culture." PhD dissertation, Purdue University, 2011.

Paz, Octavio. *The Labyrinth of Solitude and Other Writings*. 1961. Reprint, New York: Grove Press, 1994.

Pease, Donald E. *The New American Exceptionalism*. Minneapolis: University of Minnesota Press, 2009.

Perales, Alonso S. *Are We Good Neighbors?* San Antonio, TX: Artes Graficas, 1948.

Perea, Juan F. "The Black/White Binary Paradigm of Race: The 'Normal Science' of American Racial Thought." *California Law Review* 85.5 (1997): 1213–58.

———, ed. *Immigrants Out! The New Nativism and the Anti-immigrant Impulse in the United States*. New York: New York University Press, 1997.

Pérez-Torres, Rafael. *Mestizaje: Critical Uses of Race in Chicano Culture*. Minneapolis: University of Minnesota Press, 2006.

———. "Refiguring Aztlán." In *The Chicano Studies Reader: An Anthology of Aztlán, 1970–2000*, edited by Rafael Pérez-Torres, Chon Noriega, Eric Avila, Mary Karen Davilos, and Chela Sandoval, 213–39. Los Angeles: Chicano Studies Research Center, 2001.

Pitt, Leonard. *The Decline of the Californios: A Social History of the Spanish-Speaking Californians, 1846–1890*. 1966. Reprint, Berkeley: University of California Press, 1970.

"El Plan Espiritual de Aztlán." In *Aztlán: An Anthology of Mexican American Literature*, edited by Luis Valdez and Stan Steiner, 402–6. New York: Knopf, 1972.

Polletta, Francesca. *It Was Like a Fever: Storytelling in Protest and Politics*. Chicago: University of Chicago Press, 2006.

The Professionals. Directed by Richard Brooks. 1966. Sony Home Pictures, 2005. DVD.

Rancière, Jacques. *The Politics of Aesthetics*. Edited and translated by Gabriel Rockhill. New York: Bloomsbury, 2013.

The Return of the Seven. Directed by Burt Kennedy. 1966. MGM, 2002. DVD.

Rich, Adrienne. "Compulsory Heterosexuality and Lesbian Existence." In *Blood, Bread, and Poetry: Selected Prose 1979–1985*, 23–75. New York: Norton, 1994.

Richardson, Valerie. "Chicano Group Denied Funding; Stanford Acts after Refusal to Repudiate Racist Origin." *Washington Times*, May 9, 2004, final ed., A2.

Robinson, Cedric J. *Forgeries of Memory and Meaning: Blacks and the Regimes of Race in American Theater and Film before World War II*. Chapel Hill: University of North Carolina Press, 2007.

Rocco, Raymond. "Transforming Citizenship: Membership, Strategies of Containment, and the Public Sphere in Latino Communities." *Latino Studies* 2.1 (2004): 4–25.

Rocha, Edmundo. "Reconquista: A Nativist Creation." *¡Para Justicia y Libertad! Scholars and Rogues*, June 9, 2008. http://xicanopwr.com.

———. "Reconquista: A Nativist Creation." *¡Para Justicia y Libertad! XicanoPwr*, April 22, 2006. http://xicanopwr.com.

Rockhill, Gabriel. "Introduction." In Rancière, *Politics of Aesthetics*, xi–xvi.

Rodríguez, Annette Marie. "Writing Boundaries on Bodies: Constructing the U.S.-Mexican Border through Public Violence." Paper presented at the American Studies Association annual meeting, San Juan, Puerto Rico, November 2012.

Rodriguez, Dylan. *Suspended Apocalypse: White Supremacy, Genocide, and the Filipino Condition*. Minneapolis: University of Minnesota Press, 2010.

Rodriguez, Richard. *Brown: The Last Discovery of America*. New York: Penguin, 2002.

Roediger, David R. "The Color of Whiteness Studies: Studying Whiteness from an Ethnic Studies Perspective." Paper presented at the American Studies Association annual meeting, Washington, DC, November 7, 2009.

———. *Towards the Abolition of Whiteness: Essays on Race, Politics, and Working Class History*. New York: Verso, 1994.

———. *The Wages of Whiteness: Race and the Making of the American Working Class*. Rev. ed. New York: Verso, 1999.

———. "White Looks: Hairy Apes, True Stories, and Limbaugh's Laughs." In Hill, *Whiteness*, 35–46.

Rogin, Michael. *Ronald Reagan, the Movie: And Other Episodes in Political Demonology*. Berkeley: University of California Press, 1987.

Rosaldo, Renato. *Culture and Truth: The Remaking of Social Analysis*. Boston: Beacon, 1993.

Rosas, Gilberto. "The Thickening Borderlands: Diffused Exceptionality and 'Immigrant' Social Struggle during the 'War on Terror.'" *Cultural Dynamics* 18.3 (2006): 335–49.

Ruiz, Jason. *Americans in the Treasure House: Travel to Porfirian Mexico and the Cultural Politics of Empire*. Austin: University of Texas Press, 2014.

Ruiz de Burton, María Amparo. *The Squatter and the Don*. 1885. Reprint, Houston: Arte Público, 1997.

Russell, Tom. "Who's Gonna Build Your Wall?" *Border Songs*. CD Baby, No Más Muertes, 2012. CD.

Said, Edward W. *Orientalism*. New York: Vintage, 1979.

Saldaña-Portillo, Josefina. "Who's the Indian in Aztlán? Rewriting Mestizaje, Indianism, and Chicanismo from the Lacandón." In *The Latin American Subaltern Studies Reader*, edited by Ileana Rodríguez, 402–23. Durham, NC: Duke University Press, 2001.

Sánchez, George. *Becoming Mexican American: Ethnicity, Culture, and Identity in Chicano Los Angeles, 1900–1945*. Oxford: Oxford University Press, 1995.

Santa Ana, Otto. *Brown Tide Rising: Metaphors of Latinos in Contemporary American Public Discourse*. Austin: University of Texas Press, 2002.

———. "'Like an Animal I Was Treated': Anti-immigrant Metaphor in U.S. Public Discourse." *Discourse and Society* 10.2 (1999): 191–224.

Schaeffer, Felicity Amaya. *Love and Empire: Cybermarriage and Citizenship across the Americas*. New York: New York University Press, 2013.

Scheuer, Phillip K. "Swords of Bushido Become Guns in 'Magnificent Seven.'" *Los Angeles Times*, October 30, 1960, B3.

Schumach, Murray. "Producer Scores Mexican Censor." *New York Times*, May 20, 1960, 25.

Scott-Heron, Gil. "Whitey on the Moon." Gil Scott-Heron. *Small Talk at 125th and Lenox*. 1970. BGP Records, 2015. CD.

Seven Samurai. Directed by Akira Kurosawa. 1954. Criterion Collection, 2010. DVD.

Shapiro, Ann R. "Edna Ferber, Jewish American Feminist." *SHOFAR* 20.2 (2002): 52–60.

Shemak, April. *Asylum Speakers: Caribbean Refugees and Testimonial Discourse*. New York: Fordham University Press, 2010.

Shih, David. "What Happened to White Privilege?" *Arcade: Literature, Humanities, and the World*, June 9, 2015. http://arcade.stanford.edu.

Skyhorse, Brando. *The Madonnas of Echo Park*. New York: Free Press, 2010.

"Skyy Tastelessly Tries to Capitalize on Absolut's Mexican Gaffe." *Consumerist*, April 12, 2008. http://consumerist.com.

Slotkin, Richard. *Gunfighter Nation: The Myth of the Frontier in Twentieth Century America*. New York: Atheneum, 1992.

Smith, Andrea. "Heteropatriarchy and the Three Pillars of White Supremacy: Rethinking Women of Color Organizing." In *Color of Violence: The INCITE! Anthology*, edited by INCITE! Women of Color Against Violence, 66–73. Boston: South End Press, 2006.

Southern Exposure: Causes and Consequences of Illegal Immigration. Films Media Group, 2010. Films on Demand.

Southern Poverty Law Center. "Ethnic Nationalism." *Intelligence Report*, Fall 2001. www.splcenter.org.

"Southwest Border Unaccompanied Alien Children." U.S. Customs and Border Protection. www.cbp.gov.

Spelman, Elizabeth V. *Inessential Woman: Problems of Exclusion in Feminist Thought*. Boston: Beacon, 1988.

Stalling, Max. "Drunk in Mexico." *Sell Out—Live at Dan's Silver Leaf*. Blind Nello Records, 2007. CD.

Stinson, Charles. "'Magnificent Seven' Magnificent Western." *Los Angeles Times*, November 25, 1960, C15.

St. John, Rachel. *Line in the Sand: A History of the Western U.S.-Mexico Border*. Princeton: Princeton University Press, 2012.

Strait, George. *One Step at a Time*. MCA Nashville, 1989. CD.

———. "The Seashores of Old Mexico." Merle Haggard. *Somewhere Down in Texas*, MCA Nashville, 2005. CD.

Streeby, Shelley. *American Sensations: Class, Empire, and the Production of Popular Culture*. Berkeley: University of California Press, 2002.

"Teen Survivor of Hate Crime Attack at Texas Party Jumps from Cruise Ship, Dies." *Fox News*, July 2, 2007. www.foxnews.com.

"Teen Who Survived Brutal Attack Jumps to His Death." *USA Today*, July 3, 2007.www.usatoday.com.

Thandeka. *Learning to Be White: Money, Race, and God in America*. New York: Bloomsbury, 2000.

Thompson, Ivan. *Cowboy Cupid: Mail Order Brides and Other Tales from the Desert Southwest*. 1999.

Los Tigres Del Norte. "Juala del Oro (Cage of Gold)." Enrique Franco. *Herencia Musical: 20 Norteñas Famosas*. 1984. Fonovisa, 2003. CD.

Torres, Edén. "Race, Place and Chicana/o Politics in a Postnational American Studies." Paper presented at the American Studies Association annual meeting, San Antonio, TX, November 2010.

Treviño, Jesús Salvador. "Latino Portrayals in Film and Television." *Jump Cut: A Review of Contemporary Media* 30 (1985). www.ejumpcut.org.

"Trouble with Schools." *Fox & Friends*, January 23, 2015.

Turner, Frederick Jackson. *The Frontier in American History*. New York: Henry Holt, 1920.

Turner, John Kenneth. *Barbarous Mexico*. 1910. Reprint, Austin: University of Texas Press, 1969.

Uncooperative Blogger. "Drink Absolut Vodka: Bring Back the Mythical Aztlan." *Uncooperative Blogger*, April 5, 2008.

Urrea, Luis Alberto. *The Devil's Highway*. New York: Little, Brown, 2004.

———. *In Search of Snow*. Tucson: University of Arizona Press, 1994.

Usborne, David. "Storm in a Shot Glass as Advert Redraws Map of Americas." *Independent*, April 8, 2008, 1st ed.

U.S. Customs and Border Protection. "Alleged Human Smuggling Attempt in San Diego Ends with Two Dead." August 13, 2014. www.cbp.gov.

———. "April Starts Off Busy for Rio Grande Valley Sector Border Patrol Agents." April 3, 2015. www.cbp.gov.

———. "Border Patrol Agents Assist Citizens in Precarious Situations." March 11, 2015. www.cbp.gov.

———. "Border Patrol Agents Halt Human Smuggling Attempts." June 11, 2013. www.cbp.gov.

———. "Border Patrol Agents in Texas Save 4; Find Remains." February 5, 2014. www.cbp.gov.

———. "Border Patrol Agents Rescue Illegal Immigrants, Arrest Traffickers, Seize Marijuana." May 4, 2015. www.cbp.gov.

———. "Border Patrol Rescues 49 People within 24 Hours." April 24, 2015. www.cbp.gov.

———. "Border Patrol Rescues Three Individuals over the Last Four Days." April 22, 2015. www.cbp.gov.

———. "Border Patrol Rescues Two Migrants from Desert." October 17, 2014. www.cbp.gov.

———. "CBP Office of Air and Marine Make Rescues in NM, West Texas Due to Heavy Flooding." September 29, 2014. www.cbp.gov.

———. "CBP Rescues Hitchhiking Baby Squirrel." February 23, 2015. www.cbp.gov.

———. "Del Rio Border Patrol Agents Rescue Drowning Victim." August 28, 2013. www.cbp.gov.

———. "Joint Border Patrol, Office of Air and Marine Effort Saves Man's Life." January 29, 2015. www.cbp.gov.

———. "Joint CBP Efforts in El Paso Collars Sexual Offender, Rescues Lost Hiker." April 23, 2015. www.cbp.gov.

———. "Joint Efforts Save Another Life." September 22, 2014. www.cbp.gov.

———. "Laredo Border Patrol Sector Agents Make Several Significant Arrests and Narcotics Seizures during a Week's Period." May 27, 2015. www.cbp.gov.

———. "Rio Grande Valley Agents Rescue 36 Illegal Immigrants; Pregnant Woman." March 10, 2015. www.cbp.gov.

———. "Rio Grande Valley Border Patrol Agents Rescue Immigrants." May 29, 2015. www.cbp.gov.

———. "Rio Grande Valley Border Patrol Agents Rescue 35 People at Falfurrias Checkpoint." April 28, 2015. www.cbp.gov.

——. "Rio Grande Valley Sector Border Patrol Agents Rescue Two People Hidden inside Speaker Box." March 20, 2015. www.cbp.gov.

——. "Temperatures, Dangers on Rise in Arizona; 177 Migrants Rescued during Past Month." June 13, 2013. www.cbp.gov.

Vega, Sujey. *Latino Heartland: Of Borders and Belonging in the Midwest.* New York: New York University Press, 2015.

Vidal, Juan. "Spic-O-Rama: Where 'Spic' Comes From, and Where It's Going." *Code Switch: Frontiers of Race, Culture and Ethnicity*, March 3, 2015. www.NPR.org.

Villanueva, Tino. *Scene from the Movie GIANT.* Boston: Curbstone, 1993.

Vizenor, Gerald. *Manifest Manners: Postindian Warriors of Survivance.* Lincoln: University of Nebraska Press, 1999.

Watts, Eileen H. "Edna Ferber, Jewish American Writer: Who Knew?" In *Modern Jewish Women Writers in America*, edited by Evelyn Avery, 41–61. New York: Palgrave, 2007.

Webb, John C., Jr. "How One Citizen Is Feeling about Our Current Immigration Policies." *Washington Times*, September 21, 1996, final ed., A12.

The Wild Bunch. Directed by Sam Peckinpah. Warner Brothers, 1969. DVD.

Williams, Patricia J. *The Alchemy of Race and Rights: Diary of a Law Professor.* Cambridge, MA: Harvard University Press, 1991.

——. "The Hydra of Jim Crow." *Nation*, August 28–September 4, 2006, 9.

Winant, Howard. *The New Politics of Race: Globalism, Difference, Justice.* Minneapolis: University of Minnesota Press, 2004.

Winkler-Morey, Anne. "The War on History: Defending Ethnic Studies." *Black Scholar* 40.4 (2010): 51–56.

Wise, Tim. *White Like Me: Reflections on Race from a Privileged Son.* Rev. ed. Berkeley, CA: Soft Skull Press, 2008.

Yancy, George. *Look, a White! Philosophical Essays on Whiteness.* Philadelphia: Temple University Press, 2012.

Zac Brown Band. "Toes." Zac Brown, Wyatt Durrette, Jon Hopkins, and Shawn Mullins. *The Foundation.* Atlantic, 2008. CD.

Zamora, Emilio. *Claiming Rights and Righting Wrongs in Texas: Mexican Workers and Job Politics during World War II.* College Station: Texas A&M University Press, 2009.

INDEX

Lee Bebout is Associate Professor of English at Arizona State University, where he is affiliated with the School of Transborder Studies and the Program in American Studies. He is the author of *Mythohistorical Interventions: The Chicano Movement and Its Legacies* (2011).

Lightning Source UK Ltd.
Milton Keynes UK
UKOW02f1121031116
286785UK00003B/31/P